The World Bank and Africa

How can the notable increase in the intensity of intervention by the World Bank in African states be explained at a time when notions of 'partnership' and governments in the 'driving seat' have become more prominent?

This book explores the wide-ranging interventions of the World Bank in severely indebted African states. Understanding sovereignty as a frontier rather than a boundary, the book develops a vision of a powerful international organisation reconciling a global political economy with its own designs and a specific set of challenges posed by the African region. This book details the nature of World Bank intervention in the sovereign frontier, investigating institutional development, discursive intervention, and political stabilisation. It analyses the methods by which the World Bank has led a project to re-shape certain African states according to a governance template, leading to the presentation of 'success stories' in a continent associated with reform failure.

This conceptually innovative book details a political economy of the World Bank in Africa that is both globally contextualised and attentive to individual states. It is the only volume to look at the Bank's relations with Africa and will interest all students and researchers of African politics and the World Bank.

Graham Harrison lectures politics at the University of Sheffield, UK. He is an editor of *New Political Economy* and *Review of African Political Economy*, and is currently working on the concept of empire in international relations, and administrative reform in Tanzania.

Routledge advances in international political economy

The World Bank and Africa

The construction of governance states

Graham Harrison

Routledge
Taylor & Francis Group

LONDON AND NEW YORK

First published 2004
by Routledge
2 Park Square, Milton Park, Abingdon, Oxon, OX14 4RN

Simultaneously published in the USA and Canada
by Routledge
270 Madison Ave, New York NY 10016

Routledge is an imprint of the Taylor & Francis Group

Transferred to Digital Printing 2005

Typeset in Times by Wearset Ltd, Boldon, Tyne and Wear

British Library Cataloguing in Publication Data
A catalogue record for this book is available from the British Library

Library of Congress Cataloging in Publication Data
Harrison, Graham, 1968–
   The World Bank and Africa : the construction of governance
states / Graham Harrison.
      p. cm.
Includes bibliographical references and index.
   1. World Bank. 2. Africa—Economic policy. 3. Africa—Politics
and government—1960– I. Title.
   HG3881.5.W57H37 2004
   338.91′096—dc22

                                                    2003025313

ISBN 0-415-30280-3

Contents

8 Neoliberalism's revenge? 128

Illustrations

Figures

Tables

Acknowledgements

This book relies on research in Tanzania, Uganda and Mozambique. The following people gave me invaluable support during fieldwork: Nyangabyaki Bazaara, Brian Cooksey, Udo Etukudo, Deborah Katuramu, Haruna Kyamanywa, Matern Lumbanga, Daudi Mukangara, Patrick Mulindwa, John Okello, Joseph Rugumyamheto, Ernest Salla and Klaus Schmidt.

Fieldwork was funded by the Nuffield Foundation.

Bits of this book have benefited from comments and criticism from the following: Martin Doornbos, Kim Kelsall, Claire Mercer, Tony Payne, Lisa Richey, Alice Sindzingre and Robert Wade. Special thanks go to David Moore for inviting me to speak about the book's ideas at the International Political Science Association in Durban.

For Jane, Jack and Lydia.

Abbreviations

BWS	Bretton Woods System
CAS	Country Assistance Strategy
CCM	*Chama cha Mapinduzi* (Communist Party)
CDF	Comprehensive Development Framework
CG	Consultative Group
CSD	Civil Service Department (Tanzania)
CSRP	Civil Service Reform Programme
DFID	Department for International Development
DRC	Democratic Republic of Congo
EAC	East Africa Community
EDA	Effective Development Assistance
EDI	Economic Development Institute (now World Bank Institute)
EIU	Economist Intelligence Unit
ESAP	Economic and Social Adjustment Programme
FGR	First Generation Reform
GNP	Gross National Product
HIPC	Highly Indebted Poor Country
IBRD	International Bank of Reconstruction and Development
IFC	International Finance Corporation
IFI	International Finance Institution
IGG	Inspector General of Government
IMF	International Monetary Fund
IPE	International Political Economy
MIGA	Multilateral Investment Guarantee Agency
MOF	Ministry of Finance (Tanzania)
MoFPED	Ministry of Finance Planning and Economic Development (Uganda)
MPS	Ministry of Public Service (Uganda)
MTEF	Medium Term Economic Framework
NGO	Non Governmental Organisation
NRM	National Resistance Movement
PCB	Prevention of Corruption Bureau
PEAP	Poverty Eradication Action Plan (Uganda)

PRSC	Poverty Reduction Strategy Credit
PRSP	Poverty Reduction Strategy Paper
PSRP	Public Service Reform Programme
PSRRC	Public Sector Review and Reform Commission (Uganda)
PWC	Post-Washington Consensus
ROM	Results Oriented Management
SAL	Structural Adjustment Loan
SAP	Structural Adjustment Programme
SDS	Service Delivery Survey
SGR	Second Generation Reform
SIP	Sector Investment Programme
SWAP	Sector Wide Approach
TAL	Technical Assistance Loan
TRA	Tanzania Revenue Authority
UNDP	United Nations Development Programme
UPDF	Uganda Peoples Defence Forces

Part I

The governance encounter

The World Bank, governance states
and a new sovereign frontier

1 The road to governance

The World Bank and Africa

Introduction

Governance states: towards responsibility?[1]

> The World Bank's broad mission of promoting development requires it to work actively with a large number of ministries in each developing country – on environment, labour markets, health, education, judicial systems. This in turn necessitates it taking into account a wide range of perspectives. This has become even more true in recent years, as views of development have changed from a more narrow focus on solving certain technical problems, like lowering tariffs, to a broader one of the transformation of society.
>
> (Stiglitz 1999b: F582)

Africa is in the throes of a profound global project of socio-political engineering. This project, commenced in earnest in the early 1990s, goes under the rubric of governance and it encapsulates a set of integrated ideas and specific programmes. Governance can now be said to constitute a historically unprecedented reconfiguration of state forms in post-colonial Africa. The significance of governance reform is enhanced by its international dimensions: even a cursory review of governance in Africa reveals that it is intrinsically related to the actions of international agencies – most notably the World Bank.

Almost all contemporary discussions of development, poverty reduction, sustainability, international financial regulation and democratisation (to name the most salient) in Africa make an acknowledgement to governance. 'Governance' itself has become a concept as elastic as it is popular (Frischtak 1994). One effect of the general ascendancy of governance in Africa has been to produce a sub-set of states which have undergone related processes and display certain similar features, *mutatis mutandis*. These states are conceptualised here as governance states. We will come to look more closely at the defining features of governance states later in this chapter and in Chapter 3, but for now we can note that they are states which appear to have succeeded in internalising the impetus of governance. As such, they provide a unique and important point-of-departure: an analysis of cases where the governance project has (within the bounds of realistic expectation) succeeded.

But, what do we mean exactly by 'success'? As is well-known, normative phrases such as 'success' are difficult to pin down. What this book argues is that success has a great deal to do with progress towards the resolution of a set of structured tensions generated by a decade of neoliberal reform in sub Saharan Africa during the 1980s. Neoliberal reform – programmatised as structural adjustment – failed to infuse itself into the state as the founding logic of public action; it also generated destabilising effects on African societies. We will argue in coming chapters that the construction of governance states constitutes an attempt to address these problems through discursive intervention, programme lending focussed on administrative reform and capacity building, and the introduction of new resource management techniques. The World Bank has been the lead institution promoting reform in all these areas. In a phrase, governance states represent the Bank's[2] best efforts to embed neoliberalism in Africa.

'Governance' has worked to produce governance states in Africa through the articulation of a set of ideas and practices. As such, governance can be understood discursively and programmatically. It is also the case that governance is embedded in a set of global structures of political economy. As such, for all its novelty and effectiveness, governance cannot be analysed within the boundaries of its own dynamics; it operates within a broader conjuncture. Understanding this conjuncture is key to an analysis of governance states principally because the political economy of governance shapes the ontology of specific actors that promote governance reform through discursive and programmatic acts. The production of governance does not require a methodology of functionalist determination, but on the other hand, it would be naïve not to take into account the underlying power relations between groups of states, international agencies, and the structures of class relations more broadly. It will become clear throughout the book that the World Bank in particular has produced much of the impetus behind the production of governance states and it is not excessively vulgar to state that it has done this in large part merely through its ability to dispense hard currency.

How do we define governance? It will become clear that part of the reason why the term has gained such power – even seduction (Abrahamsen 2000: 47 *et seq.*) – is that it is extremely 'promiscuous': it involves itself in a wide range of political considerations. This will become clear in later chapters. Let us merely 'establish' the term with reference to the World Bank's ambitious definition. Governance involves: a more efficient public administration, the promotion of accountability, the establishment of the rule of law and a capable judiciary, and transparency (World Bank 1994b).

This is a very wide-ranging remit. This book focuses mainly on the first component, administrative reform.

To make a brief summary: governance, as a general project of political engineering that has pervaded Africa for at least a decade, has produced a set of governance states out of the varied terrain of the continent. These states have 'internalised' core features of governance discourse and practice and have won the plaudits of the World Bank and other international organisations as a result. The aim of this book is to analyse the mechanics of governance states and the interplay of the agencies involved in their construction, most centrally the World Bank, as facets of a project to embed neoliberalism.

This chapter introduces governance states by situating them within three scene-setting contexts. The two principal 'players' – the World Bank and African states – are introduced with particular attention paid to the inter-relations between the two. The more specific nature of these two players' encounter during the 1990s is reviewed, as this provides the 'moment' within which governance states have been constructed. The section on the World Bank establishes a set of its operating principles that provide us with a basic ontology of Bank agency. The section on African states focuses on the interface between states and the global political economy. The scene setting section details the development of governance politics as a successive phase from the neoliberalism of the 1980s, namely Second Generation Reform (SGR). This contextualisation will leave us in a position to raise the pertinent questions that drive the second section of the book. It will also introduce the more detailed theoretical reflections of Chapters 2 and 3.

Analysing governance states: a précis

Governance states are not hermetically-sealed national institutions, or 'models' with a tendency towards equilibrium, and to imagine that they are so would be to ignore important facets of governance states' features. In fact, governance states constitute a 'clustering' of actions and interpellations which render the notion of national sovereignty problematic.[3] In this sense, the analysis here does not start with the internal/external divide which has been problematised in International Relations theory for some time now. Governance states are global as much as they are national and, as a result, the narrative here moves from national case studies to global political economy and the politics of the World Bank. It is only within the space produced by these different levels that governance states can be meaningfully situated as we shall see in Chapter 2. This is not an easy 'space' to delimit; it is, rather, an international arena where the World Bank and governance states interact – a kind of 'international public sphere' (Cooper 2001a; Latham 2001: 73).

Governance states, it will be argued, are produced out of a confluence of forces. But this confluence is not chaotic or 'decentred' in its rationale. Rather, governance states represent a manifestation of a grander and profoundly historical problematic: the politics of the encounter between the institutions of global capitalism and African nation-states. Some of this history will be dealt with in Chapter 3 through the history of the World Bank in Africa, so here it is only necessary to sign some of the key issues that derive from the political economy of governance states.

Governance states encapsulate a process of addressing the tensions produced by an increasingly powerful set of global institutions and an increasingly powerless set of states in the African region. As such, governance states are analysed in Chapter 4 as possessing a different relation with donors to that encapsulated by the standard notions of national and global/international interests or internal and external actors. For those sympathetic to the governance project, this is a great step forward, abandoning as it does images of conditionality, external vigilance, and threats to declare a country 'off-track' (in the International Monetary Fund's (IMF) well-known punitive phrase). Chapter 5 details the forms of interventions that the Bank pursues to realise governance reform under 'post-conditionality' circumstances. Chapter 6 identifies the underlying liberal articles of faith that produce an image of governance states as harmonious or equilibrating entities. The main source of liberal governance discourse is the World Bank, which has made a strong effort to become an intellectual leader in this and other areas throughout the 1990s and into the twenty first century. But, governance states are not just the outcome of the Bank's successful liberal mission. In a later section of this chapter it is suggested that Africa's encounter with the World Bank has been particularly 'troubled' by issues of conflict and civil order. Concerns with order have coloured the nature of the construction of governance states as Chapter 7 will detail. Chapter 8 concludes by reflecting on the prospects for governance states with reference to a model outlined in Chapter 2.

Within all the chapters of this book, the processes and discourse of governance are 'concretised' through reference to specific cases: mainly Tanzania and Uganda, but also Mozambique. These countries do not constitute national case studies in the standard sense, but where necessary allow us a level of detail within our 'international public space' of governance, not amenable to a study which works at the more abstract level common to many international relations and international political economy studies. The countries also provide a prism through which the multi-level interactions of governance work: the institutional manoeuvres of ministries, appeals to national development, and the expansive globalised 'common sense' of the World Bank and others. The need for specificity is strengthened by the fact that much of the mechanics of governance are worked through a specific kind of political engineering: administrative reform. As we shall see, administrative reform programmes have emerged in all governance states, possess key common features, and allow the most intimate facets of statehood to be evaluated and reconfigured in the name of governance.[4] However, programmes of administrative reform are not presented here as isolated refuges of 'proof' against the hubris of governance-speak and political rhetoric; rather the programmes them-selves – the logic of their objectives and the language of the documenta-tion that they generate – are highly ideologised. They work to produce governance truly as a political project.

Once more to make a brief summary, governance states will be analysed by addressing the following issues: the strengths and weaknesses of governance as a form of liberal discourse; the collapse of a sovereign ontology of internal/external and the dynamics of donor-state relations and the polarities that this evokes; the origins and rationales of World Bank advocacy of governance; and the construction of governance states as a solution to the enduring instability of markets and production in African states. This requires a focus that moves between different levels of analysis: both generic and specific to certain countries; both focussed on discursive interventions and the funding of 'real' programmes of state reconstruction.

The World Bank: foundations of an international institution

As will become clear throughout this book, the World Bank is the key actor in the construction of governance states in Africa. No matter how much emphasis one puts on the ownership of governance reform by African states, it is undeniable that the similarity of governance reforms between states – the reason that one can establish a generic category of governance states – owes itself to the fact that the World Bank has ploughed intellectual and financial resources into governance states, and maintains a powerful and close relation with them. If the Bank is such an important actor – the paramount force behind governance no less – then it becomes necessary to pay close attention to the nature of World Bank action.

Although the Bank's history reveals an institution that has changed significantly in some ways (Kapur *et al.* 1997) one can discern a core empirical foundation to the World Bank's actions since its establishment in 1944. This set of core actions provides a useful starting point to an analysis of the Bank because it provides us with a sense of the Bank as an agency. The three core actions dealt with here are: to expand inter-national capitalism, to promote social change through lending pro-grammes, and to regulate or institutionalise capitalist development; but before proceeding to develop these, a review of some of the existing work on the Bank provides a context and justification for the starting point used here.

The World Bank charter lists five establishing purposes:

1   to assist in development and reconstruction,
2   to promote private foreign investment,
3   to promote long term balanced international trade,
4   to lend for project development,
5   to conduct its operations with due regard for business conditions (adapted from Shihata 1991: 62).

Broadly speaking, most writers (including this one) accept the Bank's self-representation,[5] albeit with different emphases between – and interpretations of – the five points. And, most are reasonably comfortable to take some interpretation of these five points as sufficiently robust to endure the turbulent post-1945 political economy: 'leading up to the Bank's establishment ... a number of ground rules were laid down which still govern its activities today' (van der Laar 1980: 32).

To identify a set of core actions is not to portray an unchanging international institution, a rock standing indifferently to the turbulent waters of global change. Rather, it is to take a reasonable starting point to an analysis of the World Bank, to serve as a reference against which changes in Bank actions and discourse have taken place. Also, of course, the relative strength that one gives to each of the five points and the justifications one might evoke to throw some of them out, depends on one's interpretation of the Bank's founding statement of purpose. For example, Nelson's critical and powerful study stresses the key task of capitalist global integration: 'Promoting foreign capital investment in member countries is emphasised in three of the IBRD's [International Bank for Reconstruction and Development] five statements of purpose ... and has remained central through its forty-five years' (1995: 15). For Miller-Adams, the Bank maintains an imperative of institutional survival by maintaining itself as a lending 'technocracy' (1999: 6). Nelson adopts a radical political-economy perspective whereas Miller-Adams relies mainly on a kind of Weberian institutionalism. Hopkins *et al.* make a functional analysis of the Bank that condenses the Bank's 'essence' into its work as a bank, a development agency, and a development research institution (2000: 283). The distinctions made by Hopkins *et al.* explore the ways in which the Bank can function more effectively in its core tasks, locating the World Bank in a liberal *problematique* of how to reconcile adroit public action with basically harmonious market forces. Thus, each writer must approach the Bank with a premise about the nature of its relations with other structures and processes. In this book, the neoliberal rostrums are not accepted as axiomatic and the analysis of the World Bank involves a critique of this intellectual paradigm within which the Bank operates. The three core realms of action outlined below – as facilitator of capitalist expansion, development agency and international institution – will be problematised within a particular framework which attempts to address the Bank as a political-institutional 'moment' within a broader international political economy.

The World Bank and global capitalism

The World Bank has openly and keenly worked to promote the expansion of international capitalism within its operations. Because of its institutional origins at Bretton Woods (Oliver 1975; Elson 1994) and the ascendance of an American-led liberal capitalist globalism after World War Two, the Bank has elaborated various forms of support for large-scale international capital which derives mainly from the US.[6] But the World Bank also works to promote global capitalism in a more nationally disinterested fashion (Cammack 2004): the Bank will stop all lending to any member state that violates the property rights of a transnational corporation. A substantial portion of its project lending goes to transnational companies through public tenders in what Payer analyses as a form of global fordism for international firms (Payer 1991; Bracking 2003). The Bank's enduring predilection for large-scale infrastructural developments such as dams, irrigation schemes, highway construction, etc. favour companies that can raise large packages of capital – rarely within the national capitalist class's capacity, especially in Africa. The Multilateral Investment Guarantee Agency and the International Finance Corporation, two of the institutions within the World Bank family, directly work to promote international investment (Rich 2002). The details of how the Bank has pursued its pro-international capital agenda are detailed in Payer's study:

> The World Bank has deliberately ... used its financial power to promote the interests of ... international capital ... in many different ways: by acting as an intermediary for the flow of funds abroad with taxpayers' money from its developed member countries serving to guarantee the safety of the bonds it sells; by opening up previously remote regions through transportation and telecommunications investments; by directly aiding certain multinational corporations; by pressuring the borrowing governments to improve the legal privileges for the tax liabilities of foreign investment; by insisting on production for export which chiefly benefits the corporations that control international trade; by selectively refusing to loan to governments that repudiate international debts or nationalise foreign property; by opposing minimum wage laws, trade unions activity, and all measures that would improve the share of labour in national income; by insisting on procurement through international competitive bidding, which favours the largest multinationals; by opposing all kinds of protection for locally-owned business and industry; and by financing projects and promoting national policies that deny the control of basic resources – land, water, forests – to poor people and appropriate them for the benefit of multinationals.
>
> (Payer 1982: 19–20)

One is struck by the enduring relevance of this overview: since the mid 1990s the Bank has become increasingly supportive of the free trade agenda of the World Trade Organisation (Jordan 1999; Wade 2002); it has promoted the privatisation of public utilities mainly to international companies (a recent controversy concerning the Bank's role in water privatisation being a prominent example); and its attempts to produce a clear positive statement on labour rights (World Bank 1995b) barely hide its desire to make labour cheap and flexible for business. In 1995, 56 per cent of total Bank lending went to transnational corporations (Caufield 1998: 242). In the words of a Bank official: 'Most of our money doesn't go to the South, it goes straight from Washington to Pennsylvania, where they manufacture the turbines, or Frankfurt, where they produce the dredging equipment.' (in ibid.) From the mid 1990s, the Bank has increased its direct lending and finance security to international companies through Multilateral Investment Guarantee Agency (MIGA) and International Finance Corporation (IFC), lending to Coca Cola, Elf Aquitaine, Royal Dutch Shell, Exxon, international hotel chains and beer companies (Rich 2002: 38–40).

The World Bank and development

The World Bank's key specialisation is to promote 'development'. Much of the discourse of development has been generated out of a desire to order and institutionalise the dynamics of capitalist accumulation and their social effects, to the extent that Cowen and Shenton (1996) ably illustrate a genealogy of 'custodianship' within development discourse. The notion of custodianship allows development to be thought of in terms of ordered, rational and scientific-technical public action – mainly national, but also international in the case of the World Bank.[7] In fact, much Bank technical assistance to borrowing states, has been concerned to strengthen the ability of states to act as 'good custodians' of the development process. One is struck by the universality of national plans throughout the post colonial world – communist or capitalist – and the ability of the Bank to find a 'niche' in so many of these – communist or capitalist. Custodianship is based on a degree of denial of popular will in the name of development (or perhaps more honestly modernisation) and again national states, sometimes starkly authoritarian, have relied (and rely) on World Bank support.[8]

> The underlying political rationale for the Bank's ... development projects seemed to be political stability through *defensive modernisation*. [...] Defensive modernisation aims at forestalling or pre-empting social and political pressures. If defensive modernisation is successful, it results in conservatism among the newly modernised (*sic*) and thus contributes to political stability.
>
> (Ayres 1983: 226, italics added)

The passage from Ayres illustrates the confluence of the Bank's desire to effect social transformation with a concern to regulate this transition in a way that minimises its 'disruptive' effects. This is the essence of the meaning of development for the Bank.

The Bank's own ideological evolution has closely accompanied that of development as an international political issue or concept: both were products of the early post-war period (Escobar 1995; Rist 1997). The Bank's approach to development has undergone significant changes in its half-century. Broadly speaking, the Bank commenced with a growth-oriented capital-intensive approach in which the 'problem' for development was understood primarily in terms of capital scarcity. From 1968 (and the McNamara presidency of the Bank) policy broadly moved towards a focus on poverty alleviation and redistribution, encapsulated by the Integrated Rural Development Programme (Ayres 1983; Gibbon 1992). From the late 1970s, lending became linked to a set of neoliberal macroeconomic reforms through structural adjustment lending. Most recently, the Bank has revived an interest in poverty alleviation, adhering to a set of International Development Targets that aim to half the world's poor by 2015, although the logic of the reforms behind this goal are not necessarily a departure from the 'adjustment period' that preceded it, as will be shown later. What unites each of the Bank's successive prioritisations is what – in different but related circumstances – Altvater (2002) has called the 'growth obsession'. Economic growth, measured as a high rate of Gross National Product (GNP) growth, or at least a rate above that of population growth (Crane and Finkle 1981; Das Gupta 1999), is the *sine qua non* for the Bank – today as it was fifty years ago.

The World Bank and institutionalisation

The turbulence of the Bank's development thinking should be tempered by the acknowledgement of a certain institutional continuity within the Bank, to maintain its own technical pre-eminence in a 'development community' increasingly crowded with 'experts' (Miller-Adams 1999). This generates an institutional conservatism for any reforming Bank president (Crane and Finkle 1981: 518; Ascher 1983), reinforced by its 'solidly homogeneous culture' (O'Brien *et al.* 2000: 54[9]). Contained within the Bank's institutional reproduction is a constant imperative to lend (Rich 1994; Kapur *et al.* 1997: 713; Collier 1999: 321): the intermediation of loans[10] constitutes the basis upon which all Bank development visions have been based. Cynically, one might comment that this is why all development ideals articulated by the Bank require new and often larger lending programmes from the World Bank, perhaps another kind of growth obsession. There is within the Bank an institutional ethos that strongly compels its employees to work to increase levels of lending to the extent that one long serving Bank economist stated that 'success was measured by whether you kept your lending targets or not' (in Caufield 1998: 101).

Thus, 'development' for the Bank – in spite of its twists and turns in development thinking – is concerned with the promotion of capitalism within a framework of ordered public action with the effect of reproducing the Bank's international institutional niche in lending to borrowing member states. Because the Bank has such a founding faith in the progressive nature of capitalism,[11] it imagines development to be a stable and harmonious process: the multiplier effects (or trickle down) of capital investment, the externalities of redistribution with growth, the efficiency gains of liberalisation, and the empowerment of farmers and entrepreneurs as a result of Poverty Reduction Strategy Papers. The Bank's documentation generally (with a few interesting exceptions) maintains a studied apoliticism (consonant with its own Articles) that renders development a curiously straightforward process. A detailed example of this is the World Bank's (and bilaterals') involvement in rural development in Lesotho, as studied by Ferguson (1994; see also Harriss 2002). Ferguson carefully exposes how all issues of political struggle, accumulation, historical legacy and relations with South Africa are effaced, creating a discourse of development profoundly evacuated of politics – an anti-politics machine in Ferguson's powerful phrase. Thus, the Bank acts as an institution not only in the sense that one can draw organograms of its departments and personnel; it also *institutionalises development*, rendering it as largely a technical issue rather than a political one.

Development is more or less what the Bank claims to be striving for *and achieving* in governance states. The Bank's refrains with respect to governance states are that these states have achieved a requisite level of general civic order and national integration which gives the state capacity to act. Governance states have pursued the 'correct' economic reforms with political will, and these have produced healthy rates of economic growth that are having a positive impact on general levels of well-being in that levels of poverty are falling. All of this has been achieved with the judicious support of the World Bank and other international donor/ creditors. This image of the governance state is the Bank's, even if it expands therefrom.

Africa and the World Bank's regional encounters

The World Bank has been a key actor in sub Saharan Africa's post-colonial history. Although the Bank has not been all-powerful or all-pervasive, it has been a significant force in many post-colonial national development trajectories. The history of Bank involvement in Africa began in the late colonial period (from 1950), when the notion of 'development' replaced that of 'civilisation', and colonial powers became anxious about the increasing power of African nationalism on the continent. The Bank subsequently engaged with African political economies through a number of phases, right up to the present day when it is difficult to

imagine African politics without the statements of Bank resident representatives, the regular trips of Ministers of Finance to the Consultative Group
meetings chaired by the Bank, and the ongoing horse trading that revolves
around structural adjustment and conditionality.

If one can say that the World Bank has been an important part of
Africa's politics, one can also note that Africa has been important for the
Bank's politics. More than any other region of the world, sub Saharan
Africa has served as a focal point in Bank thinking about the theory and
practice of 'development'. African states faced the most pressing challenges after decolonisation, and Bank thinking evolved with the fortunes
that African states – and the Bank itself – had in meeting these challenges.
The 'soft' institution within the World Bank family, the International
Development Association (IDA), lends a substantial proportion of its allo-
cations to sub Saharan Africa (Kapur *et al.* 1997: 731–3), and if Africa ever
escapes the debt trap and develops in a sustainable fashion, the IDA
would lose its central reason for existence. This theme of mutual interaction – albeit within a structured context of Bank pre-eminence – will be
developed throughout the book.

The global constitution of Africa as a region (1980–)

Even more fundamental in many [African] countries is the deteriorat-
ing quality of government, epitomised by bureaucratic obstruction,
rent-seeking, weak judicial systems, and arbitrary decision-making.

(World Bank 1989: 3)

Many countries in sub Saharan Africa are suffering from a crisis of
statehood – a crisis of capability. An urgent priority is to rebuild state
effectiveness through an overhaul of public institutions, reassertion of
the rule of law, and credible check on abuse of state power.

(World Bank 1997: 14)

Since the early 1980s, a huge amount of research has been undertaken on
the involvement of the International Finance Institutions (IFIs) in sub
Saharan Africa. The bulk of this literature has been concerned with the
relationship between structural adjustment and growth, and the social
impact of the former.[12] Less work has been done at a more abstract level,
which is partly a reflection of Africa's marginality to the field of International Political Economy (IPE).

Throughout the 1980s, Africa was generally perceived as marginal to
the globalisation project, and as exceptional by virtue of its instability.
This instability is a result of the region's economic decline and the crisis of
the nation-state in many parts of the region.[13] Consequently, Africa constituted a region of the global system which was, and is, highly unstable in
terms of its economic performance and its political ordering. Thus, any

understanding of the role of the World Bank in sub Saharan Africa has to take on board two levels of analysis.

In the first place, there is a 'generic' or macro level set of dynamics, based in the global mission of the World Bank to use finance and conditionality to impose or lock in neoliberal reform (Taylor 1997; Moore 1999; Gore 2000; Standing 2000). One can see this agenda in the structural adjustment programmes of most of Africa and Latin America. After the collapse of the Berlin Wall and the USSR, the Bank and IMF have become key agents in the 'reform' process of eastern and central Europe (Gould-Davies and Woods 1999; Rutland 1999). Slightly later, on the heels of the 'Asian crisis' of 1997, the World Bank, and IMF in particular, have become an important force in southeast Asia (Berger and Beeson 1998; Bullard *et al.* 1998; Robinson and Rosser 1998; Gowan 1999; Higgot and Phillips 2000; Wade 2000; Thirkell-White 2003). Overall, analysts have defined the same core agenda – often known as the 'Washington consensus' – articulated by the World Bank, IMF, Wall Street and US Treasury (Gowan 1999; Naim 2000; Standing 2000; Wade 2001a).

At the 'meso' level, one can identify patterns which are *regionally* specific, based in the particular histories of regions' interactions with the global political economy. Hence, to use broad characterisations, the Latin American debt crisis was a crisis of medium-sized economies closely interlinked with the US economy (Green 1996). The IFIs approach to Latin America was based in fears of the repercussions of economic insolvency for the world economy, and for the US in particular. IFI lending was designed to bail out economies with unsustainable levels of commercial debt, not multilateral debt 'overhang'. In Southeast Asia, IFI involvement has been closely related to the liberalisation of currency trade and capital controls and the subsequent provision of finance to stave off extremely damaging speculative runs on currencies and bank deposits.

In sub Saharan Africa, economic crisis has had little impact on global markets because – with the exceptions of Nigeria and South Africa – national economies are so small that they matter very little for the global economy. Not unrelatedly, African political economies have been beset by a *different order* of problems to those in other regions, manifest more clearly in political crises of stability. There are certain fundamentals – concerning the operational capacity of states and levels of civic order – which are more or less taken for granted in Latin America and Southeast Asia but constitute an integral part of sub Saharan Africa's crisis. As a result, the IFIs have coupled their generic concerns of neoliberal reform with a desire to stabilise states and facilitate processes of ordering and regulation within debtors' political economies (Williams 1996). This regional constitution – of an unstable capitalism and an incomplete project of state-centred ordering (Harrison 2004) – provides a key to understanding the Bank's actions in Africa and more specifically the motivation for the Bank's enthusiasm for governance states.

States, order and informal economies: a regional problematic

Historical sociologists and others have identified close inter-relations between war and capitalist modernity. Tilly (1992) identifies the way in which war facilitated the consolidation of hegemonic nation-states in Europe through the necessity to tax the citizenry, and theorists of imperialism have argued that the expansion of markets and the rise of powerful (inter)national capitals have evoked political and military conflict between global national powers (Lenin 1975). At a more detailed level, the social processes of violence and conflict can generate new forms of accumulation (Giddens 1995).

One can certainly identify a relationship between conflict, instability and accumulation in many parts of Africa. For Mozambique, Chingono identifies how the protracted civil conflict created conditions for a close relationship between conflict and accumulation, producing a grassroots capitalism characterised by extreme brutality (1996). In Uganda, civil conflict provided the opportunity for the emergence of a propertied class known as *mafutamingi* (Mamdani 1976, 1990); a relationship between conflict and accumulation remains with Uganda after civil war by virtue of its involvement in the conflict(s) in the Democratic Republic of Congo (Reno 2002). The Liberian warlord Charles Taylor wrought a fiefdom out of the centre of the country which he subsequently used to enrich himself to the extent that his so-called 'Greater Liberia' became France's second largest source for the import of hardwoods (Reno 1995). More infamously, conflicts in Sierra Leone and Angola have become substantially conflicts over access to high-value minerals, involving mercenaries, warlordism and 'blood diamonds' (Hodges 2001).

Whilst all of these examples describe markets which states cannot regulate because they are integrated into conflicts that *challenge* the state, there is also a more pervasive set of social relations of production and accumulation in sub Saharan Africa which does not destroy the state in the stark sense defined above, but rather interacts with the state, undermining its formal structures. The generic term for these social relations is 'informal economic activity'. MacGaffey's (1987; MacGaffey *et al.* 1991) detailed research in Zaire reveals how deep and complex these informal activities can be. She also reveals that informal trade does not necessarily evade the state entirely but in fact employs resources strategically to ensure factionalised political complicity for informal activity at the expense of a broader régime of regulation. The essence of Reno's (1995) conceptualisation of the 'shadow' state and economy is not an economy disarticulated from the state, but a 'shadowy' one: regulated principally through ethnic and clientelist alliances and illicit trade which reproduces itself by drawing the state into its own logic of operation. These alliances also provide resources through which state classes reproduce themselves (Allen 1995). Thus, state involvement with unofficial activity does not mean state regulation; in some cases, it is the reverse: state involvement in informal activities leads to the *state*'s informalisation.[14]

Taken together, one can make a characterisation of sub Saharan Africa as a region particularly beset with instability and 'informality', challenging the basic assumptions of statehood and sovereignty and the assumptions that constitute the premise for the Bank's generic projects. Sub Saharan Africa contains a variety of forms of market activity and accumulation, few of which are regulated and institutionalised in ways that would be familiar to national planners or development economists of whatever political stripe. It is these conditions which substantially define the engagement of the World Bank (and those aligned with it)[15] with sub Saharan Africa. This is expressed in the opening quotation in the previous section from the World Bank's *Sub-Saharan Africa: From Crisis to Sustainable Growth* (1989). External agencies involve themselves in sub Saharan Africa in order to stabilise states in conditions of greater or lesser insecurity and economic crisis. If we integrate separate notions and narratives of crisis – the debt crisis, complex emergencies, humanitarian crisis (Leys 1994; Arrighi 2002) – we can understand these particular notions as part of an over-arching relationship which defines African societies as the target of a global régime of crisis management effected through deeply dependent post colonial states (Abrahamsen 2000; Duffield 2001). The notion of an African crisis enables a raft of external interventions by donors and creditors.

Africa and globalisation: (de)stabilisation?

One central contradiction in the regionally-constituted donor-state relation is that between economic liberalisation and social-political stability. Early formulations of 'shock therapy', propounded particularly by the IMF, proselytised a régime of radical and rapid change in economic policy, the metaphor being that a sudden short sharp shock would evacuate the economy of all of its rent-seeking, irrational regulation and inefficiency, leaving in its wake a 'lean and mean' economy, forged out of the austere but ultimately beneficent fires of radical liberalisation. Milder (1996: 151) nicely encapsulates this approach as a neoliberal 'revolution', based on the drastic sudden actions of an insulated elite (revolutionary cadre) that pulls the patrimonial rugs from under the feet of vested interests and rent-seekers to lay open a scorched earth for renewed and vigorous market forces. The merits of shock therapy have been criticised in the 1990s, from a variety of standpoints (Gowan 1995; Stiglitz 1999a, 1999b). For other regions of the global political economy, shock therapy's controversy emerged from questions as to whether the therapy actually provoked economic recovery; however, in much of Africa, the dilemma was posed as a play-off between a strictly and rapidly applied liberalisation and a basic stability in the maintenance of a social fabric which might hold a national society together. This manifested itself institutionally in a slight difference of approach between the Bank and the Fund, the former being concerned with stabilisation (involving medium-term development loans for infrastructure, the sequencing of reform etc.) and the latter liberalisation (rapid fiscal and monetary liberalisation and minimal state action to ameliorate the consequences). The contradiction was, then: how to liberalise economies in a 'crisis region' without endangering the basic political stability which underpins *all* economic policy and modelling? A World Bank employee's answer would be likely to evoke the examples of Uganda or Mozambique for reasons that pertain to the features of governance states, detailed in Chapter 2.

The argument here is not to portray Africa in essentialist terms as the site of some form of primordial instability as is intimated in some accounts (Kaplan 1994). Rather, it is to suggest that the history of capitalism and the related formation of modern state structures in Africa has been violent, contradictory and incomplete (Davidson 1992; Berman 1998). As a result, unique state-forms have emerged (Bayart 1993), and the contemporary engagement of African states with global forces cannot but reflect this common historical legacy (Cooper 2001a). Let us look at intervention in a little more detail.

Mark Duffield's important work on international humanitarianism provides us with insight into this global constitution of Africa's regional problematic of stability. He analyses relief agencies and Non Governmental Organisations (NGOs) more generally as constituting a kind of globalised social 'safety net', providing minimal support for impoverished populations, ravaged by insecurity and the effects of economic liberalisation.

> In Africa, northern intervention has encouraged the emergence of a neoliberal, two-tier system of public welfare. From the end of the 1970s, World Bank/IMF structural adjustment programmes have been attempting, with highly debatable consequences, to stimulate market reform and encourage producers. For those people unable to benefit from these measures a welfare 'safety net' has emerged ..., largely as a result of NGO activity.
>
> (Duffield 1993: 140)

Duffield's overview gives us a sense of a peripheral region, regulated by a massive profusion of NGO activity, which maintains a basic social stability against the instabilities of neoliberal adjustment (see also Fowler 1994). Abrahamsen (2000) makes a related argument concerning democratisation and the involvement of international agencies. She outlines how much of the discourse of democratisation and governance, articulated not least by the World Bank, is expressed in a disciplinary ontology – of limits, stability, order, again in the face of disruptive neoliberal projects. In keeping with Duffield and Abrahamsen's important work, this book will develop a similar theme in respect to Bank involvement with governance states.

This section has introduced sub Saharan Africa as a region with a historically-produced form of state that has rendered basic state power, in the Weberian model, at most a partial achievement in many cases. This issue of state power and social stability infuses the nature of the encounter between external agencies and African states (Reno 1998; Bayart 2000; Latham 2001). The next section will relate these concerns more directly to governance states through a consideration of second generation reform (SGR). As we shall see, SGR signifies the attainment of a level of social stability and state capacity that implies – at least in a minimal sense – a resolution of Africa's *problematique* of instability and order.

From first to second generation reform: a governance manifesto

> Supporting good policies is important but it is not enough. We learned in the 1990s that process is as important as policy ... The way donors and recipients interact strongly influences the effectiveness of development co-operation. Relationships have tended to follow the preferences of donor countries, leaving recipients with little sense of ownership [...] If development co-operation is to attack poverty effectively and efficiently, donors will need to [...] provide sustained support for policy and institutional environments.
>
> (World Bank 2000/2001: 191–2)

First generation reform (FGR) is what is more commonly known as economic liberalisation. A familiar menu will already have suggested itself to the reader: devaluation, the removal of all price controls and subsidies, the abolition of state-owned marketing boards, privatisation, the removal of quotas and reduction of tariffs for imports and exports, a radical reduction in deficit financing and the introduction of user fees for social services. In sum: rolling back the state and putting faith in the market. FGR encapsulates policies associated with structural adjustment programmes (SAPs) in Africa.

While FGR clearly concerns itself with a reduction in the scope of state action; SGR is concerned with the *nature* of state action as much as its scope: institutional capacity building; civil service (or more broadly public service) reform; the introduction of new forms of information technology, finance management and human resource management; technical assistance and the facilitation of public participation in policy monitoring, evaluation and development.[16] One can readily see that SGR encapsulates a raft of policy innovations closely related to the more explicitly normative framing of governance. The ethos is that 'process' is as important as 'policy'; in other words, the generic functioning of institutions is as important as the specific actions of those institutions. The move from first to second generation reform constitutes a move from *crisis management* to *institutional development* (World Bank 1997: 152; Jones 2000: 271) which, in the light of the previous section, is immensely significant for donors. The key point to note is that, to some extent, SGR represents a renewed focus of the state. The state shifts from acting as the venal, rent-seeking 'vampire' – source of all problems[17] – to the key institution to ensure that the market functions properly. The institutional stability of the state is now the guarantor of the institutional stability and health of the market. The politics of this shift will be a principal concern of Part II of the book.

The context for SGR

SGR provides a rubric under which a series of externally-funded projects construct governance states. Normatively, SGR is presented as a subsequent stage in the process of development, a sign of qualitative transformation in the way states operate. As such, it has been presented as innovation and novelty. SGR has been analysed as a key component in a profound shift towards a 'new paradigm for development' (Stiglitz, in Standing 2000: 738). Relatedly, and in keeping with this notion of paradigmatic change, Krugman (1995) asserts that the (old) Washington Consensus died during the 1990s, which has led many journalists and 'pundits' to speak of a 'post-Washington consensus', as a kind of sea-change in intellectual thinking about the nature of development and the role of lending institutions such as the World Bank (Naim 2000). Pastor and Wise have related the development of second generation reforms out of the first as a tandem development to the discursive shift from the Washington to post-Washington consensus (1999: 36).

Other writers have questioned the extent to which recent changes in conceptualisations of development represent a paradigm shift (Gore 2000; Harriss 2002: 78), but few would deny that the discourse of substantial change has gained a social resonance, to the extent that Fine asserts that 'even before the old [Washington] consensus has been decently buried, the pretender to its throne is already grabbing at the crown in a palace revolution' (1999: 2). Both Gore and Fine caution claims of novelty by highlighting the underlying endurance of neoliberalism and the fact that, in some ways SGR expresses an attempt to deepen and extend the social relations of the free market. This sense of SGR as a consolidation of a process initiated by FGR is present in the literature on key Bank publications. In reviewing Bank documents published during the SGR period, some authors have identified how World Bank 'new thinking' is actually premissed on the acceptance of the 'first generation' fundamentals set out in the 'Berg report'. Loxley reviews *Adjustment in Africa: Reforms, Results, and the Road Ahead* (World Bank 1994a) and finds that the study is a 'throwback to the ideological evangelism of the early 1980s' (Loxley 1995: 266). Analysing the Bank's *The State in a Changing World* (World Bank

1997), Moore finds that the report 'is no radical departure from neo liberal development principles' (Moore 1999: 61). Most recently, Watkins argues that the 2000/2001 *World Development Report* 'in the space of six months ... was transformed from a statement in favour of growth with equity into a restatement of the old Washington consensus of the 1980s' (Watkins 2000: 190). The key point here is that SGR is based on the ascendance, or victory, of neoliberal fundamentals. The second generation can only flourish if the first generation has reached adulthood, and the relationship between the two is very much a gerontocracy. In light of this, our consideration of the World Bank and governance in Africa will develop an understanding of novel reforms based on a *consolidating orthodoxy* of neoliberalism which has produced a set of 'graduated' states (moving from first to second generation reform) collectively known as governance states.

Discursively, however, SGR does constitute an innovation in Bank strategy and thinking. There are two points to note by way of general context. First, structural adjustment has moved from a programme of reforms to be implemented over a defined period to a kind of rolling set of policy imperatives that aspire to embed themselves deeply within the sinews of the state. Originally, the Structural Adjustment Programme (SAP) was to be a short-term expedient, projected to last for five years (Caufield 1998: 146), but now it has enjoyed a longer reign than any development paradigm (Gibbon 1995: 140). By the early 1990s, 29 African states had undergone more than five years of continuous adjustment (World Bank 1994a: 36, Table 1.3) and there were few signs of adjustment coming to any form of conclusion. Thus, SAP developed from conjunctural necessity (associated with 'shock therapy') to something more akin to a 'structuring' or disciplining of state policy. As such, SAP has become an intimate and integrated part of 'statehood'. Managing the 'two constituencies' of domestic citizenries and Washington boardrooms (Mkandawire 1999) became a rule, not an exception. As a result, SAP is part of African political history, not a 'moment' of external intervention, as we shall detail in Chapter 2.

Second, the success of Southeast Asia could not be ignored by the World Bank (Callaghy 2001: 138). It seemed that the economic success of states such as South Korea was based not on neoliberal fundamentals, nor on 'getting the prices right', but on strong state intervention, and 'getting the prices wrong' in Alice Amsden's influential phrase. The question this raised could hardly be more important: does the success of Southeast Asian developmental states demonstrate that the Bank has been forcing the wrong diagnosis and prognosis on sub Saharan Africa's indebted states? The Bank's response, filtered through its own domination by the United States (Wade 1996), was to publish a report on Southeast Asia (World Bank 1993), and gradually to 'bring the state back in' to its policy strategies during the 1990s (World Bank 1994a, 1997).

In sum, as many states implemented one SAP after another, it became clear that adjustment was not merely about 'one off' economic reforms through the mechanism of conditionality. SAP, and the broader involvement of external agencies that it implied, reconfigured the political form of the state. SAP has become embedded in the political tapestry of many post-colonial African states. This fact, in conjunction with the increasing attention given to the nature of the state in the Southeast Asian 'tigers', gave rise to a context in which the Bank could elaborate a framework and strategy of reform more closely focussed on the institutions and processes of state. The result was a strategy of SGR within a normative framework of good governance. This context played itself out within the more specific contradictions of structural adjustment in African states as the next section will show.

SGR and régimes of adjustment in Africa

It is worth noting the ways in which the Bank's experiences with SAP and FGR led it to re-focus its attention on the role of the state, because it is 'bringing the state back in' that is the prelude to SGR. There were two key processes from the SAP period which are worth mentioning here. First, it was clear that SAP was not 'working'. Rolling back the state did not automatically produce thriving and productive markets in its wake. Economies were not recovering (Mosley and Weeks 1993; Schatz 1994), forms of illicit economic activity (and corruption) were emerging, and rates of foreign direct investment were not increasing markedly despite the opening up of African economies (Collier 1999). Consequently, the Bank paid increasing attention to the *institutionalisation* of markets. Thus, the state, pushed to the sidelines as rent seeker, re-entered the analytical frame as a 'midwife' to the re-birth of an ordered market economy.

Second, it became apparent that a different kind of executive action was required for reforms that were not merely 'stroke of the pen' changes. Much of the first generation reform involved 'quick wins' and centralised executive decisions (of the 'revolutionary' type mentioned earlier), for example concerning the deregulation of exchange rates, the abolition of subsidies, or the removal of quotas and tariffs. SGR engages with a more complex set of issues, based on the understanding that key facets of the first generation are now 'locked in' as a kind of logic to state action – neither requiring constant invigilation (although surveillance does not cease – this is one of the key functions of the IMF) or politicisation (evoking donor/creditor action, debates and statements). Reform is now understood in terms of capacity, sequencing and attitudes, all of which replace centralised quick wins with deeper, incremental reform.

As we shall see throughout this book, SGR and governance enable massive amounts of finance and intervention from the World Bank. SGR is partly concerned to construct an appropriate system of government to allow governance states to absorb and operationalise funds and technical assistance (World Bank 1999: 4).

So far, we have identified a general context of change which the Bank had to engage with as the 1990s progressed; we have also identified key dynamics from the SAP period which 'pushed' for change in the Bank's approach to reforming African debtor states. It was within this context that the governance agenda was born. SGR refers to a sequencing of externally-driven socio-political engineering techniques which provide the opportunity for governance discourse and reform to emerge. A key development that we can glean from this is that the Bank's reform agenda has gone more deeply into the 'heart' of government. The Bank is now involved in supporting reform in the civil service, or public service more broadly, a key facet of SGR. It funds workshops which aim to inculcate a different work culture in the bureaucracy; it holds regular meetings within key ministries to monitor progress; it funds the installation of new frameworks of data management within the state, often based on computerisation; and it funds various monitoring processes based in surveys. This wide range of intimate interventions could hardly be effected solely through the crude politics of conditionality. In fact, in governance states where the SGR agenda has strongly established itself, conditionality has been de-emphasised in favour of a more complex set of donor-state relations, presented by the Bank in the introductory quotation to this section and analysed in Chapters 2 and 4.

Conclusion: governance states and the realm of governance

This chapter has moved between different levels of analysis in order to provide the context within which to locate governance states. The Bank's 'developmental' mandate, embedded as it is in ideals of capitalist progress, has encountered African states and economies beset with economic and political contradictions. Informal economies, fragile formal state capacity, conflict and economic marginalisation have led the Bank to intervene heavily and radically in African states, most notably from the early 1980s. These interventions have produced a subsequent cohort of contradictions, some of which are addressed within SGRs. Where SGR has internalised itself within the routines of state processes, governance states emerge. So, how do governance states fare in terms of the issues raised in this chapter? Has the Bank succeeded in creating the ordered capitalist development it cleaves to? Have more fundamental questions of statehood and political stability been addressed? How has the Bank negotiated its preponderance and intervention with the liberal ideals of partnership? These questions are addressed in Part II. The next two chapters return to our two main *dramatis personae* (the Bank and governance states) to give them more detailed theoretical reflection.

2 Governance states in Africa

Conceptualising the encounter
between the World Bank and the
sovereign frontier

Introduction

The previous chapter provided an overview of sub Saharan Africa's regional constitution as part of the global order. But the encounter that this book is interested in is more specific: we need to focus in from the global order to the World Bank in particular and from the African region to a sub-set of governance states. This chapter introduces the latter, and Chapter 3 will introduce the World Bank in more detail.

The purposes of this chapter are threefold. In the first place, we shall specify how the concept of sovereignty can be made to serve as a way to narrate the development of governance states. This section will introduce the notion of a sovereign frontier. Second, we shall provide a historical review of the genesis of governance states in Tanzania, Uganda, and Mozambique. This provides us with a sense of agency in the construction of governance states that eludes more synchronic analyses. Third, we shall provide a more detailed description of the key features of governance states, in order to establish that there is a robust categorisation to be made between different states in the African region.

Beyond sovereignty

It is already evident that analysing the World Bank requires careful reflection. It is an institution with its own identity, but it also conditioned in crucial ways by changing discourses of development and patterns of market relations; it has also been subjected to diverse interpretations. We have also seen how this complex and powerful global institution acts in ways that are mediated through its encounters with specific regions within the global political economy in ways that are historically mediated, that is, based on previous successes, failures, and unintended outcomes.

It would be very neat, analytically speaking, to portray the Bank as a coherent institution with a simple direction or logic of action. This would then allow us to consider the Bank's actions on specific states in the standard fashion: the ontology of internal/external. It would then only require

a slight hybridisation of Realist International Relations theory to charac-
terise the Bank as a quasi-state institution – another 'black box' that
imposes its will across the sovereign boundary by virtue of its superior
power. However, the more complex ensemble of considerations that we
have outlined to define the Bank and African states in the previous
chapter raises the important question of whether the notion of sovereignty is suitable to analyse Bank interventions in African states and
societies.

These concerns are only amplified with other considerations. We have
already suggested that the Bank has been a powerful actor in African
states for the last fifty years; assuming a discrete 'starting point' for 'intervention' in a realm of sovereignty is hardly useful in this respect. Historically speaking, African politics *is* partly World Bank politics. Furthermore,
almost all of the theorising of the African state since the late 1960s has
urged us to consider sovereignty as either fragile, problematic or non-
existent. This is perhaps the only theme that endures and unites writings
on African politics. We can briefly reflect on some examples. Early post-
colonial analyses, taking from Hamza Alavi, Nicos Poulantzas, dependency theory, and radical African scholarship (a good example being the
University of Dar es Salaam throughout the 1970s) argued that the state
was 'overdeveloped', 'dependent' and subject to neo-colonialism or imperialism (Rhodes 1970; Charney 1987; Fanon 1990). Rodney encapsulates
the perspective of this writing: 'Today in many African countries foreign
ownership is still present, although the armies and flags of foreign powers
have been removed' (Rodney 1972: 31).

Within the International Relations literature, Jackson's influential work
argues that sovereignty is juridical rather than empirical (1990; Jackson
and Rosberg 1982). Sovereignty is maintained by the states system, even if
its 'Weberian substance' is very weak. The picture that Jackson paints is of
states that are dependent on the international system for their recognition
and affirmation; domestic sovereignty may well be a different matter.
Clapham terms the kind of sovereignty that this produces 'letterbox sovereignty': whoever opens the diplomatic mail retains internationally-
constructed juridical statehood (1996: 20).

Writing in the late 1980s developed an awareness of the ways in which
African societies disengaged, evaded and undermined the state, especially
as economic crisis set in during the seventies. This perspective focussed on
illicit trade, the 'revenge'; of civil society (Bayart 1986) and peasants
taking the 'exit option' (Hydén 1980). Relatedly, recent arguments have
been made about the 'extraversion' of the state (Bayart 2000) whereby
states are extremely weak *vis à vis* the global system, relying on 'ruses'
(Hibou 1998) and globalised 'shadow economies' (Reno 1995) to engage
with global forces. One could add to this brief review, but it serves to
emphasise that one cannot start with a concept of sovereignty and then put
it to work on the Bank–state encounter in Africa: it is empirically too pro-

visional and theoretically too contested. The content of sovereignty, even in its fundamentals, is still unclear.

The fact that sovereignty as commonly understood is absent from Africa does not necessarily mean that we should abandon the concept. The question is its heuristic value: whether it provides us with a productive focus to analyse the interaction of governance states and the World Bank. It is worth noting that by the time the concept has been through the various approaches outlined above, it has already gathered a series of caveats that need to be borne in mind concerning the external sources of sovereign power, the incomplete or tenuous nature of state monopolies over violence, and the lack of state 'presence' throughout a national territory. The concept of sovereignty necessarily posits a state of self-containment or inviolateness that exists before intervention which, as noted above, is not relevant to the Bank's 50 years of lending, technical assistance, policy advice, conditionality and general politicking. Sovereignty readily appears to be encumbered rather than strengthened by the caveats that have accreted to it.

If not sovereignty, then what? One of the reasons why this concept endures despite its heavy clothing of provisos is that, conceptually, outside the notion of sovereignty, there are only spaces and grey areas. Furthermore, the concept of sovereignty is frequently *evoked* by states and institutions, and it maintains a powerful presence in political discourse. Sovereignty does connote issues of power and control that are extremely relevant to the Bank's intervention in governance states. One can read Ugandan president Yoweri Museveni's political speeches as one of the most eloquent invocations of sovereignty in contemporary Africa, but he is by no means alone.[1]

In essence, it is the ontology of the notion of sovereignty that needs attention. Modern sovereign states are intrinsically territorial (Krasner 1999: 20), cartographically defined before they gain their social and political content. But it is the notion of boundaries that has been most problematic for African states. Freund (1998: 79) describes the creation of the modern boundaries of African states – a result of the Treaty of Berlin (1884/5) – as 'handshake over new African boundaries at European conference tables'. Many African societies related to these delimitations far more effectively than Western academe, crossing them, using them to their advantage, and respecting them provisionally when the state succeeds in compelling them to; in other words treating sovereignty as a *frontier*, not a boundary.

Palan makes the distinction between boundaries and frontiers as follows: 'Geographers distinguish between the concept of boundary and frontier: boundaries are lines, frontiers are zones' (2000: 1). A sovereignty 'zone' is not linear; it defines a *space* within which different actors can work to define sovereignty in different ways, and it produces a less severe delimitation of one territory from another. In other words, a sovereign frontier is formed by the interaction of forces therein, rather than by the delimitation between one space and another. The notion of a sovereign frontier moves us away from the limiting concerns of 'external imposition', 'national independence', 'self-determination' and so on, that often insinuate studies of the encounter between African states and external agencies. It means that we do not have to 'solve' the apparent contradiction that the Bank both undermines sovereignty (as a boundary) through conditionality and strengthens it through its lending to states. Instead, we can understand the Bank as working within the sovereign frontier to constitute a specific role for governance states as mediators of African societies' interactions with global forces. Also within this frontier, governance states evoke national sovereignty as a discourse to support their own actions against the Bank, with the Bank, or perhaps against classes and social groups within their own national spaces. The conceptual expansion from a 'line' to a 'zone' allows us to consider the 'content' of sovereignty – its construction, discourse, the interplay between actors – more fully than would be possible if we were merely concerned with the extent to which an imagined boundary has been defended or violated.

These reflections on sovereignty are central to our analysis of governance states. Governance states are constructed in large part through the actions of international organisations, led by the World Bank. As such, the nature of the sovereign frontier in these states is pivotal. The next section will introduce governance states more fully. Rather than approaching these states through narratives of statehood and intervention, the focus will be on the historical development of the sovereign frontier. The Bank, African states and other actors have involved themselves in this frontier; there have been periods where the frontier resembles a boundary more closely, and periods where the frontier is characterised by extreme turbulence. It is a frontier that is immanently neither 'national' nor 'global'; in fact it is the liminal properties of the sovereign frontier that interest us. By taking this approach in the next section the key properties of governance states will become apparent.

The history of governance states

Post-colonial sovereigns: development and socialism

Tanzania and Uganda gained their independence in 1961 and 1962 respectively; Mozambique gained its independence in 1974 after an armed struggle of liberation against the Portuguese (Isaacman and Isaacman 1983; Mondlane 1983). Each post-colonial state was very much a product of the nature of the late colonial period when European colonial powers opened up limited aspects of state power to Africans, and of the nature of African nationalism in each state (Mamdani 1976: 147 *et seq.*). Tanzanian nationalism was expressed through a variety of different organisations

(Coulson 1982: 101 *et seq.*; Mueller 1981), some strongly based in local considerations, but from the eve of independence, the force of nationalist demands was channelled through the Tanganyika African National Union (TANU), the party that inherited the state and has remained in power until the present day.[2]

Ugandan nationalism had not effectively unified around a single political organisation by the time of independence. Instead, three socio-political blocs – expressions of regional, class and confessional differences among the Ugandan elite – produced three political parties that contested elections.[3] Milton Obote's Ugandan Peoples Congress (UPC) won the post-independence elections in coalition with Kabaka Yekka (KY). Shortly after this victory, Obote set about confining the political space for the opposition, until a single party constitution was promulgated in 1966, abandoning KY. In that year, the so-called 'post-box constitution' was instituted, the nick-name deriving from the fact that the constitution was issued by Prime Minister Obote without any discussion in the Ugandan Parliament. The constitution banned political parties and ended the Buganda monarchy, both sources of independent political power. In 1971, Idi Amin came to power through a *coup* when Obote was out of the country, establishing a populist and initially developmentalist (Nabuguzi 1995: 196) régime that became increasingly brutal from about 1973 (Mutibwa 1992).

In 1974, the *Frente de Libertação de Moçambique* (Frelimo) inherited power by virtue of its guerrilla struggle in the north of the country (Munslow 1983). The Lusaka Accord between the Portuguese government and Frelimo stated that Frelimo was the legitimate expression of the will of the Mozambican people. From 1977, Frelimo boldly set out a 'Marxist–Leninist' development framework in which Mozambique would transform itself into a developed socialist economy. The key aims of the Mozambican state were to create communal villages, state farms and develop a state-owned industrial sector (Egerö 1990; Hanlon 1990).

Each of these countries experienced a centralisation of power around a single political organisation that had established sufficient power in the run-up to independence to monopolise the state afterwards. The party-state form that emerged in all three countries, although distinct and different in many ways, produced similar political patterns and processes. Interestingly, despite different ideological currents, histories and social bases, each party-state declared an affinity with socialism. Tanzania's first president, Julius Nyerere, made the most eloquent expression of this political alignment, marrying a concept of African 'familyhood' with socialism's developmental promise (Nyerere 1967; Legum and Mmari 1995). It is also well-recognised that Mozambique's first president, Samora Machel[4] professed a strong desire to establish socialism in Mozambique (Machel and Munslow 1985; Christie 1989). It is less well recognised that Obote also declared a 'turn to the left', after his monopolisation of power.

None of these states was socialist in any easily recognisable sense. Rather, socialism provided a very effective discourse to integrate a range of state strategies oriented towards the maintenance of power and the prosecution of development strategies. It is clear, however, that some states took socialism more seriously than others: Uganda's socialism was weakly formulated and made relatively little difference to policy;[5] Mozambique's socialism infused all aspects of state action and led to radical and concerted programmes by the state (Saul 1985). Nevertheless, one can understand the emergence of socialist language as a discourse to express a desire to consolidate state power and use that power to order, engineer and materially develop the societies within post-colonial state spatial boundaries, even if these forms of public action were implemented with greater or lesser amounts of effort.

Uganda, Mozambique and Tanzania each became single-party states immediately or shortly after independence. This allowed a specific social elite to capture power, and this always involved the marginalisation of other elite groups from the state. In Uganda's case the northern based and protestant elites were marginalized, as well as those within and around the Bugandan monarchy (Apter 1997). In Tanzania regionally-based petty bourgeois farmers and traders were marginalized, detained, and/or co-opted into *Chama cha Mapinduzi* (CCM), which displayed a strong corporatist tendency (Yeager 1982: 53). In Mozambique, Frelimo interned political opponents, banned opposition parties and deposed the chieftaincy system (Geffray 1991). The story in each case is one of a desire to centralise and consolidate the power of an elite born out of party through control of the state. Control of the state rapidly became the all-or-nothing focus of politics in each country.[6]

Socialism legitimised this jealous control of the state: opposing elites could be named as 'counter-revolutionary'; state-party mandate could be presented as the 'will of the people'; external intervention could be portrayed as 'imperialist'.[7] 'The masses' could be evoked as a kind of silent but legitimising constituency for a range of state actions that, in reality, were executed with negligible input from the masses, or in some cases (most strikingly during villagisation in Tanzania and Mozambique) against the wishes of peasant communities.

Socialism enjoyed a high level of attractiveness throughout the post-colonial world in the 1960s and early 1970s because it seemed to provide a framework through which to tackle 'late development' (White *et al.* 1983). The template was set by Josef Stalin: the Plan.[8] Each of our three cases embraced the Plan, rolling over three, five or even ten years. The Plan allowed states to set out bold indicative investment schedules, weighted towards social provision and investment in state-owned industries (the latter most prominent in Tanzania). 'Development' became a strong signifier of state legitimacy in each state; it was articulated as a series of top-down state interventions to integrate societies into the state's remit, to provide social services (most importantly basic health care and education), to produce powerful icons of modernity such as large industries and infra-structural investments, and to further the integration of peasant farming into the formal economy dominated by the state (Bernstein 1981).

The sovereign frontier of these states during this period varied from case to case. During this period, these three states could not readily be cat-egorised apart from other states in Africa. Mozambique's Portuguese colo-nial legacy marked this country apart from the other two, and although Tanzania and Uganda were products of British imperialism and were both members of the East African Community (EAC), there were substantial differences in each country's relations with external agents.

Uganda initially maintained close commercial relations with Britain and portrayed itself as a moderate and open political economy. General Western attitudes towards Uganda were that it represented a more 'responsible' and potentially progressive state: the first Five Year Plan relied on external sources for 48 per cent of its finance (Mamdani 1976: 264; Brett 1995a: 313). In 1968, 74 per cent of the 'professional' cadres within the civil service were expatriates (Tata 1996: 135). However, Obote's gradual 'shift to the left' from 1967 cooled Uganda's relations with Western external donors and led to an increase in Soviet assistance. In 1971, Idi Amin seized power for the military, rapidly crushing sources of opposition (within society and the Army itself). Amin maintained the essentials of the developmentalist model set out by Obote, but the expan-sion of state infrastructure in the early 1970s, bolstered by the alienation of Ugandan-Asian property from 1972,[9] collapsed into a situation where the state was vastly overextended, public service employees were substan-tially demotivated, civic order had evaporated, and routine human rights abuses were effected by the military (Omara-Otunnu 1987). Once Amin came to power, relations with the West worsened rapidly and Amin aligned Uganda with certain Arab states.

Tanzania maintained a similar relationship with Britain as Uganda for the first five years after independence.[10] After the Arusha Declaration in 1967, which set out a socialist vision for Tanzania's future, Tanzania's rela-tions with external donors changed. Nyerere was a strong supporter of the Non Aligned Movement, and maintained a strong sense of Tanzanian and African nationalism which led the Tanzanian state to develop relations with a wide variety of actors. Tanzania's *ujamaa* socialism was supported by progressive NGOs, Scandinavian states (Elgstrom 1999) and China (Ping 1999).[11] During the presidency of Peter McNamara, the World Bank also gave significant support to Tanzania, for example funding the (*ujamaa*) Village Management Training Project. In 1969, Tanzania broke diplomatic relations with Britain over Rhodesia, as well as cutting ties with the USA and West Germany over matters relating to political non-alignment.

The heavy involvement of external donors in the *ujamaa* project[12] meant that, despite its strong nationalism, Tanzania became heavily dependent on external sources of funding for its national-socialist project. The conditions that the Tanzanian government set in the sovereign frontier were that agencies could only involve themselves if they adhered to the parameters of Tanzanian socialism. This led some agencies to involve themselves in projects with unintended consequences that they would not ordinarily accept. For example Oxfam supported the villagisation project, despite the compulsion and the deleterious social effects of this programme (Jennings 2001). The World Bank supported agricultural projects, again under the rubric of *ujamaa*, which was premised on the expansion of the state into the economy. In sum, the powerful discourse of Tanzanian nationalism and *ujamaa* captured the sovereign frontier and set formative conditions for the entry of other agencies; but, in spite of this, Tanzania became increasingly dependent on external sources of resources.

Mozambique parallels Tanzania in some respects.[13] It also declared a non-aligned approach to foreign relations, receiving external support from the Soviet Union and China, as well as other states in the Soviet bloc such as East Germany and Romania. The 'high modernism' of Mozambique's socialism was perhaps most clearly expressed in the Romanian-supported 400,000-hectare scheme – a 'factories in the field' design for agricultural development. Mozambique also developed close relations with the so-called like-minded states (Scandinavia and Canada) (Littlejohn 1988). The World Bank had no presence in Mozambique at this time. But, Mozambique's sovereign frontier was far less stable than Tanzania's because of the ongoing civil conflict in the country which involved a complex array of external actors. Most obviously, South Africa supported the anti-government guerrilla force, Renamo (Fauvet 1984). Beyond this, an array of conservative groups also supported Renamo (Jordan 1983; Vines 1991). Frelimo received military support from the Soviet bloc, and suffered hostile relations with the US. In essence, the rural insurgency prosecuted by Renamo (which involved a strategy of destruction and violence rather than a 'hearts and minds' political campaign) drew Mozambique heavily into the security politics of the Cold War and South Africa's regional war against radical nationalism in the region (Birmingham 1992). As such, Mozambique's sovereign frontier has, like Tanzania's, been pervaded by external agencies, producing a high level of dependency on outside sources of funding, but the frontier has been policed by the Mozambican state not only through concerns with national/socialist development, but also concerns with security. Military aid constituted a large component of external funding, especially from the Soviet Union.

All three countries (Uganda only up until 1971) developed an increasing reliance on external sources of funding.[14] Each state managed, relatively effectively with hindsight, to produce a stable frontier within which regulations and discourses of development and socialism induced external agencies into a statist paradigm. The key economic lever that maintained this state of affairs was the maintenance of government-controlled exchange rates, leading to overvalued currencies in all three cases. Never-theless, these broad characterisations should not detract from the diversity between the three countries in this period; and indeed, the commonalities that these three share were also present in many other African states.

The crisis of developmentalism

Whatever stability states managed to construct within the sovereign fron-tier was substantially eroded by 1979. This was a result of inauspicious changes in the global economy which began in 1973 but 'peaked' in 1979 with the second oil price hike, a fall in coffee and other agricultural export prices and the onset of recession in most of the world's major capitalist economies (Lawrence 1986; Szeftel 1987). We will return to these changes in Chapter 3, but for now, let us reflect on the three case studies and the ways in which sovereign frontiers moved into flux after a period of relative stability.

Amin was ousted from power in 1979 and, after a brief interlude, Obote returned to power in elections that were not clearly free and fair. Amin had brutalised Uganda's people and destroyed its national infrastructure; Obote's contested election led to more conflict in which the Ugandan army acted at least as brutally as it had done during Amin. The global slowdown only served to underline this persistent decline: Uganda's terms of trade fell from 158 to 45 between 1977 and 1981 (Mamdani 1990: 432).

Tanzania also suffered a series of external shocks over the same period: the deleterious consequences of the break-up of the EAC in 1976, a drought in 1979, flooding in 1980 and the entry of Tanzania into the Ugandan conflicts from 1979. Each of these tipped a high level of depend-ency into a full-blown economic crisis. These external 'shocks' impacted on a national-socialist project that was suffering under the weight of its own contradictions. From 1974 to 1976, the Tanzanian government carried out a nation-wide compulsory villagisation programme, producing villages with heavy demands for social provision, disrupting existing peasant pat-terns of production (Shao 1986) and reproduction from the late 1970s and into the 1980s. Investment in parastatals continued at high levels, but pro-ductivity remained low throughout the 1980s.

In Mozambique, the optimism of the early 1970s did not last into the 1980s. A Decade for the Victory over Underdevelopment was declared in 1979, to commence in 1980, but was all but abandoned by 1983.[15] In 1983, Mozambique was refused membership of COMECON, which would have opened up large amounts of financial and military support from the USSR. Villagisation had produced many of the same problems as it had in Tanza-nia (Casal 1988), and the authoritarian nature of villagisation also exacer-bated the Renamo war (Geffray and Pedersen 1986).[16]

These brief overviews could be given a lot more detail, but the central point here is that each of these three states suffered profound blows to their national-developmental programmes. For Uganda and Mozambique, basic issues of public order, rather than public action for development, became most pressing; in Tanzania, political order was maintained to an impressive extent, but the economics of *ujamaa* socialism became increasingly unsustainable.

The palpable failure of national-developmental programmes, a conjuncture of global and national changes, rendered states less powerful and consistent actors in the sovereign frontier. Indebtedness and reliance on external agencies became more intense, and as economic growth slowed, these flows of resources came to reflect a shift in power in the sovereign frontier. External agencies tended to involve themselves in the three cases less through a framework of state-defined national planning and more as 'donors' to states that increasingly resembled mendicants. The discourse of developmentalism and national-socialism weakened into a discourse of contingency, assistance and – significantly – conditionality.

Conditionality expresses a principle that diffused itself throughout the sovereign frontier and radically changed the nature of state relations with international organisations. One can starkly represent conditionality as a kind of reversal: donors once involved themselves in countries through conditions set by African states; during the 1980s, donors involved themselves in African states on the conditions set by external agents upon African states. The World Bank and the IMF were the architects of this shift in the sovereign frontier. The conditionality that reconstructed the sovereign frontier constituted a set of policy changes, both central to the economic thinking of the World Bank and IMF. These policy changes were packaged into Structural Adjustment Programmes (SAPs).

For Tanzania, the economic problems of the late 1970s produced a very high level of aid dependency (Yeager 1982: 77). Tanzania received a standby credit with the IMF in 1979.[17] This was a standard credit that any member of the IMF could draw on if necessary; it came with relatively few strings attached, but it did set off a volatile contest of authority between the Tanzanian government and the International Finance Institutions. Nevertheless, Tanzania maintained a high degree of public order and general loyalty to the state throughout the 1980s, when the economy declined drastically. The ideology of *ujamaa*, and Tanzanian nationalism more generally, remained robust and relied substantially on the powerful imagery and status of Julius Nyerere. As such, the government was extremely chary to implement SAP policies with the World Bank and IMF as authors. Tanzania's sovereign frontier was characterised by a contest between external conditionality, substantive economic weakness, and a persistent defence of the national-developmental model. The awkward resolution of this contest was that the Tanzanian government implemented many of the policies contained within SAPs, but under its own authorship and without IFI funding: in 1981 it announced the short-lived National Economic Survival Plan (NESP), and from 1982 to 1983 it implemented its 'home-grown' SAP (Stein 1992). These 'Tanzanian' SAPs served to defend the discourse of national development in the sovereign frontier even if, in effect, many aspects of World Bank policy had been introduced.

Thus, the first half of the 1980s was characterised by high levels of tension between the IMF and the Tanzanian government. The NESP included a number of liberalisation measures, but an accord with the IMF was blocked by apparently fundamental disagreements over devaluation, which became a symbol of national sovereignty (Malima 1986; Singh 1986; Loxley 1989). As Tanzania's home grown reforms failed, the economy went further into crisis, and bilateral donors (as they have done elsewhere) premised their contributions on a reconciliation with the IMF (Stein 1992: 70). In 1986 a standby agreement was signed, followed by the implementation of a Structural Adjustment Facility and an Economic Recovery Programme (ERP), funded by the World Bank. This signing in 1986 took place after Nyerere retired as president, symbolising the ideological shift in power away from *ujamaa* and towards conditionality. In sum, Tanzania defended the nationalist-developmentalist nature of the sovereign frontier relatively effectively, producing a period of turbulence in Tanzania's external relations through the 1980s. But, by the end of the decade – in 1989 a second Bank-funded SAP, named the Economic and Social Adjustment Programme (1989–1992) was implemented – the régime of conditionality had gained ascendancy.

Mozambique's national socialism was clearly unsustainable from the early 1980s. As well as suffering external economic shocks and the contradictions of an authoritarian and rapid social engineering that went with socialist modernisation, the Mozambican government had to contend with the Renamo war, fuelled as it was by South Africa's strategy of destabilisation. At no point during the 1980s did the Mozambican government have full control of the national territory; much of the social provision that Frelimo invested in during the second half of the 1970s was destroyed or left to decay as a result of actions by Renamo. The financial cost of the war for the Mozambican state has been estimated to be as high as $15 billion (Hanlon 1991: 40–2).

Mozambique was not a member of the World Bank or IMF until 1984.[18] Like Tanzania, Mozambique maintained a strong ideological hostility to the IFIs, based in notions of socialism, national development and sovereignty. But, also like Tanzania, Mozambique simply could not continue to prosecute its programme of socialist development. This square was circled by implementing a hybrid structural adjustment programme under the authorship of the Mozambican government without IFI funding – the Economic Action Programme (1984–1986). Mozambique used the mechanism of 'autobiographical' SAP to defend a claim to national self-determination in regard to development policy, even if the content of that policy had been set externally.

As mentioned earlier, Mozambique failed to join COMECON in 1983. This was a pivotal moment in Mozambique's diplomatic relations, marking a shift away from the eastern bloc and towards a rapprochement with Western states. The 1984 Nkomati Accord signed with South Africa to establish mutual non-aggression (subsequently violated by South Africa) was partly a signal to the US of a changed attitude. Mozambique suffered a terrible drought and famine in 1984, but the US conditioned food aid on a 'moderation' in Mozambique's foreign policy (Abrahamsson and Nilsson 1995: 107). Also, as already noted, in 1984, Mozambique joined the World Bank. In the late 1980s, the right-wing government in the US warmed to Frelimo, and an equally doctrinaire Conservative government in the UK actively supported Frelimo in its war against Renamo (Vines 1991). This reveals how the considerations of diplomacy, security and the war strongly influenced Mozambique's sovereign frontier, marking it apart from Tanzania in important respects. Mozambique's capitulation to a régime of conditionality within the sovereign frontier was a result of the pounding the state received from the Renamo war, and its reconciliation with the West derived not just from the World Bank and IMF but also from increased security co-operation and the influx of emergency relief NGOs (Hanlon 1991; Saul 1990).

Just as importantly, the Renamo war continued throughout SAP. Mozambique implemented its first Bank-funded SAP – the ERP – in 1987. The effects of the ERP exacerbated the social disaster created by the war (Marshall 1992). The exacerbation of the human costs of war by budgetary cut-backs the inflationary effects of devaluation and the removal of subsidies (O'Laughlin 1996) led Frelimo to contest the sovereign frontier through a defence of the high prioritisation of social welfare that Frelimo's socialism contained. Thus, although the language of socialism was only employed domestically and more in the fashion of a ritual than as a concerted focus for state action, Frelimo contested the actions of the IFIs by representing itself as the defender of Mozambique's social well-being.

Uganda under Obote's second régime (Obote II) ushered in a modest warming of relations with the West. From 1982 to 1984, Uganda implemented a World Bank-sponsored SAP[19] four years before SAP was implemented in our other two cases. This involved the 'usual package of policy requirements' (Brett 1995a: 314), backed up by external assistance estimated as high as $1 billion. (ibid.: 315). On paper, the SAP appeared to produce positive economic effects in its initial years, but by 1984 the increasing levels of civil disorder led the government of Uganda to violate the conditions of the programme mainly through increased military expenditure, and the World Bank withdrew.

In 1986, the National Resistance Movement (NRM) came to power, after Obote's overthrow and a short-lived series of intermediate military régimes (Mutibwa 1992). The NRM established an impressive level of civic order and rule of law after such a protracted period of instability and violence (Brett 1994). Initially, the NRM cleaved to an economic model based in the kind of nationalist developmentalism which was crumbling in Mozambique and Tanzania,[20] including *re*valuing the currency and rationing (Bernt Hansen and Twaddle 1998: 7). The close relations between the World Bank and the government of Uganda under Obote II rendered the NRM leadership (which had been fighting Obote II and perceived the Bank as supporting its enemy) ideologically hostile to structural adjustment.

Nevertheless, as a result of the economic devastation that Uganda had suffered (effectively since the late 1960s)[21] and the inauspicious global context, Uganda's moment of economic *dirigisme* was brief and ineffective as a template for economic recovery. By 1987, a group within the NRM leadership, closely focussed around President Museveni who established a cabal of key people (within the powerful Presidential Economic Council) with whom he consulted, mooted the adoption of neoliberal policy reform as the only way to re-establish the Ugandan economy (Langseth *et al.* 1995). By 1987, Uganda adopted a World Bank-funded SAP (Economic Recovery Programme) and a Structural Adjustment Facility (SAF) loan from the IMF. In 1989, Uganda embarked upon an enhanced SAF. Thus, Uganda entered the 1980s with a sovereign frontier that engaged the state with the World Bank and its régime of conditionality and it left the decade in the same situation but under a different régime. The interval between these two moments was very unstable as a result of civil war and a failure of the state to establish a minimal degree of law and order. It was only in the late 1980s that an orderly patterning of relations within the sovereign frontier became a real possibility.

Taken together, the three countries arrive at an interesting conjuncture by the end of the 1980s. In spite of their different post-colonial trajectories, each of the three arrived at the same point. In the 1960s, like most countries in Africa, these three embarked on national-developmentalist programmes strongly based in the expansion of state intervention. This model was fatally wounded as a result of its own contradictions, civil conflict, and changes in the global economy. After a period of instability and contestation within the sovereign frontier, each adopted a SAP in the mid 1980s. These SAPs were implemented more or less willingly and with varying degrees of policy 'slippage' (Mosley *et al.* 1991). By 1989, all three had just embarked upon a second round of adjustment measures – Tanzania's ESAP, Mozambique's Social and Economic Recovery Programme (SERP), and Uganda's rapid 'catch-up' to an Enhanced Structural Adjustment Facility under the IMF with a continuing Bank SAP running concurrently. The sovereign frontier for all three cases had irrevocably moved from nationalist developmentalism to neoliberal conditionality.

Re-stabilising the frontier

> Opportunities for reform often arise from economic or political crises
> that inspire ... political elites to demand changes in the status quo and
> search for new solutions to long-standing problems.
>
> (World Bank 2003: 57)

It should be emphasised that the denouement of the 1980s was not the
smooth establishment of a new and generally-accepted politics within the
sovereign frontier, based on conditionality and the increasing pre-
eminence of the World Bank and IMF. Rather, the 1980s demonstrated
that the previous political form of national developmentalism had collapsed, and that the nearest potential discursive and programmatic
replacement was that maintained by the World Bank and others. Mozambique, Tanzania and Uganda all desired a re-stabilisation of their sovereign frontiers, but they were also keenly aware that the World Bank
'model' involved a substantial reduction of state influence within the frontier. In other words, re-stabilisation came at the price of a massive increase
in IFI power in the frontier. The choice was, in essence, instability or the
preponderance of the IFIs. Governance states constitute an attempted resolution of this dilemma.

The early 1990s witnessed the playing out of the tensions inherent in re-
stabilisation. Divisions emerged within ruling elites as the Bank consolidated its power in the frontier, stimulating nationalist sensitivities. In
Mozambique, a ruling party renowned for its unity developed a schism
between so-called 'old' and 'new' factions, the latter resigned to the Bank
model of political economy, the former still evoking the ideals of national
self-determination and socialism (Simpson 1993). In Tanzania and
Uganda, the key post of Minister of Finance became a symbol of tensions
and their resolution: there was donor pressure to oust Kigoma Malima as
Finance Minister in Tanzania (Bigsten *et al.* 1999: 31) and in 1992, in
Uganda, the Minister of Finance was sacked under pressure from the IFIs
(Brett 1995a: 320). Both Ministers were perceived as hostile to liberalisation. Tanzania's tensions concerning the restabilisation of the sovereign
frontier were particularly sharp. In 1993, Tanzania's Economic and Social
Adjustment Facility (ESAF) was suspended, followed by a general freeze
on donor funds for reform in 1994. This was a result of a deterioration in
state-donor relations that revolved centrally over corruption but it also
reflected a more general hostility within the Tanzanian government
towards external intervention in Tanzanian 'sovereign' affairs (Helleiner *et
al.* 1995). In 1995, Benjamin Mkapa was elected to the Presidency, ushering in a moderate and reformist executive, bent on rapprochement with
the IFIs. In 1996, the IMF renewed its cancelled ESAF and a consolidation
of a stable working relationship with external agencies was established
(Helleiner 1999).

As in Tanzania, so in Mozambique and Uganda. Moments of conflict are succeeded by the strengthening of pro-reform elements within the ruling elite and a strengthening of support for those elements by the IFIs and others. Perhaps Mozambique's most visible rupture and rapprochement commenced in 1995, when Sergio Leite, an IMF economist visiting Maputo in late 1995, asserted the need for wage constraint in order to avoid inflation, in spite of the fact that at least two thirds of the population were below the absolute poverty line. The IMF publicly stated that it was considering declaring Mozambique 'off-track'[22] in its macroeconomic fundamentals as a result. The Frelimo government condemned Leite's comments, as did some other donors and groups within Mozambican civil society.[23] The protest over Leite's comments produced a measured opposition to the IMF by the Bank and a tangible warming to the Mozambican state by the same. In February 1997, World Bank President James Wolfenson made a visit to Mozambique, symbolising the Bank's desire to maintain a strong relationship with Mozambique. He responded to Leite's comments thus: 'if people don't have a living wage, its hard to come down and attack them for corruption ... It's a two-way problem' (*Mozambique-file* March 1997). Wolfenson's words – less dogmatic and combative than any previous statements from the World Bank or IMF – pre-empted a change of mood in the next Paris Club meeting of bilateral donors (chaired by the Bank) and led to increased financial support for the Frelimo government (Harrison 1999a).

In Uganda, once Museveni had sided with the reforming clique, drastic public ruptures, such as those in Mozambique and Tanzania, were unlikely. Museveni's recent rise to power through a military organisation allowed a relatively high degree of conformity, demonstrated most clearly in the way the NRM managed the return of Asian property to its Ugandan-Asian Diaspora. In one sense, the former instability in Uganda allowed it to 'catch up' with Mozambique and Tanzania: the NRM faced very little resistance from long-entrenched, stable and ideologically settled cliques within the apparatus of the state (Langseth 1996).

In sum, by the mid 1990s, the uncertain and occasionally unstable sovereign frontier constructed around conditionality began to 'settle' (Figure 2.1). SAP became part of state routine; neoliberal rostrums moved significantly towards attaining hegemony within the economic bureaucracies, and external agencies gave increasingly strong support to adjusting states. In effect, external finance became the way to reproduce the state and the elite that depended on access to its institutions (Williams 1994). In the 1990s, Tanzania relied on aid for 30 per cent of its entire GDP (Bigsten *et al.* 1999: 3); Uganda relied on aid for 53 per cent of its public expenditure from 1990/1 to 1998/9 (Reinikka and Collier 2001) and 55 per cent of Uganda's national budget relied on external funding in financial year 2002–2003 (*Africa Confidential* September 2003). Since 1986, Mozambique has received $8 billion in external aid, an average of about $600 million

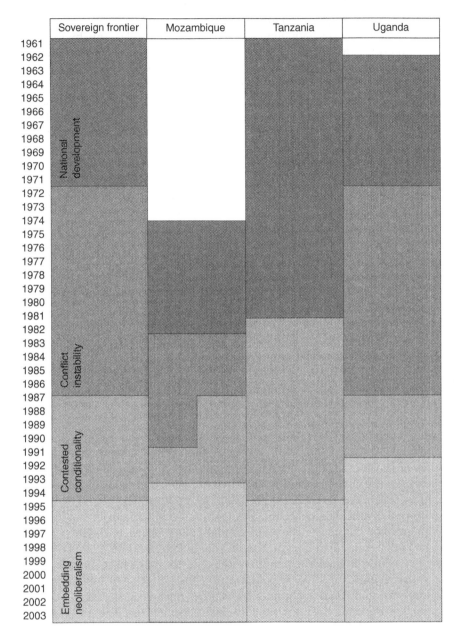

Figure 2.1 Governance states and the sovereign frontier: a timeline.

per year or 17 per cent of GDP; in the late 1990s 50 per cent of govern-ment spending and 75 per cent of public investments were funded exter-nally (World Bank 2000b: 4). This situation depended in its very constitution on the World Bank and IMF.

Governance states: key features

The narrative given in the previous section resembles a teleology: three states with very different political trajectories moving towards a single des-tination which allows us to draw them into a single categorisation. It should be clear, even from the brief political histories painted above, that these three countries were not embarked upon a single linear pathway towards attaining the condition of governance states. Nevertheless, it is the argu-ment of this book that the different political issues that emerged within each state were shaped by a global context, and that the resolution of these issues produced a historical 'narrowing' of difference between these three states – not in all aspects of political change, but certainly in respect to the reconstruction and modification of their sovereign frontiers. As we shall see in Part II, one key development in the World Bank's understanding of gov-ernance states has been to make strong differentiations between states in Africa by way of defining 'good' and 'bad' reformers. It is very clear that, for the Bank, Tanzania, Uganda and Mozambique are the three 'best cases' in Africa[24] in its gradation of reform success. In other words, the Bank (and many other external actors) perceives these states as 'select' and relates to them accordingly. It has now become an intrinsic part of these three states sovereign frontiers that they are defined as 'governance states' (not a phrase the Bank has ever used), set apart in some respects from other countries in the continent. This has produced a substantial modification in the régime of conditionality which will be detailed in Chapter 4.

What remains for this chapter is to make a clear account of the key fea-tures of governance states. There are four main components. In the first place, as implied above, these states have attained a 'showcase' status. Each of these three, but especially Uganda in the 1990s and Tanzania in the 2000s, has been evoked as proof that SAP works, that the World Bank has 'got it right', and that the contradictions within the sovereign frontier produced by conditionality can be resolved. Attaining this status has meant going through a 'trial of fire': the contemporary Highly Indebted Poor Countries (HIPC)[25] (those which have graduated from conditional-ity-based lending) underwent an average of six structural adjustment pro-grammes over the period from 1980 to 1991 (Loxley 2003: 124). Bank documents on each of the three countries reinforce this showcase status; the reports from 'Paris Club' and Consultative Group meetings generate a hubris along the same lines. One can see the same representations more strongly in the *Financial Times* country surveys and other country reports within elite media. For example:

This year [1999], the Washington-based international finance institutions have declared Tanzania to be the best macroeconomic reformer in Africa.

(Hydén 1999: 142)

an overall assessment is that today many bilateral donors see great potential in Tanzania.

(Bigsten, Mutalemwa, Tsikata and Wangwe 2001: 309)

[Tanzanian president] Mkapa has become the Western donors' latest African hero.

(*Africa Confidential* 24 November 2000: 4)

Uganda [is] the first and best-performing of the poor countries due to receive accelerated debt reduction.

(Bird 2000: 222)

Uganda is a star and a role model in international development for other countries, not only in Africa but also in the rest of the world.

(Clare Short, quoted in *New Vision*, 29 July 2000)

Mozambique has made enormous strides since the end of the war in 1992 ... Today the country is at peace, a market economy is in place, and substantial progress has been made on a challenging reform agenda, all leading to a growth rate the highest in the world.

(World Bank 2000b)

These three countries have constituted an apex atop of a continuum established by the World Bank largely as a result of research that has argued that policy-based lending (conditionality) has failed and that future lending should be undertaken *selectively* based on the policy environment of the debtor state (Collier 1999: 325; Burnside and Dollar 2000; Deverajan *et al.* 2001). This research argues that aid only 'works' in states where the institutional environment is generally effective, thus rendering governance states as *post hoc* aid successes. The external support for these three cases is easily seen in a massive profusion of externally-funded initiatives, all aimed at constructing and reconfiguring governance states (a pairing which will be returned to in Chapter 6). Uganda was the first country to receive enhanced HIPC status; Tanzania was the second, having been 'fast-tracked'; Mozambique gained HIPC status in 1998 and reached an 'accelerated' completion point in 2001.

Second, each of these three states experienced economic growth during the 1990s at rates that compare favourably with the continent generally (Table 2.1).

These rates of growth occurred after a period of protracted economic

Table 2.1 Rates of economic growth

GDP growth (annual percentage)	1998	2001	2002
Sub Saharan Africa	2	3	3
Mozambique	12.6	13.8	9.9
Tanzania	3.7	5.7	5.8
Uganda	5.6	4.6	6.3

Source: *World Bank Development Indicators* database, 2003, retrieved from http://devdata. worldbank.org/data-query/.

instability, stagnation or decline. This stagnation has in fact been a general trend for the entire continent. Of course, 'paper' improvements in economic indices are limited as to what they can tell us about the reality of economic change. The Bank has a rather dubious history of modifying its statistics and being unclear in its interpretation of data (see Chapter 6, note 3). However, the effect of these ostensible economic turnarounds is considerable. These three states allow the Bank (and others) to paint a picture of economic recovery for the first time since structural adjustment began in Africa in 1980. This both provides the Bank with justification for its interventions, and it generates a certain amount of extra political sway for the governments of these states. Officially 'healthy' levels of GNP growth binds these cases together and underpin much of the edifice of 'selectivity'.

Third, each of the three governance states have undergone some form of controlled political transition which has produced narratives of 'new beginnings'. Uganda's 'new beginning' is clearest: it commences with the victory of the NRM. Tanzania's moment of renewal is marked by the accession of Benjamin Mkapa to power in 1995; Mozambique's 'moment' is the end of civil war and elections in 1992 and 1994 respectively.[26] Bank documents each use these events to bolster a narrative of renewal, or a return to 'normality'. There is an imagery of the phoenix behind all of this – a governance renaissance forged out of the fires of previous instability, resistance to conditionality, and economic decline, something to which we will return in Chapter 6. One example of this, quite naïve in its patronising formulation, is a research report titled 'Tanzania: is the ugly duckling finally growing up?'[27] The common new beginnings (imagined or real) between governance states have been affirmed by the ascendance of 'reformers' within the state. Governance states require nothing less than the transformation of the culture of statecraft and the replacement of personnel that do not have the skills and motivation to pursue neoliberal reform agendas.

Fourth, governance states are stable and ordered states. In Chapter 1, it was noted that stability had constituted a key consideration in the way in which World Bank policies were 'regionalised' by the encounter with Africa. It remains the case today that large parts of Africa suffer from contested authority, military conflict, and an absence of public provision of infrastructure. The term 'collapsed' states was popularised very much with reference to Africa (Zartman 1995; Gros 1996). Tanzania is distinguished in its success in maintaining national integrity and state order; Uganda has made remarkable (but not complete) progress in reducing levels of violence and re-integrating its national territory. Mozambique's peace process and elections amazed all observers in the degree to which armed conflict ceased, demobilisation succeeded, and a new polity formed which allowed a former guerrilla movement to act (or try to act) as an opposition party (Manning 1998). In other words, these countries all have a strong degree of stability or have achieved a striking restabilisation after periods of seemingly intractable civil conflict. As we shall see especially in Chapter 6, the stability of governance states is not merely a question of order, but also of the social formation of stable ruling elites and 'bureaucratic structures that are insulated from political interference' (World Bank 1997: 160) in their determination to implement key aspects of the neoliberal programme.

These four features define governance states and draw our three cases together. They also provide distinctions which explain the specific relationship that these states have with the World Bank and other donors, as will become clear in Part II. What remains for this section is to give a more detailed account of the World Bank's actions within the sovereign frontier.

3 Conceptualising the World Bank

Governance and global régimes

Introduction

As we have already noted, governance expresses the rising influence of the World Bank in Africa from the 1980s to the present day. Governance states gain their sense of commonality through an increasingly powerful shaping of the sovereign frontier by the Bank once the nationalist-developmental sovereign frontier collapses. Chapter 1 established a basic set of operational 'imperatives' for the Bank, but these do not take us very far in understanding why the Bank has intervened so profoundly to re-shape a set of African states in ways that 'materialise' governance in certain African states. This chapter provides a theoretical framework to explain the emergence of governance in relation to changes in the World Bank's engagement with African states' sovereign frontiers. In doing so, the Bank's historical positioning within the international political economy will be detailed. As Chapter 2 demonstrated, today's governance states emerged confidently after independence under the banners of nationalism and socialism, lost that confidence during the 1970s, and pushed themselves bruisingly through a transition to conditionality. Here we can see that the Bank went through related processes. We will see how this historical experience led the Bank towards governance as a way to 'embed' the neoliberalism of the 1980s.

It is striking that the rise of governance has focussed unprecedented critical attention on the Bank. Until recently, theorising the Bank's expansive remit was limited. It is notable that the majority of research on the Bank before the 1990s was very 'dry' in that it rarely challenged the Bank's own assumptions and contained little reflection on theory and critique. Work was 'in-house'[1] and oriented towards making the Bank function more effectively within its own terms, what Cox (1996: 525) would dub 'problem-solving theory' with its innate conservatism (van der Laar 1980; Ascher 1983; Ayres 1983; Commins 1988). Other research focussed on specific aspects of World Bank programmes, making it unnecessary to conceptualise the Bank as an agent with a theoretically-informed ontology (Crane and Finkle 1981).[2] The Bank itself has promoted the depoliticisation of its interventions, producing a technicist discourse to evade critical analysis of its actions (Ferguson 1994; Harriss 2002). But, since 1990, interest in critically-oriented theorisations of the nature of the World Bank has emerged. These theorisations lend themselves to a distinction between two theories of Bank action, which will be engaged with in the next two sections. In doing so, we will have the beginnings for our own understanding of the Bank's elaboration of governance as a means to 're-embed' neoliberalism.

The World Bank as 'liberalism in action'

Although much of the text of the Bank's explicitly political work remains vague (Marquette 2001) and at times rather simplistic,[3] most authors recognise common contours to the Bank's political thinking which falls under the rubric of good governance. As already noted, effective governance, according to the World Bank, encompasses a series of institutional characteristics and parameters, notably transparency, predictability in decision making and the rule of law (World Bank 1992, 1994b). It also defines the limits of state action through a conceptualisation of the citizenry and civil society organisations. It is good governance that has attracted the attention of many researchers in politics and political economy to the Bank with unprecedented enthusiasm, and it is mainly within the realms of governance that writers move in order to construct critical analyses of the Bank.[4]

It is worth starting with an early contribution by Williams and Young (1994) which sets out an acute and critical appraisal of good governance and the Bank. Like most other authors examined in this chapter, Williams and Young are struck by the *scope* of the Bank's ambition. In a later article, David Williams begins by characterising good governance as the Bank's 'grand vision' (Williams 1996: 157), a vision that he subsequently identifies as involving the radical re-invention of the state and the identities of individuals in African societies (Williams 1999, 2001). But it is not merely the epochal potential of the governance agenda that the Bank has articulated, but its close relation to a certain ideology or, perhaps better, a certain form of philosophy-doctrine. For Williams, the key point is that governance is an expression of liberalism. Liberalism here refers to the political philosophy of universal individual rights derived from rational and self-interested selves and associated forms of state.[5]

Liberalism constitutes a field of norms and practices that provide a subjectivity through which individuals within the World Bank act. Liberalism is therefore, at least in part, constitutive of the World Bank's agency, pervading its complex institutional machinery and policing the ways in which governance is problematised and operationalised (Williams 1996: 160–2.). As such, liberalism acts as a 'working ideology' for the World

Bank (Williams and Young 1994: 92), and good governance provides this working ideology with an integrated and normatively attractive image.

The nub of Williams' work, then, is critically to evaluate the World Bank's expansive governance agenda as an expression of the intrinsic qualities of liberalism as an ideology-in-action.[6] The World Bank's 'institutional ontology' as an agency steeped in liberalism means that its actions necessarily promote the expansion of liberal capitalism throughout the world. Expressed in typically liberal terms which connote a non-antagonistic set of processes and relations (freeing people/institutions, dialogue and partnership, providing incentives, positive sum gains, checks and balances and so on), the Bank's project is in fact both procrustean and authoritarian. The Bank aims to *impose* liberalism on all societies within which it intervenes, whether these societies like it or not. Moving beyond this establishing critical point, Williams proceeds to argue that the Bank's universalising mission produces further contradictions: it relies on techniques of disciplining to effect supposedly natural or voluntary social changes; it intervenes in debtor societies in an extremely nebulous and detailed fashion in order to create liberal selves and appropriate institutions to police them; it affirms cultural pluralism but tailors this pluralism to the boundaries of liberal civil society;[7] and these interventions give the lie to the formal system of state sovereignty upon which the Bank is founded (Williams 2000).

In sum, the critique that Williams has developed portrays the World Bank as a form of 'liberal imperialism', using its immense control of resources to forge liberal selves, societies and states out of a plurality of cultures while hiding behind an ideology that denies its own authoritarianism through the evocation of governance as natural progress, partnership, neutrality and so on. This critique is powerful and very theoretically engaged. Anyone who has studied the Bank's actions and literature in specific places cannot help but be mindful of the framework Williams sets out. But, this approach has weaknesses as well. These weaknesses, which will be elaborated presently, relate closely to Williams's epistemology, notably, his desire to locate liberalism as the primary *problematique* in understanding the Bank.[8]

Liberalism and history

Liberalism is an ideology that has been at the centre of Western political thought for at least two hundred years. Despite lively and complex debates within the liberal tradition concerning issues such as harm, the role of the state and the relationship between rights and equality, the basic foundational ontology of liberalism has remained strong and constant (Barry 2001). Nevertheless, the nature of political power – in liberalism's heartland as well as elsewhere – has changed radically during the last two centuries.

Liberal ideology, embedded in a more generalised faith in Enlightenment thinking and wedded to discourses of Christian mission, national supremacy and patriarchy, framed the nature of colonial projects in sub Saharan Africa from the early 1800s. The missionaries justified their actions of 'salvation' in strikingly liberal ways: introducing literacy and education, proselytising individual salvation, and condemning 'pagan' cultural practices from the wearing of amulets to practices of polygyny. It is beyond the scope of this author authoritatively to give an account of the inter-relations of liberal thought with the encounter between Europe and Africa,[9] but the general brush strokes given above focus our attention on an assumption in Williams' work: that the World Bank's good governance agenda is novel, that is, it represents a form of *historical rupture* – more or less profound – that introduces Williams's critique as timely and contemporary. But the reader cannot help but ask questions concerning the lack of a more historicised theoretical framework. In the previous chapter, it became apparent that any contemporary change in the sovereign frontier was the result of previous successions of interplay within the frontier. But, we can also see a studied ahistoricism in Williams' text itself. This is clearly the case when Williams makes an interpretation of Adam Smith (Williams 1999: 85–9). Williams argues that Adam Smith's economic theory is based on an assumption of an essential and natural individual proclivity towards reflexive self-interest, but that Smith has to confront the fact that this form of individual agency must be constructed or at least invigilated by encompassing institutions. The reason for this consideration of Smith is to articulate a contradiction which is then used to highlight the World Bank's own problematic constructions of *homo oeconomicus*. Smith first published *Wealth of Nations* in 1776. In this period, the developed capitalist societies were *already* engaged with non-capitalist, non-liberal societies throughout the world. Set in its time, *Wealth of Nations* was itself a *globalising* treatise, articulating a liberal argument for international political economy against mercantilism, defining England's relations with its colonies only as 'somewhat less illiberal' than the others (in Fieldhouse 1967: 5). It is also the case that Smith's analysis is historically contextualised in a second sense. The notion of *laissez-faire* was produced partly as a critique of states born out of war and forms of *réntier* accumulation (Desai 2002: 24). Smith was very much engaged with the difficulties of understanding transitions to new political forms in early modern Europe, leaving himself space to consider absolutist states as well as possibilities of more constitutionalised liberal states in the process (Salter 1992). Thus, in part, Smith was engaging with the political and legislative issues of his day. It seems strange, then, not to explain the complex historical interlude between Adam Smith and late twentieth-century governance, an interlude in which state forms and the West's relations with its post-colonies has changed as much as it has stayed the same.

Of course, one might ask whether Williams needs to fill this 'gap' in order to defend his arguments. It is perfectly possible for his analysis to remain coherent without doing this, as long as 'classical' texts of the liberal and neoclassical genre remain apposite to an analysis of the Bank in the present day. But there are two more specific points that derive from this 'gap' which are more directly germane to his arguments.

First, it leaves the novelty of good governance substantially under explained or interpreted: why governance and why now?[10] For a certain strand in political economy, the agenda of good governance is substantially shaped by the failures of *previous* forms of Bank intervention. Gibbon has given a number of historically embedded accounts of good governance and the Bank, based on a framework in which the Bank is seen as trying to manage the underlying contradictions of an aid régime established during the implementation of structural adjustment programmes throughout the global South (Gibbon 1992, 1993, 1995). Beckman sees the rise to prominence of civil society as a component of the broader travails of the Bank's neoliberalism (Beckman 1993). Moore analyses the Bank's 1997 *World Development Report*, situating good governance in a 'neo statism' which constitutes an adjustment within a neoliberalism already consolidated over a decade (Moore 1999). Williams may or may not agree with these arguments, which share important common judgements about the Bank, but these accounts strongly suggest that good governance was historically constituted in important ways, whether we understand that constitution in terms of the Bank's determination within a capitalist global system or within a realm of ideological and discursive change. So, if one agrees that Williams can reflect on Adam Smith and interpret the Bank through the *Wealth of Nations*, does this mean that the actions of imperial states in the West during other periods during the last 200 years can be interpreted in the same way? Whether the answer is 'yes' or 'no', we return to the question of the specificity and novelty of governance and find Williams's epistemology weak in this respect.

Second, and relatedly, there is a need to deal with the repercussions of Williams's partially-hidden epistemological relativism. The force of Williams's critique derives from the dualised image it constructs – of a liberal imperialism and a non-liberal subject of intervention. Although this dualism is not fully defined, it remains as the ontological tension that allows the Bank to be analysed as an agency of disciplinarian intervention. This then creates a profound social tension between the Bank and the societies into which it interjects:

> [The World Bank is] attempting to transform existing institutions, attitudes, norms, and patterns of conduct. Resistance to the reconstruction of persons and governments should not be seen as simple ignorance of the necessary conditions for peoples' material well-being; rather, resistance should be seen as *arising out of pre-existing attitudes, norms, and patterns of conduct.*
>
> (Williams 1999: 97–8, emphasis added)

The implication here is that non-liberal selves are being forged into liberal ones. If this was not the case, then what purpose would Williams's analysis serve, or at least what would justify Williams's critical tone? But this opposition is not historically tenable because Western political agencies have been intervening powerfully in African societies since the late 1800s, ushering in forces of proletarianisation, resistance against state regulations, migrations, new forms of taxation and chieftaincy, different articulations of local community and nation/world, new syncretisms of religious belief and practice and so on. But it is out of this lurching and violent history that we are to extrapolate a non-liberal self with some form of immanent opposition to liberal forms of identity. One can imagine how, say, lineage societies have been variously, partially and reciprocally integrated into 'modern' social practices over the generations. Societies might maintain a substantial internal coherence based in historically embedded mores and beliefs; they might 're-invent' traditional identities; or they might embrace liberal codes of social interaction; but no society is untouched by 'modernity', expressed through international currencies, firms, traders, radios and government offices. And once we see liberalism's historical record in Africa as a multi-generational and complex series of inconclusive encounters (Berry 1993) we have to question the mileage that Williams can get out of the ontological bipolarity which powers his critique. Even if previous brutal episodes of Western liberal 'mission' have not produced ready-made liberal individuals, they certainly have introduced sufficient social turbulence and hybridity to render the notion of non-liberal selves and communities problematic.

Returning to the Williams quotation above, it is noteworthy that in general conversation during research on the Bank by this author in Uganda and Tanzania, people would criticise the Bank for acting in cahoots with the highest echelons of government. This also came across periodically in letters and editorials in the daily newspapers. This suggests that previous constructions of social identity, based in notions of civic nationalism, have left a *liberal* and civic legacy that now opposes the Bank's *modus operandi* caricatured in regal-feudal terms. The purpose of this point is not to make a grand counter-claim to Williams as much as to suggest that the opposition of liberal and non-liberal selves, owing to a certain ahistoricism, excludes any consideration of the fact that 'the liberal project' has been around for a good while and has already created 'hybrid' selves that are a good deal more complex than the characterisation 'non liberal'.

The question of the epistemology of history also closely relates to that of *how* change happens, that is, the issue of agency. In Williams's view, agents are individuals whose acts are an expression of the broader cultural-normative field within which they exist. It is easy to read Williams's critique as part of a history of the expansion and consolidation of liberalism itself.[11] Liberalism represents an Idea whose historic destiny is a synergy between the liberal mind and social structures. The historical significance of the development of liberalism is indeed difficult to underestimate; in fact it is so embedded in Western culture as to become practically invisible or 'common sense'. Much of liberalism's 'imperial' propensity derives from its self-denial as an ideology with specific geographical and historic origins. But all of the foundations of liberalism – and a good deal of the cardinal debates within this diverse philosophical tradition – cannot be understood without a full cognisance of these historic origins in a broader sense than that of the realm of ideas.

For example, one reading of Adam Smith is as an invective against early modern states: not so much an advocacy of the invisible hand (Smith actually does not advocate a nation of pin factories) as a critique of the Old Corruption in early modern Europe. One can interpret this as a historically-contextualised expression of an establishing feature of capitalist societies: the need for state regulation of some form but an immanent hostility to the latter. Relatedly, Ricardo's theory of comparative advantage is not merely a statement of the positive sum effects of free trade but a critique of the mercantile state system and the militarism produced therein (Biel 2000: 25–6). J. S. Mill's secular statement of positive liberty is based on assumptions of modernity that precludes 'backward states' (Mill 1982: 69).[12] It seems that, more or less explicitly, all liberal philosophers and political economists have expressed their ideas not merely in the abstract, but also as intellectual acts of their time, that is, as expressions of the moment, whether that moment be the decline of mercantilism, the reformulation of European states or the construction of empire.

This means that it is of limited value to conceptualise liberalism's globalising imperative without an understanding of the historiography of the rise of the modern state and capitalism as a global system and their changes over time. For example, although Adam Smith is echoed in the *World Development Report* (2003: 171), perhaps the most striking contemporary revival of a classical liberal thinker is Immanuel Kant. Irrespective of the intrinsic merits of Kant's liberalism, his recent prominence surely owes itself to contemporary problematisations of globalisation (via notions of cosmopolitanism) and concerns with international conflict (Kant's liberal peace). Relatedly, it is interesting to read E. H. Carr's (1938/1995) study which, engaging with a specific and unique twenty years of history, argues for the demise of the liberal idealism. This example only serves to illustrate that liberalism might provide a basic genotype of a large body of thought, but its historical articulation is very much contingent upon changing forms of power, violence and economic relations.

In sum, we can take the force of Williams's insightful analysis of the Bank, but bear in mind the importance of a historical perspective that relates ideas and their articulation to political economy.

The World Bank as 'agent of capitalism'

This brings us to the work of Paul Cammack, for whom the Bank is a key component in the globalisation of the neoliberal revolution. The preface 'neo' is an important sign to distinguish the work of those who see ideology not as a force-in-itself (Williams's liberalism), but as an expression of a broader set of social relations. Most analyses in this vein avoid an Althusserian method of an economic base, an ideological superstructure, and a final instance, but instead analyse ideology as part of a changing capitalist political economy with sufficient nuance to endow neoliberalism with a 'material' force of some kind (Gill 1995).

It is the defining context of a virile, global neoliberal capitalism that, for Cammack, establishes his critique of the World Bank. Following on from the sense that capitalism has entered a significant new period since the collapse of the Soviet Union and the Keynesian model in Western societies, the Bank has taken advantage of a 'window of opportunity' to become a key agency in redefining the global architecture of capitalism. What interests Cammack is the increasing prominence of an anti-poverty agenda within the Bank: the bold banner on the Bank's homepage – our dream is a world free of poverty – the rise of the concept of pro-poor growth, the flagship World Development Report for 2000, *Attacking Poverty*, and a range of more specific programmes and techniques such as the Poverty Reduction Strategy Plans that all HIPCs are required to develop in order to benefit from debt rescheduling. Cammack reviews all of these recent developments and interprets them as a substantive social project to promote the expansion of capital: a capitalist manifesto, in fact (Cammack 2002a: 127).

This capitalist manifesto has as its internal logic the central objective of proletarianisation, in Cammack's words 'deliver[ing] an exploitable global proletariat into the hands of capital' (Cammack 2002a: 125). Thus, many of the key themes in the Bank's anti-poverty campaign, including the components of good governance, are in fact devices to expand and consolidate the originary class relations of capitalism. Cammack reviews each of the World Development Reports[13] of the 1990s and reveals how each of them defines an integrated class agenda: to enlarge private markets (*The Challenge of Development*); to regulate the ecosystems within which capital operates (*Development and the Environment*); to forge a proletariat robust enough for wage labour (*Investing in Health*); to extend capital into infrastructural provision (*Infrastructure for Development*); to consolidate the subjection of labour to international capital (*Workers in an Integrating World*); to define the institutional imperatives to establish capitalism in transition economies (*From Plan to Market*); and to legitimise and regulate markets (*The State in a Changing World*) (*op cit*.: 127–30).

The insight that provides the starting point for this critical interpretation of the Bank's perennial 'big ideas' is Marx's analysis of poverty within capitalism. Capital requires a 'reserve army of labour' in order both to discipline existing labour, and to ensure a tendency for wages to fall towards their minimum based in socially necessary labour time. Furthermore, as capitalism develops and endures crises, it periodically expels the labour that it has drawn into the workplace, as the organic composition of capital rises and as competition produces recessions. In other words, capital actively and tendentially produces a proletariat that is available for work (Cammack 2002c: 194–8). The repercussions of this for Cammack are striking: the World Bank's mission is not a world free of poverty but a world in which poor people are pushed into the workplace: 'what is presented as a "pro-poor" strategy is in fact a pro-capital strategy' (Cammack 2002c: 200) and 'under the guise of attacking poverty, the World Bank is attacking the poor' (Cammack 2002a: 134).

In sum, for Cammack, the Bank's anti-poverty agenda represents an integrated mission to pursue the collective interests of capitalism. The last quotation in the paragraph above introduces a related point which brings Cammack into a similar realm to that dealt with by Williams. The notion of attacking the poor is an extremely strong formulation, which goes beyond the argument that pro-poor strategies are a smokescreen for a more essential objective. The notion of *attacking* the poor derives from Cammack's understanding of proletarianisation, closely following Marx's own. Proletarianisation is seen as the creation of 'free' labour. For Marx, the adjective 'free' contains an irony in that the formal independence of individual labourers – to work or not to work, or to work for different employers – is underpinned by the capital relation which gives labourers no independent means for reproduction and produces a labour market in which capital in general can exploit workers, regardless of their mobility between firms. Cammack signals the importance of this double-edged freedom by beginning one article with an account of the power of hunger to motivate a worker. Here, Cammack is engaging with the dissonance between the liberal rhetoric of the Bank (he is particularly concerned with the notion of empowerment) and the substantive context of vast inequalities in the structures of power within which the Bank is embedded. In a sense, one might take the notion of disciplining people to be free from Williams and embellish it as forcing people to be *free to labour for wages* in Cammack's perspective. Consider the following:

> The disciplinary context [of World Bank reforms] would now be presented as natural and inevitable, effectively beyond human control, and the practices necessary to sustain it would be turned on their heads, and presented as instances of opportunity, choice, and self-realization.
> (Cammack 2002c: 200)

But the paradox for Cammack is that the compulsion behind the Bank's notions of empowerment, freedom etc. is not its authoritarian forging of liberal selves as much as the narrowing of choice to within the boundaries of dependence on wage labour – 'the ultimate form of disempowerment' (Cammack 2002c: 201).

Marx without class?

Cammack's critique has the merit of drawing our attention to the fact that the World Bank constitutes a central institution of global capitalism and that, therefore, any critique of the Bank must also explicitly rely on a broader critique of capitalism. There is also a focus on political economy here which allows us the possibility of understanding the World Bank's actions *materially* as well as ideologically. As mentioned at the end of the review of Williams, so much of the Bank's ideology of liberalism is tied up with changing notions of state action, market form and international order that a critique of the Bank as an ideational agency remains rather limited, especially within a historical frame. But does Cammack bring us towards a political economy of the Bank?

Capitalist essentialism

Cammack's analysis is keenly aware of the process of class creation and the Bank: his writings collectively portray a global agency in pursuit of global proletarianisation. But in another sense, Cammack's methodology is less Marxist than it might appear. At certain points in his argument, Cammack needs to relate the Bank's actions to its motivations, and it is here that the analysis looks a little weak. If the World Bank is acting consistently over a decade to pursue a class project, how do these class interests constitute themselves as real social forces or institutions that determine the scope and nature of development action? In part, Cammack relies on implication and circumstantial evidence; where this is not sufficient, we are told that the Bank is acting in the interests of 'capitalism': putting the 'core disciplines of capitalism in place' (Cammack 2002c: 194), or making a bid to lead the project of 'capitalist exploitation of labour' (Cammack 2002b: 165–6). This certainly corresponds with the notion of the Bank as the dynamo of primitive accumulation, and there is a wealth of empirical evidence that one might draw on to back up the claim (Payer 1982; Gowan 1995; Nelson 1995),[14] but the notion of 'capitalism' or the general interest of capital constitute very broad swords with which to slay the Bank.

Capitalism, as Cammack argues, does contain within it certain core imperatives: the extraction of surplus from wage labour being the key element, from which are derived the expansion of the commodity form, the expanded circulation of capital, the consolidation of systems of law that ensure markets and property[15] and so on. But capitalism is also extremely differentiated institutionally and historically, as Cammack recognises in earlier writing (Cammack 1990). One would have thought that when studying an international organisation acting across an extremely complex and uneven global social terrain, the reliance on an essential capitalist imperative would limit the insights that Marxism might bring to our analysis of the World Bank.

This limitation comes across most clearly when Cammack reviews the *World Development Reports* from 1990 onwards. Here, he dissects the *Reports* in order to expose their capitalist essentials.[16] One can't help but imagine a World Bank 'staffer' reading extended excerpts from Cammack and *agreeing* with him. The Bank makes no secret of its capitalist imperatives: after all, they are written into its originating constitution: to promote free trade and investment (see Chapter 1). But, a World Bank sympathiser might respond – 'Yes, the Bank is really concerned to promote global capitalism and not necessarily good governance, but, so what?' Cammack's response would be (on the assumption that he would follow Marx) that capitalism generates poverty. This point allows him to argue that the abolition of poverty would necessarily involve the abolition of capitalism (Cammack 2002c: 195). It is at this point that the level of generality becomes palpably uncomfortable because social patterns of impoverishment and accumulation are much more complex than 'the expansion of capitalism'. In certain historical circumstances – most obviously Southeast Asia but also in sub Saharan Africa for a time (Warren 1980; Sender and Smith 1986) – the expansion of capitalist social relations has proven to be beneficial for general social well-being.[17] Furthermore, existing class relations in a particular society might create social circumstances in which primitive accumulation can improve the life chances of the most impoverished or disempowered. Here, Cammack seems to have internalised the Bank's populist category 'the poor' to represent a mass of individuals who have as their binding characteristic possession of their own small scale or familial property and therefore an under-specified relative autonomy from capital. That these people are poor is implicit; that a consolidation of capitalism would make them poorer or perpetuate their poverty is also implicit: by 'converting the world's poor into proletarians, stripped of alternative means of survival, obliged to offer themselves to capitalists for work ... the World Bank is attacking the poor' (Cammack 2002a: 127, 134).

Contra Cammack, the argument here is that the social or 'developmental' effects of the development of capitalist social relations are historically contingent and not deductible from capital's general laws. There is a need to analyse capitalism's effects on poverty through an analysis of prevailing class relations, market forms and public action. This will certainly reveal relations of exploitation and accumulation, but the effects of this on social well being will depend on the nature of emerging markets for labour and commodities, the structuring of capitalist institutions and the nature of inter-relations between global markets and local production.[18] A template in which fundamentally 'the poor' are proletarianised and remain poor hardly captures any of this.

Cammack does in fact make some distinction within the category 'the poor': floating, latent and stagnant. The latter category (taken from Marx's analysis of relative surplus population) contains those whose 'conditions sink below the average normal level of the working class' (Cammack 2002c, quoting Marx: 196). Bringing these categories to his analysis of the World Bank, Cammack notes that

> [w]hat the World Bank envisages in its grand plan for reducing absolute poverty by half by 2015, is an efficient global labour market in which the existing proletariat will 'float' easily in and out of work, and the 'latent' proletariat ... will be 'freed' and fully proletarianised. And, despite its headline claims to the contrary, it recognises that a third layer of the absolutely poor will continue to exist beyond these two, as a reservoir for further workers, and a valuable source of discipline for the rest.
>
> (Cammack 2002c: 197–8)

This is the closest Cammack gets to disaggregating 'the poor', and crucially, the quotation can be interpreted to mean either an increase or a decrease in poverty depending on the changing size of the 'reservoir' category. The 'grand plan' to reduce poverty might mean bringing some of those in the 'stagnant' category into other categories: proletarianised but (at least economically) better off. It might be that 'if there is one thing worse than being exploited, it is not being exploited' (Kay 1975: 10). The problem is that Cammack works too closely with the Bank's broad categorisations and takes on stratifications (not class categorisations that Marx employs), leaving one with little sense of the effects of Bank-promoted capitalism in indebted societies. Marx himself recognises that capitalism's fundamental contradictions – alienation, exploitation, crises – are only historically sustainable because of related progressive mechanisms – the unprecedented capacity of capitalism to develop the forces of production, to increase labour productivity, and the expansive compulsion of competition.

Agency and 'logic'

There is a curious sense of a lack of agency in Cammack's writings. The Bank's declarations are critically interpreted by Cammack as functions of a globalising neoliberal capitalism but – in the tradition of functionalism – an awareness of agency and motive do not come into close focus. Consider the following passage:

> It was clear ... that proletarianization *was to be sold* as an 'opportunity' that would allow the poor to 'take advantage' of their lack of other assets by selling their labour power on the open market ... *They were*

to be obliged to sell their labour power, while the Bank would support its efficient extraction by promoting targeted investment in health and education. Ten years on, the *logic* is the same, but the attempt to disguise it is more elaborate.

(Cammack 2002c: 199, emphasis added)

The passive nouns leave one with a sense of agent-less functionalism: a logic under which the Bank functions, inducing effects upon 'the poor'. Is it that the Bank's higher echelons have a capitalist world view? Are power factions of capital 'capturing' the Bank's developmental agenda? Does the structural power of capitalism exert direction over Bank policy making? Is the Bank acting *as* capital (a homologue of state theories within the New Left that saw the state as a kind of collective capitalist), or is it an *agent* of capital? Or, are all of the above true? Of course, it would be very unfair to impose all of these questions on Cammack's writing, but it is difficult to see how his approach defines a starting point to engage with them. In fact, unease with Cammack's 'capitalist-logic' approach reminds one of Booth's incisive review of neo-Marxist development theory generally:

[the] basic problem with Marxist theory as an input to development sociology . . . is its metatheoretical commitment to demonstrating what happens in societies in the era of capitalism is not only explicable, but also in some sense *necessary*.

(Booth 1985: 773, emphasis in the original)

Collectively, Williams and Cammack deal a substantial body blow to the World Bank's increasingly ostentatious claims and representations during the 1990s. But each critical approach to the Bank has limitations: the ahistoricism of a 'liberal' Bank and the functionalism of a 'capitalist' Bank. Furthermore, Williams and Cammack don't refer to each others' work, despite the fact that each raises issues that the other needs to deal with. The rest of Part I will attempt to set out a framework within which to provide a context to assimilate the strengths of each of the critiques. The aim is not to 'better' these contributions, but to make a theoretical statement that engages them in the same critical terrain. This is done in the hope that others (including the authors critically reviewed) will find something in this framework that allows a closer dialogue between each critical approach. This framework does work to contextualise the chapters in Part II of this book. It does this by generating an answer to the question: 'Whence governance?'

Both Williams and Cammack have been stimulated by a sense of novelty: the Bank has entered a qualitatively new period in which governance, anti-poverty programmes or the 'Washington Consensus' have propelled the Bank into new forms of action. Strikingly, neither of the approaches seriously provides a historical context for these innovations. This is not merely to say that each critique is not properly introduced, but to raise the issue of the way we theorise history itself. Cammack's ahistoricism allows him to neglect a century or more of uneven and violent proletarianisation in the global South despite the fact that these processes often created the poverty that the Bank now aims to relieve. Of course, the Bank itself practices a studied ahistoricism, forgetting its own actions and their repercussions in previous decades, forever in search of a 'new' global future-vision of developmental capitalist harmony (Moore 1999: 62; Rich 2002). Thus, it is imperative to deny the Bank the luxury of iterative novelty and locate it within a historical context which problematises the Bank's actions.

Historicising the World Bank: international organisations and capitalist régimes

This section takes Williams and Cammack as the cardinal influences on this book's understanding of the Bank. Williams's attention to the discursive and Cammack's focus on the capitalist political economy are elaborated here through a historicisation of the Bank's engagement with Africa. The key dynamic that shapes the World Bank's actions is that of regulation – one of the three 'fundamentals' noted in Chapter 1. The regulative imperative produces régimes of action for the Bank which, to some extent, integrate with the sequencing of the sovereign frontier.

We will take each period and briefly comment on the three column headings in order to draw out the interlinkages between the global economy, global architecture and development. To the extent that the three 'regions' relate to each other, a legitimising ideology of global development can be forged.

Table 3.1 The World Bank, global political economy and developmental architectures: a schema

Period	Global regulative régime	National economic context	World Bank's regulative strategy
1950s–1973	Embedded liberalism and BWS	Planning and statism	Statism and economic growth
1973–1979	Economic slowdown and instability, BWS	Weakened planning and statism; debt-led development	Statism and poverty reduction
1979–1990	Global recession; disciplinary neoliberalism	Economic crisis, roll-back of the state	Structural adjustment and conditionality
1990–present	Moderate economic recovery, PWC	Good governance	Good governance; embedding neoliberalism

The 1950s to 1973: developmentalism and embedded liberalism

Global regulative régime

For sub Saharan Africa the 1960s were – comparatively speaking – the decade of optimism. In the morass of retrospective critiques of the post-colonial states, it is often forgotten that African economies generally grew at comparatively high percentage rates during the 1960s. This state of affairs was integrated into the broader contours of the global political economy. Africa's decade of development was reflected in the UN's declaration of a Decade of Development from 1960 to 1970. Other changes in the regulative infrastructure of the time reveal a clear construction of a 'developmentalist' agenda: the World Bank's subsidised loan institution the International Development Agency (IDA) was created in 1961; in 1960 the Organisation for Economic Co-operation and Development (OECD) was created, which a year later created its Development Assistance Committee to integrate the aid policy of member states; in 1964 the UN Conference on Trade and Development (UNCTAD) was created with a strong 'Third Worldist' agenda (Harris 1986; Williams 1991); in 1965 the UN Development Programme was created.

Furthermore, the 1960s constituted a period of unprecedented high and stable capitalist expansion (a 'Golden Age'), and an intensification of the internationalisation (not globalisation) of markets. Ruggie (1982) characterises this period as one of *embedded liberalism*.[19] Embedded liberalism refers to the way in which an expanding liberal international economy was 'embedded' in (Western) domestic national societies. Forms of protectionism and social service infrastructure provided the conduits through which Western states legitimised a liberal global order within specific national societies, all under the stabilising hegemonic influence of the United States. The international market was regulated to ensure domestic stability: currencies were tied to gold reserves through a fixed dollar price and the IMF provided short-term finance to states to correct short term exchange rate imbalances. In fact, market regulation was the *essence* of the Bretton Woods System (Helleiner 1994: 25 *et seq.*). Embedded liberalism thus provides us with a reasonably robust regulative form: the fixing of currency prices and controls on indirect foreign investment to ensure global economic stability which would ensure the free and stable movement of goods, direct investment, and services throughout the non Communist world. The regulation of currencies and finance allowed developed states to maintain Keynesian national planning and some form of social provision (Armstrong *et al.* 1991: Chapter 9). It was unthinkable that markets should be free (Ruggie 1982: 396); rather, they should be regulated to ensure that societies enjoyed social legitimacy within individual nation-states.

National economic context

This legitimacy manifested itself in sub Saharan Africa principally through the ideology of developmentalism: if states could plan, regulate, and invest in the correct manner, economies would grow and political stability would be assured (Moore and Schmitz 1995; Berger 2001). This was the common sense of a generation of development economists and modernisation theorists who contributed to the social ideals we found in the sovereign frontiers of governance states at that time. A key feature of almost all post colonial economies was development planning. Development economists, state planners and politicians all believed that strong, effective state action was the key to development. Whether a government declared itself communist or capitalist, national plans of one kind or another became the guiding faith of public action, often based on indicative investment, output targets, and large infrastructural or other project investments, what White terms pervasive intervention (White 1984). Furthermore, state-led development constituted the main claim to legitimacy of governments who faced popular expectations that, once the colonial oppressor had left, ordinary people's lives would improve (Davidson 1992). Thus, 'developmentalism' was not just an economic strategy but a political ideology, allowing governments to stake a claim to legitimacy.

The World Bank's regulative strategy

The World Bank emerged to play a key role in sub Saharan Africa, and many other parts of the southern hemisphere. The Bank was heavily involved – mainly through concessional project lending – in supporting large scale infrastructural investment in post-colonial states which were planning rapid economic growth. Development was 'done' through central state institutions: rural marketing boards, ministries of planning or industry and so on. In this age of neoliberal 'common sense', just as we must remind ourselves that it was not always the case that everyone thought that the market should be free, we should remind ourselves that it was not always considered that high levels of indebtedness were economically damaging. High levels of debt might be a sign of an expanding economy: debt-led infrastructural investment would create the conditions for increased output, and debt would be paid off within the period of maturity. The 1960s was a decade of 'development optimism' in which international lending was a mechanism to allow the 'Third World' to 'catch up' with the West. Indeed, during this period, the Bank paid scant attention to capacity to repay debt, and concerned itself mainly with increasing levels of lending (Caufield 1998: 92–8). More specifically, Bank lending manifested itself in a raft of large-scale, state-led development projects: dams, road, rail, electricity infrastructure, port projects, irrigation schemes, and large scale agrarian mechanisation. For example, the World Bank lent and supported Tanzania's statist modernisation projects to the tune of $1 billion, according to a confidential World Bank report (*Financial Times* 27 July 1994).

In sum, we can identify a global régime of embedded liberalism, based in a desire for the free movement of capital and goods, underpinned by currency stability, Keynesian national planning in developed capitalist states and state-led development in the post-colonial regions. The World Bank, a key institution of the Bretton Woods System, provided the capital and 'expertise' to pursue the latter component of the embedded liberal régime. 'Development' was both an expression of the Bretton Woods architecture and an ideology, legitimising a dispensation between market and public action.

1973–1979: debt and economic slowdown

Global regulative régime

In 1973, the first hike in oil prices took place. This had a profound impact on the structuring of the global political economy. The global price of oil rose from $3.22 per barrel in 1973 to $34 per barrel in 1982. As most African states were oil importers, this created a drain on their external accounts: from 1973 to 1982, Africa's external balance of trade moved from a small surplus to a $6 billion deficit (Singh 1986: 104).

The global economy had undergone two other profound changes in the early 1970s. First, the American government devalued the dollar, thus severing completely the link between the dollar and gold, reflecting a deeper loss of economic competitiveness and dominance by American capital (Rupert 1995; Brenner 2001). This in turn led to the collapse of fixed exchange rates. Second, the restriction of oil supply by the Oil Producing and Exporting Countries (OPEC) produced a surplus of dollars in the oil states that were then ploughed into the Eurocurrency market for dollars, a market which effectively escaped the banking regulations imposed within US territory (Germain 1997: 92–3). These changes produced a period of economic slowdown and instability, coupled with an increase in international liquidity.

It is noteworthy that the economic turbulence created by the end of the gold–dollar link, and its implied decline in American power, did not usher in the collapse of the Bretton Woods system *tout court*. This led Ruggie to argue that US hegemony was not as important to the embedded liberal régime as hegemonic stability theorists would have it. Germain also notes the change and continuity of the Bretton Woods régime through the early 1970s by stressing the ongoing centrality New York as the Primary Financial Centre, dealing with a shift from direct to indirect investment (1997: 82 *et seq.*; Brenner 1998: 119–20). Although weakened by the delinking of the dollar, the BWS persisted as a means to regulate finance. Nevertheless, the relative decentring of the global system of states away from the United States[20] allowed the Bank a greater scope to interpret its establishing agenda and innovate upon its developmentalism as experienced during the previous 20 years or so. Indeed, Block argues that it was 'supranational institutions' that regulated the international economy in the wake of the devaluation of the dollar (Block 1977: 211 *et seq.*).

National economic context

The oil price hike worsened the external terms of trade for oil importers, but primary commodity prices continued to rise (Mistry 1989: 17), allowing a continuation of the statist development model.[21] Thus, sub Saharan Africa's development prospects were profoundly dampened, and although the pace of economic growth slowed in Africa as a result of the downturn in the global economy, this did not lead to a strong change in direction concerning the global regulative architecture or its associated development strategies. African states continued along the same path as set out briefly above, resorting to international creditors, including the World Bank, and to the printing presses of their national banks. From 1970 to 1978, sub Saharan African external debt rose from $9.02 billion to $49.6 billion (Owusu 2003: 1657). It was during this period that it became apparent that the post-colonial régime of accumulation contained serious contradictions. Governing elites appeared in a less appealing light: authoritarian, concerned often with prestigious large-scale investments and far less with the modest concerns of workers and peasants, overly-bureaucratic, obsessed with petty regulations, and corrupt (van de Walle 2001). The legitimacy afforded by economic growth evaporated as economies slowed and projects failed.

World Bank's regulative strategy

Just as states were prepared to continue with the strategies of large scale planning and investment, so was the Bank willing to continue lending for large scale projects, paying very little attention to the issue of efficiency or returns on investment loans, as an internal World Bank audit (the Wapenhans Report in 1992)[22] later discovered. From 1969 to 1981, annual Bank lending rose from just under $2 billion in 1969 to over $12 billion in 1981 – the same period as the global slowdown took place (Miller-Adams 1999: 140). Increased lending was also integrated into a growing concern with poverty alleviation by the World Bank, leading to an emphasis on basic needs and credit for 'small farmers'. This signified a shift in the meaning of development from economic growth to a concern with basic needs and absolute poverty (Ayres 1983; Gibbon 1992: 194). The Bank also widened its project lending to urban development, health and education and population planning (Crane and Finkle 1981).

Again, the Bank's approach was partly a response to a broader set of changes in the global political economy. Changes in patterns of private finance, originating from the growth of Eurodollar markets and the supply of 'petrodollars' from the Middle East, produced strong incentives to lend *private* finance on to post-colonial states. Thus, the Bank had to maintain a sense of identity and purpose as an international lender during this period of increased private flows to the southern hemisphere (mainly Latin America).

The result is clearly summarised by Gibbon as follows: 'Its [the World Bank's] own status as a major provider of loans could only be preserved by greatly raised levels of lending' (1992: 196).[23] In other words, the Bank followed the trend in private finance to increase lending to post-colonial states, despite the economic slowdown in sub Saharan Africa and the increasingly shaky state of the 1960s development model. Furthermore, the development of the 'petrodollar' market allowed the Bank to identify new sources of capital after the end of the 'long boom' in the West: '[the Bank] was able to counter this blow ... by turning, not to the West, but to OPEC states as a source for the Bank's commercial borrowing' (Finnemore 1997: 218).

The Bank played another role in managing economic slow down. Payer (1991) argues that Bank project lending during this period constituted a kind of international demand creation for Western (and more specifically American) transnational corporations. Loans boosted demand in the Third World generally for Western goods and capital. This allowed companies access to overseas markets at a time when aggregate levels of demand were levelling off in the domestic economy. All large contributors to World Bank funds receive a 'surplus' in procurement contracts that their home companies receive (Payer 1982: 36); between 1990 and 1992 the US enjoyed 14.4 per cent of all derivative procurement business arising from the expenditures of the World Bank, leading the ranking of Western recipients (Bracking 1999). The increasing concern over levels of debt and their sustainability in the early 1970s were counterbalanced by steady and ongoing loans by official governmental and multilateral creditors, eager to maintain levels of demand in the Third World for Western exports and markets for Foreign Direct Investment (Payer 1991: 59). Bracking calls this a 'Keynesian global multiplier' (Bracking 2003).

The period from 1973 to 1979 was characterised by a gradual decay in the previous regulative form summarised as the Bretton Woods System. In this context, the Bank by-and-large maintained the model that it had developed during that previous period[24] and integrated it into its own responses to changes in the global economy. This uneasy state of affairs was held together by the ongoing amassing of debt by most African states, marrying an exhausted national development model with a global political economy moving towards a more radical change in its regulative architecture. Once levels of debt became unsustainable, setting off the debt crisis, there was not enough available finance to 'suture' the incompatibility of a debt-led model of intervention and regulation with a failed economic paradigm. One can see this period as a whole as an interlude during which the legitimising discourse of development of the previous period declined markedly.

1979–1990: the era of structural adjustment

Global regulative régime

By the time of the second OPEC oil price hike in 1979, the developmental project was in tatters. Levels of debt had become sufficiently high to make it difficult to imagine how some states could ever escape from indebtedness. The international economy, which had expanded constantly during the 1960s and slowed in the 1970s, was now clearly in recession. The 'long downturn' (Brenner 1998: 138 *et seq.*) that commenced in 1973 was addressed from 1979 by a strong shift towards monetarist economic management within the United States and the UK, with other states moving (more or less willingly – see especially France in 1981) in a similar direction over the next decade or so. Perhaps an initial event which starkly announced the shift in the 'policy logic' of regulation was the substantial rises in interest rates from 1979 in the US which in turn had severe recessionary effects in the West (Brenner 2001: 24 *et seq.*).

Globally, the rise of monetarism produced a radical change in forms of regulation. The IFIs came under strong pressure – especially from the US (Wade and Veneroso 1998) – to act as institutions to consolidate and 'lock in' a neoliberal architecture. The neoliberal project involved just as much concerted political intervention as did the previous embedded liberal project which is why Gill (1995) calls is disciplinary neoliberalism. In Cox's words, the 'hyperliberal [read: neoliberal] ideology has become entrenched in international institutions, backed by American power' (Cox 1996: 31). The IFIs increased their capacity to intervene and invigilate, re-making themselves as the active champions of the regulative revolution, re-framing 'development' as economic liberalisation and bringing this ideology into the indebted states of the world (with the exception of the United States itself, of course!). There was no region of the world more vulnerable to these global regulative changes than Africa.

National economic context

The economic slowdown in the West produced magnified crisis and vulnerability in the global South, especially Africa. Recession in Western economies dampened demand for primary commodity exports from the post colonial economies creating a decline in Africa's external terms of trade from 160.2 in 1980 to 110.5 in 1990.[25] Sub Saharan Africa's share of Foreign Direct Investment (FDI) declined from its already very marginal levels. Total external debt has increased from $60,641 million in 1980 to $177,400 million in 1990, imposing severe pressure on public expenditures – social spending declined by 26 per cent from 1980 to 1985 (Riley and Parfitt 1994: 139). The details of the crisis that this produced in Africa are complex. In his magisterial overview, Szeftel summarises as follows: 'The crisis of accumulation which has beset the world capitalist order [since the debt crisis] . . . has been particularly severe in its impact on the poorest and most peripheral societies' (1987: 87). Metaphors such as the 'lost decade' of the 1980s or the 'death of development' signal the evaporation of purposive public action and a succession of *ad hoc* and crisis management measures which themselves became integrated into structural adjustment.

World Bank's regulative strategy

Thus, the incipient tensions of the previous period were brought to a conclusion – not just globally, but also within the institutions of the World Bank. The Bank could no longer continue project lending to political economies that were reaching economic and social crisis. The result was a change in Bank strategy, starkly presented in the 'Berg Report' (World Bank 1981), and closely integrated into the rise of neoliberalism after 1979 in the West (Stern and Ferreira 1997: 537 *et seq.*; Gibbon 1992: 198). The 'Berg Report' set out a critique of the post-colonial state as a bloated, rent-seeking set of institutions which distorted price mechanisms in order to feather the nests of political elites. The solution was, in simple terms: less state, more market.

This over-arching new agenda was implemented through the creation of Structural Adjustment Loan (SAL)[26] in 1980. Moving from project support to macro-economic restructuring, the Bank lent on the condition that states would implement the new orthodoxies of neoliberal economics: low rates of inflation, devaluation, high rates of interest, divestment of state property, an economy open to global markets and capital and a general reduction in public expenditure. In essence, the fragility of African states after 1979 created an unprecedented opportunity for external regulative intervention, expressed through those institutions most heavily involved in sub Saharan Africa: the World Bank and (later) the IMF.

As mentioned in Chapter 2, SAPs were effected through the mechanism of conditionality: credit would only be forthcoming if governments implemented the 'correct' policies. This produced a very different relationship between the World Bank and indebted states to that of the debt-led development model: it reconfigured the sovereign frontier as a zone 'policed' by the IFIs and others. The conditionality mechanism created considerable tension between governing elites and the Bank. We have seen this most clearly in Tanzania: during the early 1980s the tension between conditionality and the Government was most clear in Nyerere's resistance to the devaluation of the Tanzanian shilling, manifested in his broadsides against the IMF (or the 'International Ministry of Finance', as he dubbed it). Similar tensions between African governments and the IFIs existed throughout Africa, manifest in the tendency of 'adjusting' states to evade or abandon the policy reforms that the Bank and Fund made conditions of loans (Mosley *et al.* 1995). So-called SAP riots (Walton and Seddon 1994) in some cities only served to sharpen the tensions between states and the Bank. Finally, as noted in Chapter 1, adjustment did not usher in any clear signs of economic recovery in sub Saharan Africa. Perhaps one of the most successful *intended* consequences of structural adjustment was the erosion of (formal) state capacity, the effect of which was to make management of the economy and society increasingly difficult (Moore 1999). In sum, imposing neoliberalism produced its own delegitimising contradictions: it was effective as a strategy to ensure a global neoliberal revolution in development thinking (and to reconfigure sovereign frontiers), but it failed as a strategy of economic development. For Africa as a whole the average annual GDP growth rate was 3 per cent from 1965 to 1975; it was negative during the 1980s (Mkandawire and Soludo 2000: 7).

In sum, the 1980s encapsulated an effort to resolve the problems of economic slowdown and a weakening of global regulative architecture manifest from 1973. The shift towards neoliberalism attempted to re-establish profitability as a prerequisite to reinvigorated growth. It produced a political and institutional response from the IFIs (strongly pushed forward by the US) which established neoliberalism as a synonym for 'development' and, through its own techniques of intervention, universalised neoliberal reform throughout a wide range of states facing more or less severe economic crisis. Table 3.1 shows a closer integration between the Bank's development praxis and the logic of neoliberal regulation more broadly for this period. But, the 1980s was not a period of harmonisation – far from it. It is clear that the neoliberal revolution failed to legitimise itself within African states: it produced economic instability, was perceived as an external imposition (demonising the World Bank and IMF in the process), and made indebted economies increasingly indebted and extroverted to a largely hostile global economy. It is the *failure* of the neoliberal project of the 1980s that provides the 'opportunity' for the construction of governance states.[27]

Embedding neoliberalism

The current period is described here as one of embedding neoliberalism. The World Bank and others are attempting to expand a socially embedded neoliberalism into governance states. This evokes the first period of Table 3.1, in that it presents régime-like features, and it is worth reflecting on this a little more. One of the most-referenced pieces of work concerned with régimes has been John G. Ruggie's 'International Régimes, Transactions,

and Change: Embedded Liberalism in the Postwar Economic Order'
(Ruggie 1982). Ruggie's aim is to theorise international régimes of economic management in the post-war period, but he actually begins with the
World Bank and IMF. He defines a Bretton Woods régime based in the
regulative structures of the Bank and IMF, and lasting from 1946 until
1971.[28] The régime is characterised by regulations that have as their
guiding imperative the stability of international trade and investment.
Equally importantly, this international régime defines a realm of domestic
economic policy making which also conditions international markets.
Domestic economic policy is underpinned most crucially by the maintenance of fixed exchange rates by developed states' central banks. Official
rates are only changed through agreement with the IMF and with short-
term borrowing from the latter to manage a shift from one currency value
to another. The central argument that Ruggie makes is that the relative
autonomy of domestic economic policy making underpins the international régime. Each domestic economy (especially throughout the
1960s) strives to create full employment and generalised social provision –
Keynesianism and social democracy. These policy fundamentals are what
allow states to legitimise themselves *and the market*. In other words, taking
from Polanyi, it is only when markets are embedded in society that they
can attain stability, and it is this stability – at the level of the nation-state –
that provides the building blocks for a global régime of free trade and
investment. Ruggie neatly condenses this argument in the epithet *embedded liberalism*: a global faith in the market regulated by the requirement of
states to ensure that markets maintain a basic legitimacy within the societies that sustain them. For Ruggie, the Bretton Woods régime is produced by embedded liberalism as a global-domestic structure of economic
management. The régime itself attains a comprehensive social presence,
not just constitutive of the state system or the hegemony of the United
States, and one can see this in the persistence of aspects of embedded liberalism after the devaluation of the dollar and beyond even the oil price
rises of 1973/4. Thus, Ruggie argues that embedded liberalism persists
beyond the collapse of US dollar standard and the incremental instability
of the Keynesian model that proceeds the oil shock.

Before considering how this model relates to the Bank in the present
day, it is worth noting that Ruggie's model does partially speak to the two
critiques reviewed in the first two sections of this chapter. One distinguish-
ing feature of Ruggie is his attention to norms at the international level.
He refers to a liberal 'generative grammar' that allows international
régimes to consolidate themselves (Ruggie 1982: 381). This grammar is
based in both a liberal faith in the market mechanism and an acceptance
of domestic state responsibility to ensure market legitimacy. These norms
are therefore not merely epiphenomena, but social forces in their own
right, reinforcing an international language that works even beyond the
fall of the economic underpinnings of Bretton Woods. Relatedly, Gill and

Law emphasise the importance of the normative in the 'historic bloc' constructed by the US during the Bretton Woods period (1993: 96 *et seq.*). What Ruggie, Gill and Law and others are able to do is theorise norms not merely as expressions of liberalism (although they are clearly constituted by the latter), but also as a component part of a historically specific patterning of international political economy.

Although Ruggie starts from Polanyi's *Great Transformation* (1957), he can also be read as taking régimes of *accumulation* as his starting point: perhaps more Regulation School[29] than Polanyi. The domestic model that Ruggie locates centrally within his analysis of the international is based on industrial peace through corporatism/co-determination, demand-led industrial expansion and accumulation, and near-full employment. The same régime is interpreted by Silver and Arrighi as the post-war 'labour-friendly' régime for developed capitalist states (Silver and Arrighi 2001: 55). Finally, Ruggie's understanding of régimes allows for the acts of states, especially globally ascendant ones. It should be noted that he refutes the realist interpretation of Bretton Woods as a product of American hegemony, but implicitly he bases the régime on a consensus between *developed* capitalist states:[30] a coalition of a small number of states within which the US clearly was a first among equals.[31] In sum, we can interpret Ruggie's model as encompassing theoretical space for ideology, accumulation and the inequalities of the state system.

From embedded liberalism to embedding neoliberalism

The current period, commencing in the mid 1990s can be understood as analogous to the 'embedded liberal' period, at least in respect to our interest in governance states. The decline of national development during the economic instability and slowdown of the second half of the 1970s provided no opportunity for a socially-sustainable interaction between the Bank, African states, development models and global political economy. The starkly imposed neoliberalism of the early 1980s pulled African economies into line with a changing global context, but it did so in a fashion that provoked instabilities within the sovereign frontier.

The Bank's efforts from the mid 1990s can be understood as a project to embed these neoliberal interventions in the sovereign frontier. The neoliberal fundamentals have not been abandoned in the process; instead a range of more explicitly political interventions have focussed on an engineering of states and societies towards compatibility with a free market open economy. The politics of this embedding will be detailed in the next section. One key aspect of this politics has already been dealt with: the tendency towards selectivity by the Bank. Thus, we can understand governance states as the Bank's 'best case' of embedded neoliberalism. Governance states are defined by their close relations with donors, their growing economies, and their stability. They are represented as rejuvenated, but they are very much the outcome of a strategic reflection on a previous period of neoliberal failure. The 'lesson' learnt by the Bank is not that neoliberal economic policy is damaging or contradictory, but that greater attention needs to be paid to the state as an 'embedding agent' and the stability of the sovereign frontier. The next section will investigate how the Bank has done this.

Summary of Part I

Chapter 1 introduced the key interests of this book. It has outlined the salience of governance for the World Bank and African states; it has introduced the key agencies in the construction of governance states – African states and the Bank itself. In doing so, it has outlined the way in which the Bank has necessarily engaged with Africa as a region with a specific concern for the ordering of social change. This has lent the Bank's involvement in Africa a certain kind of 'statism' not present in other regions. This can be seen most clearly in the present period, which is introduced in general terms as the move from first to second generation reform. Chapter 1 leaves us with a sense that the Bank has been a vitally important actor in post-colonial African politics, shaping the continent's integration into other global processes and relations. The second chapter looks at the repercussions of this state of affairs for the concept of sovereignty. Sovereignty is found to be something of a chimera, which severely limits its heuristic potential in analysing African states' interactions with other agencies. The rest of the chapter develops the concept of a sovereign frontier to introduce a more flexible and constructed zone of power between states and other agencies. The development of the sovereign frontier for three governance states allows us to see how this frontier has developed in these cases in a particular way. It reveals how the nature of external intervention in the sovereign frontier has stabilised from the mid 1990s, providing an important innovation in the politics of Bank involvement in Africa. This brings us to a deeper consideration of the Bank itself. In this chapter we have considered the motivations and patterning of Bank action in more theoretical detail. Having highlighted the importance of liberal ideology and the formative context of the dynamics of global capitalism, this chapter has developed an analytical framework through which the Bank's actions can be understood as a sequencing of efforts to regulate economic change in light of broader changes in the global political economy. This narrative, shadowing the sequences related in Chapter 2, brings us to the notion of embedding neoliberalism. This is the primary motive shaping the Bank's increasingly political interventions under the rubric of governance. In sum, the World Bank is embedding neoliberalism in a selected number of governance states which have recently witnessed a restabilisation of their sovereign frontiers. The question for Part II is: how has it done this?

Part II

Constructing governance states

Institutions, discourse, security

4 Introducing post-conditionality

> While Government was, in some circumstances, driven by the require-
> ments of conditionality . . . it has demonstrated that once it is persuaded by
> the merits of the proposed [adjustment] strategy, it is willing to implement
> the policy promptly and comprehensively. There is no reason why sound
> economic management should be driven by the conditionalities attached to
> donor assistance.
>
> (Emmanuel Tumusiime-Mutebile, former Permanent Secretary and
> Secretary to the Treasury, Ministry of Finance Planning
> and Economic Development 1995: 1)

Governance and post-conditionality

This chapter looks more closely at the sovereign frontier of governance
states. There are two aspects of the portrayal of governance states in
Part I which pose an apparent paradox. Governance states are characterised by an especially high degree of external influence – from the
World Bank, IMF and a range of other donors and creditors. But, governance states are also characterised by a certain 'post-conditionality' in
their sovereign frontier politics; that is to say, the period during which
donors constantly policed reform through the threat of a freezing or
withdrawal of funds has passed. In other words, the main mechanism for
external intervention in the sovereign frontier – conditionality – loses
some of its salience at the same time as external agencies become more
preponderant. This chapter looks in detail at the nature of donor
involvement in the sovereign frontier of governance states to reveal how
the fundamental conditionalities of neoliberalism have been accompanied by what is called here post-conditionality politics. Post-conditionality
politics is both more interventionist and less starkly coercive; it alludes
to a range of terms and tropes such as 'partnership' and 'participation'
which have clear liberal provenance and provide a very strong discursive
field within which to articulate post-conditionality politics. This is what
Tumusiime-Mutebile is referring to in the quotation that commences this
chapter. These terms will be the focus of attention in Chapter 6. The rest

of this chapter will detail post-conditionality as a new set of relations within the sovereign frontier. One can only understand these relations and their generation through the consideration of specific cases; thus, in Chapter 5, we return to Tanzania and Uganda from the mid 1990s in order to understand the institutional forms of World Bank influence on governance states.

Governance as punishment and reward

In Chapter 1, we noted that the shift from first to second generation reform was premised on a need to make African states act more effectively to ensure the execution of neoliberal reform. The normative expression of SGR is good governance, a term that has become the common sense of donor communities in all indebted African states. We have relied on the World Bank's definition of governance so far, but it is apposite here to broaden our understanding of governance in light of the theoretical contributions of Williams and Cammack. Williams understands governance as a repertoire of techniques of social engineering and discipline to forge liberal states and societies. As we shall see in Chapter 6, the liberal origins of governance are clear, and have important repercussions on how governance reforms are created and represented. For Cammack, governance is an ideology to express the need for states to act more concertedly as public agents for the creation of capitalist property relations. In Chapter 7, we shall relate this argument to the specific challenges of state action in unstable societies. Both of these representations of governance provide insights into the meaning of governance for this book, but neither necessarily applies exclusively to governance states. Indeed, both Williams and Cammack refer to cases in other continents as well as Africa.

It is important to recall that many generic aspects of Bank action and ideology express themselves in different ways within the sovereign frontiers of particular states. Governance is indeed a generic normative statement about the nature of public action, but that normative content evokes different judgements on different states. Many donors employ 'governance' to construct a kind of moral hierarchy of states – from 'good' to 'bad' governance. Closely related to this selectivity are a series of supposedly 'technical' or scientifically-constructed indices, ranking civic freedom, levels of corruption and levels of security of investment.[1] In other words, governance is a term that allows external agencies explicitly to rank and judge states (with more or less discretion) with reference to political factors. Interestingly, the cases of Tanzania, Mozambique and Uganda generally do not fare well on the 'positivist' governance index-rankings; nevertheless, they enjoy very favourable judgements by the Bank and others as effective reformers. There are reasons for this, relating to the construction of 'showcase' reformers, which will be investigated in Chapter 5. The main point here is that governance is *judgemental* and, consequently, the generic concerns of governance can be employed to 'reward' or 'punish' African states. Consider the judgemental words of a creditor official regarding Uganda: 'If Uganda can do it, *no other government has an excuse*' (in Reno 2002: 430, emphasis added). In this view, culpability for reform failure lies with individual states, not the Bank.

The distinction between governance-as-reward and governance-as-punishment might be a crude one, but it does serve to explain how universal concerns to reconstruct states as liberal agencies, capitalist midwives, and 'embedders' of neoliberalism can create specific political processes in a selected group of governance states. This is clarified through a brief comparison with a nearby state which has been perceived as ridden with 'bad' governance: Kenya.[2]

Kenya undertook a series of unstable liberalising reforms during the 1980s as the steady rates of economic growth that it had experienced since 1964 faltered. Reforms were supported by external agencies which perceived Kenya as a strong economy, especially in comparison with Tanzania and Uganda. Economic liberalisation was often subject to reversals and budget and balance-of-payment deficits remained throughout. Fraud and corruption accompanied Kenya's liberalisation, leading donors to evoke governance as a way to pressure the Kenyan government to implement civil service reform (Cohen 1993) and anti-corruption strategies. Poorly-implemented liberalisation, corruption and (for bilateral donors) increasing political violence as a result of pressures for multipartyism (Fox 1996), led donors to give Kenya a 'warning' at the Consultative Group meeting of 1991. This led Moi to revise the constitution and allow multi-party elections (1992), but the Kenyan government carried out a destabilising campaign to undermine the opposition (Fox 1996; Southall 1999; Anderson 2002). At the same time, a major scandal (Goldenberg scandal 1992/3) emerged in which it was revealed that $500 million had been embezzled from government accounts for fictional contracts. In 1997 the European Union and IMF broke off lending schedules in protest against continuing and pervasive corruption. The Bank's resident representative in the late 1990s, Harold Wackman, made public comments which were strikingly different from the gentle support from Bank representatives in Tanzania and Uganda (for example, see *Africa Confidential* 20 March 1998).

We can see how Kenya's governance reform was inconsistently implemented under strong and explicit conditionalities: donor-state relations were pervaded by tensions and stand-offs. Furthermore, reform was implemented during periods of economic crisis and the purposeful destabilisation of Kenyan society by the state, principally for electoral purposes. Kenya clearly did not possess the conditions that set governance states apart from other states in Africa and as a result, 'governance' was integrated into the conflictual relations of Kenya's unstable sovereign frontier.

In Mozambique, Uganda and Tanzania, governance is integrated into a stabilised sovereign frontier described in this chapter in terms of post-conditionality. Taking the periodisation of Chapter 2, we can understand post-conditionality as the attempted resolution of the coercive nature of conditionality on governance states. As we shall see, governance reform is employed more in the fashion of a 'carrot' than a 'stick'; the conditioning of funding on effective implementation which is closely monitored is replaced by the allocation of funding as an *incentive* to carry out reforms ... which are *still* closely monitored![3]

The fact that governance reform – as reward or punishment – is at least as closely monitored as reforms during the conditionality phase draws our attention to the fact that post-conditionality politics is not acted out on a *tabua rasa*. To recall a phrase from Chapter 1, SGR can only be born on the consolidation of FGR and, as such, aspects of the conditionality régime persist as the foundation upon which governance and post-conditionality are constructed in governance states. One can see this in two respects. As just mentioned, the external monitoring of policy and reform remains as prominent as ever,[4] even if these processes of monitoring are articulated less strongly as a means to discipline. Second, although we use the term post-conditionality to depict a certain state of affairs in governance states' sovereign frontiers, it is also the case that conditionality has not disappeared from these states' involvement with donor-creditors. Rather – as we shall see – it is that these conditionalities are not constantly evoked and mooted as points of conflict between states and donors; they are more 'contextual', increasingly resembling the implicit 'common sense' or foundation for all aspects of public action. Perhaps conditionality becomes all the more effective once it does not need constantly to be named and politicised.

Post-conditionality in Uganda and Tanzania

Post-conditionality régimes are historically generated often on the back of a previous period of economic crisis (Uganda 1986–1989; Tanzania 1979–1986; Mozambique 1980–1989) or conflict and capitulation *vis à vis* the IMF and World Bank (Tanzania 1980–1990; Mozambique 1984–1989). One can make the point more clearly with reference to Uganda and Tanzania's experiences with the World Bank and IMF.[5]

Tanzania's relations with the IMF during the late 1980s were extremely unstable and occasionally hostile (Biermann and Wagao 1986a, 1986b; Biermann and Campbell 1989). In Tanzania by 1986 a standby agreement was signed with the IMF, followed by the implementation of a Structural Adjustment Facility. As noted earlier, it was only after Nyerere's departure that a full structural adjustment programme was implemented.

Having implemented ESAP in 1989, with heavy World Bank, IMF and bilateral support, Tanzania's economy began to produce positive rates of growth – from 1992 to 1994 an average of 3.6 per cent – and, from 1995, much of the 'logic' of economic policy making under ESAP had become incontestable within the Tanzanian state.

In Uganda, by 1987, after a year of economic instability and decline exacerbated by dirigiste economic planning, the National Resistance Movement (NRM) implemented a SAP with IFI sponsorship, removing a hostile finance minister under advice from the IMF along the way. Also like Tanzania, Uganda's economy began to recover, averaging a GDP growth rate of 7.4 per cent from 1994/5 to 1998/9. By the start of the 1990s, the economic logic of adjustment was internalised within the state. As Brett, writing in 1994, summarises: '[c]ommitment to the political and economic discipline demanded by structural adjustment is probably more widely accepted by the leadership now than ever before, and thus [is] less dependent on continuing external ... pressures' (1994: 54). This tendency has continued from 1994 as Uganda's rate of economic growth has remained relatively high.

Both states were involved in a period of tension and tussle with the IFIs as they compromised their crumbling economic nationalism for external funds. Both economies experienced a recovery, internalised neoliberal reform, and as a result came to a 'post-conditionality' stage in their relations with external donors. Now, less pressure is put on these two states to ensure that inflation remains low because the respective finance ministries do this anyway: many of their higher-ranking personnel have received training based in monetarist economics and their accounting systems are based on fiscal prudence. The power of Ministries of Finance over other ministries is considerable, and low rates of inflation maintain a post-conditionality state in which donor funds are forthcoming: the best example of this state of affairs is the fact that Uganda and Tanzania are both receiving debt relief under the HIPC scheme after 3–6 years of effort at structural adjustment reform.

'Post-conditional' interventions: a new approach

The argument so far is that we can no longer understand donor relations with Uganda and Tanzania simply within the framework of economic conditionality which characterises the politics of the sovereign frontier under structural adjustment. The term I have given to my attempt to conceive of donor-state relations here is 'post-conditionality'. What does this mean exactly?

1   Implementing structural adjustment measures is far less of a 'political' issue than it was previously: IFIs no longer bring their considerable influence to bear on fundamental but routine economic policy. This is not to

say, then, that neoliberalism is no longer the dominant ideology behind economic policy, but that this is far less of a *political* issue than previously. In a sense, neoliberalism has made a transition from *doctrine* (openly colonizing the state terrain through the IFIs) to *ideology* (far less contested, integrated into the every-day language of policy making). Speaking of Tanzania's post-conditionality focus on Poverty Reduction Strategy Papers (PRSPs), one Tanzanian NGO referred to it as 'structural adjustment in disguise' (quoted in Whitehead 2003: 9; see also Craig and Porter 2003).

2   Donor-state relations within the post-adjustment régime are not defined by conditionality in its directly coercive sense: 'do what the IFIs say because the costs of doing so are not as great as the costs of not doing so'. Rather, IFIs employ the disbursement of funds to *promote* further changes – mainly to state institutions through administrative reform and capacity building programmes. In respect to governance, as mentioned above, this involves a movement away from threats to withdraw funds unless a country reduces its levels of corruption or opens up political space to the opposition, towards a desire to fund, say, a human rights watchdog institution or new anti-corruption agencies. It also involves a greater degree of donor interest in SGR programmes, as outlined in Chapter 1.

3   Post-conditionality politics is *selective*; it is not a régime which has swept across all of sub Saharan Africa. In effect, the Bank's engagement with different states is becoming more differentiated, as one would expect because donor-state relations are now historically embedded in each state over a period of decades. Joseph identifies the current trend in which one can locate the selectivity of post-conditionality:

> The retreat [of interventionism] from Africa has been replaced by a selective international reengagement with the continent, especially to support strong economic reformers and governments able to contribute to order and stability in their subregions.
>
> (Joseph 1999: 69–70)

Joseph takes Uganda as his key exemplar throughout the text. The OECD Emerging Africa project (which includes Tanzania and Uganda) also selects key reforming states, supporting the Bank-funded research that establishes selectivity as a principle for effective aid disbursement.

The Bank has in fact been developing a politics of 'cherry picking' in sub Saharan Africa since *Reforms Results and the Road Ahead* (1994a) in which debtor states are divided into 'good' and 'bad' adjusters. The reliability of these divisions is questionable (Schatz 1994; Mosley *et al.* 1995), but the *political* effect of this division is powerful: it lays culpability for the general failure of adjustment to work on the states themselves, not on SAP, or the nature of global economic change (Sender 2002). Tanzania and Uganda constitute cherries, along with a small group of other states, such as Ghana and Mozambique which have experienced relatively high rates of GDP growth (although Ghana less so recently). These countries are showcased as examples of what a state can achieve if it 'gets the basics right' (the innovation on Berg's[6] getting the prices right). The more the IFIs invest capital (financial and political) in these states, the more committed they become to ensuring that they remain positive examples. This has repercussions for administrative reform, as will be discussed in Chapter 5.

4   Within post-conditionality régimes, it becomes far less insightful to make distinctions between external and internal interests. As already mentioned, much of the neoliberal logic close to the heart of the IFIs is *also* close to governance states' technocrats, auditors and economists. This is not to argue that post-conditionality politics is a happy affair of dialogue and partnership even if this is how the Bank represents it (Chapter 6). Rather, contradictions and tensions still emerge and are central to post-conditionality politics, but they are not adequately explained by the notion of external intervention and coercion. We will explore some of these contradictions in respect to administrative reform below.

5   Post-conditionality régimes are still based on the politics of donor dependency. In fact some have argued that Uganda is best understood as an 'international Bantustan' (Himbara and Sultan 1995; but see Doornbos 1996). Others have made similar claims regarding Tanzania (Shivji 2003) and Mozambique (Plank 1993). The point here is that post-conditionality politics does not mean an end to donor intervention; rather it is that intervention is not exercised solely through conditionality and adjustment, but to a significant degree through a *closer* involvement in state institutions and the employment of incentive finance. This constitutes a less visible but perhaps more powerful role for donors.

The three faces of administrative reform in sub Saharan Africa

Administrative reform is the central policy focus of governance reform. Bearing in mind the nature of SGR and its focus on institutions, one can readily see how capacity building, personnel management, training, new public management techniques etc. provide the instruments for the construction of governance states. As such, administrative reform is profoundly political. This section reviews three 'faces' of administrative reform which locate it within the politics of governance (Table 4.1).

Administrative reform as structural adjustment

Let us now explore the notion of post-conditionality politics with a closer focus on donor involvement in administrative reform. The World Bank

Table 4.1 Components of administrative reform in bank-supported programmes

Component	Comments
Retrenchment	Key policy. Implemented early. Closely linked to SAP.
Consultancies	Implemented early, as part of SAP. Mainly Western personnel to effect cut-backs and retrenchment.
Simplification of procedures	Especially for revenue collection and regulating DFI – part of SAP.
Public sector wage decompression	Second generation. Aims to reduce relative benefits of corruption; associated with governance.
Training	Workshops and seminars for those at apex of departments. Aims to produce stronger governance 'ethos' in bureaucracies.
Decentralisation	Second generation – relies on established state capacity. To increase accountability/instal decentralised fiscal régimes.
More rigorous audit	Key policy, implemented early part of SAP, but auditing techniques developed and routinised through Ministries of Finance.
Introduction of incentives	Productivity-related increments, focus on output, 'results oriented management'. Demands political will and state capacity – second generation and relates to marketisation of administration.
New systems of information management	Second generation. Computerisation, more publicity for legislation, part of aim to increase transparency.
Divestment/contracting out/competitive tendering	To introduce market forces and increase efficiency. Early privatisation poorly managed; replaced by more institutionally sophisticated management of privatisation, as well as increasing use of contracting and creation of semi-autonomous executive agencies.

Sources: Lindauer and Nunberg 1994; World Bank 1994b; Adamolekun and Pinto 1995; Schacter 1995; Olowu 1999.

and a range of bilateral agencies, along with the United Nations Development Programme (UNDP), have been involved in administrative reform in sub Saharan Africa since the early 1990s. In the first place, administrative reform was an integral part of the adjustment and conditionality period proper. Structural adjustment involved substantial retrenchment programmes and the implementation of privatisation schemes – both part of the aim to roll back the state. These processes of retrenchment needed to be managed very carefully, bearing in mind the politically sensitive nature of employment within the state apparatus. As a result, civil service departments or public service commissions have carried out functional reviews, reviews of payrolls, and implemented pension, compensation and retraining programmes – all heavily donor-funded. Thus, administrative reform comprised a component of SAP – as a parsimonious concern that state be able to execute their own 'rolling back'.

Administrative reform as market ideology

Taking their theoretical point of departure from institutional economics and new public management (Harriss *et al.* 1995; McCourt and Minogue 2001; Hope 2001), the second face of administrative reform is concerned with creating states which effectively support the expansion and consolidation of market social relations. Associated reforms include: the creation of agencies and privatisation, the introduction of new resource management systems designed to minimize costs; technical support to make institutions more effective in defining and maintaining the rule of law (support for the judiciary, constitutional and legislative revision and updating).

Furthermore, new public management introduces the market into administration. This might involve 'direct' marketisation such as contracting out public services, or it might involve indirect reforms such as introducing market-like incentives to managers within bureaux. With respect to the latter, a key facet of all administrative reform is the consolidation of output oriented budgeting and results oriented management, both of which attempt to introduce financing mechanisms which 'price' public services according to a measure of productivity. Institutional economics is concerned with the 'imperialism' of economics (Fine 2001), and with ensuring that public institutions serve the market more effectively (Bayliss and Fine 1998). As such, the complimentarity of government to the market is important, as well as the presence of incentives and efficiency in administration. Both new public management and institutional economics provide ways to analyse the state and imagine its reconfiguration; both theories markedly deny the need to analyse the economy or imagine its purposeful reconfiguration. The market is seen as a realm of immanent possibility; this separation and differential judgement is a key feature of Bank discourse and will be returned to in Chapter 6.

Administrative reform as governance

One can also understand administrative reform as part of the broader SGR–governance agenda; that is, based on the belief that states can play important formative roles in facilitating market-based growth. This face of administrative reform brings us closest to governance, and the reconfiguration of states under the auspices of the World Bank. Good governance involves transparency in public decision making and accountability in the effects of policy. Both of these objectives have translated into administrative

Table 4.2 Administrative reform in Tanzania and Uganda

	Uganda	Tanzania
1987	IGG formed PSRRC established [UNDP, WB, bilats] Penal Code (Amendment) Statute	
1988	IGG statue created	
1989		PSR as part of ESAP
1990	*Civil Service Reform Programme* [bilats, IDA] PSRRC reports	Prevention of Corruption Act (1971) amended Presidential Circular No. 1 on Corruption
1991	Creation of Capacity Building Secretariat [in MFP] [IDA]	Renewed Prevention of Corruption Bureau Prevention of Corruption Act amended *Civil Service Reform Programme Launched* [UNDP]
1992	Creation of Institute of Public Accountants Leadership Code Statute PSR from PSRRC	
1993	Decentralisation Act Policy of Technical Assistance [UNDP] Public Enterprise Reform and Divestiture Statute	Prevention of Corruption Act amended CSRP implemented Parastatal and Public Sector Reform Commission created [IDA etc.]
1994	W/shop on Ethics, Transparency etc. [EDI] Creation by IGG of National Integrity Committee Creation of TI Uganda Creation of Action Plan (out of PSR) Institutional Capacity Building Project [WB] Anti-Corruption Programme	
1995	New Constitution	Creation of Presidential Commission on Corruption Service Delivery Survey [EDI] Public Leadership Code of Ethics Act
1996	Establishment of Human Rights Commission [bilats]	Presidential Commission on Corruption appointed End of first phase of PSRC Tanzanian Revenue Authority created [WB] Personnel Management and Information Unit created
1997	Human Rights Commission Act Local Government Act Movement Act Poverty Eradication Programme *Launch of PSRP* [UNDP, DfID, IDA]	TRA created PCB strengthened
1998	Public Enterprise Reform and Divestiture Statute 9	Second phase of PSRP
1999	Judicial Inquiry into Corruption in the Police Force Referendum and Other Provisions Act Public Sector Management Project [IDA etc.]	
2000		*Launch of PSRP* [WB]

reform policies aimed at changing the way state institutions work: a greater use of public information programmes, programmes to run service delivery surveys (SDSs), decentralisation and a focus on output orientation for example. This relates to the World Bank's particular predisposition: 'The Bank has taken a technocratic approach, aiming governance reforms at the encouragement of economic growth, rather than democratic politics' (Bratton and Rothchild 1992: 254).

Understanding administrative reform as driven by a governance agenda means that reform is not merely the marketisation of the state, but also a means to realise liberal designs of 'proper' public action and bureaucratic behaviour. As we shall see in Chapter 6, norms of governance work very powerfully to drive governance reform with reference to liberalism's normative representations of politics as positive-sum, pluralised and representative.

In sum, administrative reform has been generated from three integrated sources: structural adjustment itself, the rise of a globalised 'common sense' of new institutional economics and new public management and the governance agenda of transparency and accountability.

In Uganda and Tanzania, administrative reform has been a key component of post-conditionality politics. Large administrative reform programmes have been funded by donors in both countries during the post-conditionality period, as is shown in Table 4.2. The key dates for Uganda are 1990, when the Civil Service Reform Programme (CSRP) was initiated and 1997 when the Public Sector Reform Programme (PSRP) succeeded it. In Tanzania, a CSRP was launched in 1991, and the PSRP commenced in 2000. Table 4.2 also lists other significant institutional innovations, and adds in parentheses the involvement of donors. The overall impression is of a state highly active in institutional innovation and administrative reform, involving heavy donor funding.

Let us retrace our steps. The World Bank's generic championing of governance has filtered through the tendency to act selectively *vis à vis* African states, producing sovereign frontiers for governance states that involve external agencies heavily, but with less explicit coercion and conditionality. Programmatically, this conjuncture has generated a profusion of support for programmes of state restructuring: administrative reform, public sector reform and technical assistance. This is the essence of governance practice for the World Bank and it draws our attention squarely to the structures and processes of governance states themselves.

5 The mechanics of post-conditionality

'New' ministries

What impact do administrative reform programmes have on the state, working as they do within a régime of post-conditionality? In the following sections, I will trace some of the salient features of the post-conditionality governance state in Uganda and Tanzania. This will involve less attention to the technical aspects of change, for example the extent to which a new personnel management system is 'working', and more attention to changes in political structures and processes. In the first section, we will look at the changing role of the two key ministries in respect to donor-funded administrative reform programmes: the Ministry of Finance and the Ministry of Public Service. In Uganda, these ministries are: the Ministry of Finance Planning and Economic Development (MoFPED) and the Ministry of Public Service (MPS) respectively; in Tanzania the ministries are: the Tanzanian Ministry of Finance (TMF) and the Civil Service Department (CSD) respectively.[1]

Ministry of Finance

The Ministry of Finance has become the hegemonic ministry within both countries. This is a key feature of the post-conditionality state because it relates directly to the ascendance of neoliberalism within the state; that is, the overall concern with supply-side economic management and the more effective raising of taxes. It was the Ministry of Finance that became the agent to reduce the amount of fungible money running through the sinews of the state, to reduce money supply, to increase interests rates, to reduce the budget deficit, and of course to arrange repayments on debt. In Tanzania in 1986, negotiations with the IMF were held in strict secrecy: even Ministers and the Central Committee of the ruling party were kept out of the loop. Instead, the Party 'gave its consent to the Ministry of Finance to come to an agreement with the IMF' (Campbell and Stein 1992: 15).

But the Ministry of Finance's power does not just derive from its centrality to structural adjustment. In the post-conditionality régime, it remains the central institution. In the first place, it is the Ministry of Finance that serves as a conduit between the state and donor/creditors. In both Tanzania and Uganda, all agreements for project and programme funding are signed with the Permanent Secretary of the Ministry of Finance, regardless of the implementing Ministry. Uganda's MoFPED houses the Aid Liaison Unit, responsible for co-ordinating all donor funds:, 'all donor-funded projects – the only significant source of capital spending in the system – were managed centrally by the Ministry of Finance and Planning' (Brett 1994: 68, 70). As a result, all donors, bilateral and multilateral, make real efforts to maintain good relations with the higher echelons of the Finance Ministries. This involves regular contacts with the ministry and a degree of information sharing not found in other parts of the state. It is also relevant to note that in Uganda the Ministry of Finance and the Ministry of Planning and Economic Development were merged in the key year of 1992,[2] to create a 'super ministry' principally concerned with the tasks of financial management rather than planning and development.

In Tanzania, the formal implementing partner for the Public Service Reform Programme (PSRP) is not actually the Civil Service Department – despite the fact that this is the institution that executes the programme – it is the Tanzanian Ministry of Finance (TMF) (interview, *Economist*, UNDP, July 2000). The Ministry of Finance took over the co-ordination of the Poverty Reduction Strategy Paper from the Vice President's Office, signifying this ministry's ascendance and centrality to the management of donor-state relations (Evans 2001: 1–2).

All bilateral donors negotiate their aid programmes with the Ministry of Finance, many referring to it as the 'point of entry', regardless of the nature of the aid programme. USAID in Tanzania shares early drafts of its programmes with the TMF (interview, Assistant Director, USAID, August 2000). The Ugandan USAID counterpart summarised the situation there by saying that when Tumusiime-Mutebile (then the Permanent Secretary and Secretary to the Treasury in MoFPED) was out of Kampala, all the donors panic because all of their projects go through him (interview, Democracy and Governance Advisor, USAID, July 2000). Thus, the Ministry of Finance maintains its paramount position as the conduit through which donors pump money into these two governments.

The Ministry of Finance has received funding for its *own* administrative reform programmes. These have involved two components, generally known as 'soft' and hard' reforms, or those concerned with personnel and skill and those concerned with systems and technology. In terms of 'soft' reforms, it is noteworthy that Ministries of Finance have received a disproportionate amount of training and technical assistance, that is externally-funded posts for experts (almost always expatriates). Donor assistance allowed MoFPED to establish a Masters degree course at Makerere University, taking in 20 employees per year; donors fund research groups within MoFPED with a view to improving the technical competence of economic planning and policy making, and the World Bank and UNDP have introduced incentive schemes into MoFPED to enhance performance and motivation (Lamont 1995: 16–19). In Uganda,

> the Ministry of Finance, Planning and Economic Development is the most powerful ministry and has a lot of technical assistance. Other weaker ministries have little technical assistance, for example the Ministry of the Interior has not got computerized systems, so it doesn't have reliable information.
> (Interview, Commissioner, MoFPED, July 2000)

The perceived expertise within the Ministry of Finance gives it an image of power within other ministries. This is reinforced by the larger and better maintained premises and the high level of computerisation of the ministry.

In respect to 'hard' reforms, both ministries have introduced new systems of budgetary management, with donor funding. In Uganda, MoFPED introduced cash budgeting, which ties all ministries to a strict régime of expenditure based on cash subventions rather than deficit financing. Stronger budgeting systems are being implemented as part of the IDA financed Economic and Financial Management Programme (I and II) within MoFPED. In Tanzania, the Platinum System budgetary management software package has been introduced in order to give the TMF greater control over the requests for budgets from all other ministries (interview, Chief Secretary and Head of Public Service, August 2000). In effect, these are improved technologies of control, yielded by the Ministry of Finance to ensure fiscal prudence throughout most of the state. In Uganda, in 1999, the original budgets set out by the Ministry of Finance for all ministries, departments and agencies were reduced mid term unilaterally by the MoFPED (interview, Chair of Parliamentary Committee on Legal and Parliamentary Affairs, July 2000), one effect of which is to reinforce the hegemony of this ministry. In fiscal year 1991/2 MoFPED unilaterally cut expenditure for the last quarter by 70 per cent for all ministries (Bigsten and Kayizzi-Mugerwa 2001: 23). Additionally, MoFPED's relative technical competence has led it to dominate policy making in all areas (Lamont 1995: 22).

Both the hard and soft reforms, the centrality of the Ministry of Finance to the donor groups, and the relatively high level of skilled personnel in their better-kept offices provide the Ministry of Finance with a certain ideological leadership. This leadership provides an important source for the dissemination of neoliberal ideas within the state. Other ministries make requests for their budgets to the Ministry of Finance, and in Uganda each ministry's accounting officers (those who control budgets) are centrally appointed by the Secretary to the Treasury (interview, Chair, Public Accounts Committee, July 2000). This makes all ministries constantly aware of the power of the Ministry of Finance and its central concern – fiscal prudence.

Civil Service/Public Service

Administrative reform programmes are actually executed by the Ministry of Public Service (MPS) or Civil Service Department (CSD). What impact has the rise of administrative reform as a key component in the post-conditionality régime had on this institution? In the first place, the profile of the ministry has been increased. The first component of administrative reform in both Tanzania and Uganda was retrenchment, and this involved the MPS/CSD, along with the Public Service Commission, executing a pro-gramme of weeding out 'ghost' workers, updating employee lists, selecting employees to be retrenched, and administering a severance package. In similar fashion to the role played by the Ministries of Finance, donor money pumped into the Ministries of Public Service allowed it to project its own agenda into other line ministries. Some donors see a division of labour between the Ministry of Finance and the MPS as the two central executing ministries which donors deal with: one manages the money, the other the personnel. In Uganda, as part of the first Civil Service Reform Programme (CSRP, see Table 4.2), the Management Services Department of the Ministry of Public Service carried out a restructuring report on the Ministry of Health as part of the CSRP (Ministry of Public Service 1995); in 1993 a major seminar was held under the auspices of the MPS, involving ministers and permanent secretaries on the management of change in respect to civil service reform; and a functional staff review of all min-istries was made by the MPS as part of the CSRP (Ministry of Public Service 1993: 30). Thus, the reform programmes, and the donor resources that came with it, allowed the MPS and CSD to rejuvenate themselves and effect changes in ministries. Both Uganda and Tanzania have established Inter Ministerial Technical Committees, chaired by the MPS and CSD which oversee civil service reform.

Changes in each ministry have also been significantly contingent on each country's political history. In Uganda, under the CSRP, the MPS was significantly dynamised. Its main tasks in this period were to implement a new system of personnel management which essentially involved reducing employee numbers, decompressing wages and improving records manage-ment through computerisation. There were significant successes in these areas, and large amounts of donor money were involved in the early stages mainly aimed at funding retrenchment packages. The MPS also had the clear political support and interest of Museveni, to the extent that the retrenchment process went fairly smoothly, a result of the open and powerful support of the President for what was bound to be a difficult reform to implement (interview, Director of Administrative Reform, Min-istry of Public Service, July 2000).

> [During the CSRP] Uganda has made considerable progress in its move towards a more effective public service. This has been largely due to the strong political support for the programme from the President and the highest level of government. Political support has been essential to implement some potentially very unpopular, but necessary, reforms particularly the downsizing of the service.
>
> (Administrative Reform Secretariat 1997: 2).

But, after these reforms, other aspects of the CSRP – notably those concerns with instituting a new Results Oriented Management (ROM) throughout the ministries – went into abeyance. This was one reason for the design and implementation of the PSRP which aims to re-dynamise the administrative reform programme (interview, Governance Advisor, Department for International Development, July 2000), but some fear that now administrative reform is not a political issue in the same way as HIPC, the Poverty Eradication Action Plan,[3] or regional security, it will be very difficult to get this project off the ground. By 2001, at least one donor was concerned that the MPS was under-spending and not providing information that would have allowed the release of further tranches of grant support. This was interpreted by donors as a sign of failing ministry resolve to carry out reform, especially in Output Oriented Budgeting and Results Oriented Management.[4]

If Uganda's trajectory of reform is one of an explosive and effective beginning, followed by the tailing off of change, Tanzania's trajectory is in many ways the reverse. Although civil service reform began with the same process, of successful retrenchment, strongly funded by donors, subsequently, there has been a cautious build-up of preparations for the PSRP, initiated in 2000 and lasting until 2011. This will involve many of the same aspects as the Ugandan programme (Table 4.2) – principally ROM and a focus on customer service. Comparing the literature produced by both ministries, one gets the impression that the Tanzanian reform programme is more detailed and realistic in its time-frame. The 'working ethos' of interviewees in the CSD indicated a desire to ensure that reform proceeded in a measured and cautious fashion, according to 'Tanzanian' schedules, rather than donor ones.

The World Bank has been proactively funding the actions of the finance and public service ministries. In doing so, the Bank is intimately involved not only in the reconfiguring of governance states but in the very processes of public management. The repercussions of this are that the 'techniques' of state action are changing as well as the forms of government, most clearly in Uganda. This will be taken up again below.

In sum, the sovereign frontier of governance states are not easily described in terms of conditionality. The Bank has made more intimate and differentiated interventions into governance states. This has produced two cardinal institutional developments. First, the internalisation of neoliberal economic policy by the Ministry of Finance in conjunction with the rising prominence of the latter, has removed the economic 'fundamentals' from explicit political discussions. Second, the 'governance agenda' which aims to restructure states as facilitators of open, vibrant, progressive market-based growth has been articulated through capacity building projects, mainly handled by rejuvenated Ministries of Public Administration. This agenda reveals a progression from the first to the third phase of administrative reform mentioned earlier in the chapter (see also Table 4.2).

The post-conditionality state: donor/creditors

The post-conditionality state has two key features: the rise of Ministries of Finance as powerful producers of neoliberal orthodoxy, and the rise of public service ministries as the executors of administrative reform programmes. These institutional changes relate to the post-conditionality régime: internalising neoliberalism so as to locate conditionality in the background and a concern with governance in the positive sense of programmes for administrative reform. The second aspect of the post-conditionality state that requires some elaboration is the relationship between state and donors in the sovereign frontier.

The first point to bear in mind is that conditionality is still a central aspect of the donor-state relationship. For example, in Uganda, the World Bank set out 86 specific policy reforms for 1991/2–1993/4 (Killick 1997: 484). The coercive logic of conditionality remains, as it does for all of sub Saharan Africa, but the direct threat of a withdrawal of finance is removed from the political scene. State-donor politics is far more 'collegial' than it has been, for example in Kenya or Zambia in the late 1980s and 1990s, Zimbabwe in the mid 1990s, or for that matter Tanzania during the early 1980s. Consultative Group meetings statements present a donor approach which is mainly concerned with consolidating an already accepted reform logic through the provision of further loans and grants. It is therefore not satisfactory merely to make the opposition of donor and state via the mechanism of conditionality in order to understand the post-conditionality state.

It is equally important however, to bear in mind that public action in both Tanzania and Uganda are *extremely* aid-dependent. In the mid 1990s, NGOs contributed 64 per cent of the running costs of health services in Uganda (Ministry of Public Service 1995: 4); funding for the PSRP is projected to have 90 per cent of its funding come from donors (Administrative Reform Secretariat 1997: 85). In 1990, aid constituted 30 per cent of Tanzania's entire GDP (Bigsten *et al.* 1999: 2–3). In fact, rather than conceptualising donor power as a strong external force on the state, it would be more useful to conceive of donors as *part of the state itself*. This is what distinguishes the sovereign frontier of governance states from those of other African states. It is not just a result of the fact that so much of the budgeting process is contingent on the receipt of donor finance. It is also a result of the way programmes and even specific policies are designed and executed. In Tanzania and Uganda, there are donor sub-groups which meet every fortnight or every month, depending on the group. There is a group for each major ministry which receives donor funding. Donors select from within their own groups a chair – most often a larger donor with a particular specialism. In Tanzania, the governance sub group is chaired by the UNDP; in Uganda the same group is chaired by the World Bank.[5] The permanent secretary of a particular ministry is invited to the sub group meetings. The meetings discuss policy progress, monitor the disbursement of funds and consider further funding options. They are a routine part of the way the government works, and the higher echelons of the civil service routinely produce information for donors – both within the sub group meetings and as part of the donors' desire to maintain a closer monitoring of their money. In Uganda, the USAID governance advisor attends about five sub group meetings per month (interview, Governance and Democracy Advisor, USAID, July 2000). The innovation of collective donor funding (Sector Wide Approaches) also involves intense and routine donor involvement (Brown *et al.* 2001).

Donor Ideological Hegemony I: international orthodoxies

Individual donors select aspects of country programmes which fit with their particular development ethos. For all external agencies, ideals of development are informed by the governance rubric. Uganda, Tanzania and Mozambique each produce country strategy plans (CDF or PRSP) and present these to donors in order to elicit support, and donors can subsequently feel assured that overall ownership rests with the government itself. The country strategies are clearly produced by African officials with an eye to the international orthodoxies within which donors work, currently an emphasis on pro-poor growth, based on basic social provision and market friendly policy. This might be the orthodoxy that officials themselves believe to be the most effective way to ensure progress, but it is also the case that a country strategy which effectively taps into international orthodoxies of development and governance stands a much better chance of being funded by donors and, as we have seen, there is not a great deal that these states can do in the absence of donor funding. This has led some cynically to call country strategies 'shopping lists' to present to donors. Therkildsen gives a careful account of this process in respect to Tanzania:

> The preparation of a policy paper is important for ministerial fund raising. Due regard to perceived donor preferences will therefore be taken by the ministry in question. It may even request technical assis-

tance to draft the policy. This helps to explain the ... observation that many senior officials and ministers do not take an active part in the policy making process. As principals assessing the quality of policy work, they need only ascertain that their subordinate agents help to produce policy papers and plans that attract donor funding. This is a key indicator of a job well done.

(Therkildsen 2000: 66)

Much of the innovation in pro-poor budgeting in Uganda suffers from the same problem (Williamson and Canagaraja 2003). So, the argument here is that it is not very instructive to try to separate an external and national interest (if it ever was). Donor influence there certainly is, but it does not necessarily work against a state, and the state itself does not have any distinct *a priori* opposition to the global hegemony of neoliberalism and governance. This is not to agree with the World Bank and others that the new donor politics is one of partnership, ownership and states being in the 'driver's seat' (see Chapter 6). It is rather that the state is reflecting and internalising a more complex state of affairs than a dichotomy of national-external opposition in post-adjustment régimes. As we shall see later in this chapter, this state of affairs produces its own significant contradictions, even if we cannot understand these in terms of just external intervention and the violation of some notion of sovereignty.

Donor Ideological Hegemony II: methods of governance

Donor influence does not just manifest itself through the power of money and the integration of donors into the routines of government. Chapter 6 will show that the discourse of the World Bank concerning governance and administrative reform contributed to the strength of its interventions. The key themes of this discourse are very much present in Uganda and Tanzania's policy documents: participation, ownership, citizens as customers, etc. But, governance states also encapsulate a deeper change which derives from devices of reform promulgated by the Bank and other donor-creditors and which might be called the methodology of governance. With donor funding comes a new set of regulations concerning the technique of the policy process. Donors look for and fund corporate plans within ministries, departments and agencies – based on logical frameworks which set out specific policies, executing agencies, timeframes and funding requirements. One can see this most readily in the CSD's *Quarterly Reports* where a key aspect of the governance methodology, the matrix, is ever-present (Cammack 2001). Also, projects and programmes have to be audited more intensely: until recently a programme which involved a number of donors would require the production of numerous audit reports on money spent, one for each donor.[6] Donor-funded technical assistance ensures that state cadres have the capacity to take on innovations in policy technique. The Tanzanian public service produces about 2,400 quarterly reports per year for external donors (Kelsall 2002b: 599). In Uganda, some ministries have set up budget groups to ensure that new monitoring and accounting techniques are applied (interview, Governance Advisor, Department for International Development, July 2000). Uganda represents the most advanced case in this respect, changing its budget processes from an unstable dirigisme in 1986 to cash budgeting, to an Integrated Financial Management System (IFMS) that has provided the opportunity for the ideal mechanism of external funding for a governance state: general budgetary support with the assurance of a vigorous and transparent auditing and surveillance procedure (Adam and Gunning 2002; Williamson and Canagaraja 2003). Tanzania is moving in the same direction: it has a three-year Medium-Term Expenditure and Finance mechanism and Public Expenditure Reviews each year; it is also committed to the introduction of an IFMS as part of its PRSP (United Republic of Tanzania 2001). Tanzania and Uganda both have budget support mechanisms that allow donors to provide finance to a general budget and track pro-poor expenditure.

Relatedly, the presence of expatriate personnel on donor-funded contracts reinforces both the international orthodoxy of reform and the new methodologies of donors. Both Uganda and Tanzania have received considerable amounts of expatriate technical assistance, although this author could not find any aggregate numbers of expatriate personnel within the state.[7] In Uganda, the Danish governmental donor agency DANIDA had 22 advisors of one kind or another within the state in 1998. Expatriates have headed the Uganda Revenue Authority and NPART, the body which has managed the alienation of state property. In Tanzania, World Bank and DfID funding has ensured a heavy expatriate presence within the CSD, including a Chief Technical Advisor, although the Government of Tanzania wishes to phase out medium-term contracts for expatriate technical advisors in favour of shorter and more specific contracts. One technical advisor within the CSD, interviewed for this book, saw his job explicitly as acting as a conduit for new internationally-accepted management techniques.

In sum, the donor state relation is too intimate and inter-related to be understood as a dichotomy. Donors do not just impose conditionalities; they also work in routinised fashion at the centre of policy making. Donor funded technical assistance introduces not new policies but new methodologies of governance based on corporate plans, surveys and closer budgeting/monitoring techniques. It now remains to critically analyse the post-conditionality régime.

The contradictions of post-conditionality politics

Money is power: the role of the World Bank

This old aphorism is certainly not part of the Bank's lexicon, despite its obvious truth. As mentioned earlier, dependence on donor funds underpins the integration of donors into policy processes. Within the donor group, the resources that the World Bank controls gives it a (dis)proportionate influence within governance states. This is a result of two factors: first the simple fact of the size of the Bank as a multilateral international finance institution; second the politics of the World Bank's country offices. One can see this financial preponderance in Table 5.1. Extrapolating from this, we get an idea of the Bank's centrality to the financial régime of governance states. For the donor sources noted in the table, from 1992 to 1996, the Bank released $872.8 million EDA to Tanzania, and $571.2 million to Uganda. The World Bank is the largest donor, releasing a constant stream of grants and credit, as well as debt cancellation and grants through other lending mechanisms such as the International Finance Corporation.[8] A very relevant example: the World Bank's Project Appraisal Document which prepared the way for Bank funding of Tanzania's PSRP, set out that the Bank would provide $94 million, over twice as much as the Government of Tanzania's funding and a third larger than all other donor contributions (World Bank 1999: 1).

Furthermore, each country office has a resident representative who is evaluated substantially according to the amount of programme funding he or she can arrange. Therefore, a principal aim of the resident representative is to spend money during their residency.[9] The Bank has the means and the motivation to 'lead' the lending process.

The size of the Bank, and the politics of residency make the Bank a willing and able lender. For example, from 1992, the Bank pledged $928 million to Uganda (Kasekende and Atingi-Ego 1999: 623).[10] Over the same period, the IMF pledged $168 million, and total bilateral pledges reached $1,498 million (ibid.). One immediate point here is that this results in Uganda and Tanzania contracting substantial new loans during the HIPC period, making a nonsense of the whole notion of HIPC as a 'solution' to severe indebtedness. Oloka-Onyango and Barya sum this situation up nicely with respect to Uganda, but it remains true for Tanzania as well: 'with the "fresh start" provided by the [HIPC debt] relief, Uganda – like a discharged bankrupt – will be game for a new round of borrowing' (1997: 129). 'After having about one fifth external debt written off in 1998, the Ugandan government immediately increased borrowing and had a bigger debt by 1999 than before' (Allen and Weinhold 2000: 870).[11] For Tanzania, the net present value of debt in 2015 will be three times larger than it was in 1999, the year before Tanzania gained HIPC status (Danielson 2001: 2).

Another repercussion of the Bank's financial sway is that it can impose

Table 5.1 World Bank EDA in comparison with selected bilateral and multilateral donors

	1992		1993		1994		1995		1996	
	TZ	*UG*	*TZ*	*UG*	*TZ*	*UG*	*TZ*	*UG*	*TZ*	*UG*
France	1.45	4.9	0.0	4.8	0.0	3.5	0.0	10.3	0.0	13.7
Germany	0.0	23.0	0.0	37.9	0.0	29.5	0.0	47.2	0.0	40.1
The Netherlands	0.0	15.1	0.0	23.1	0.0	25.5	0.0	31.8	0.0	32.6
The UK	0.067	40.1	3.454	64.0	10.6	52.0	2.817	85.4	0.0	62.2
The USA	0.0	22.0	0.0	57.0	0.0	51.0	0.0	49.0	0.0	29.0
The EU	–	156.1	–	29.6	–	53.5	–	106.3	–	46.1
The IMF	–	51.8	–	0.0	–	48.2	–	51.0	–	0.0
The World Bank (IDA)	237.8	115.5	155.9	102.8	183.2	157.7	159.8	110.7	136.1	84.5

Sources: Bigsten *et al.* 1999: Table A5; Kasekende and Atingi-Eto 1999.

Notes
Effective development assistance (EDA) = grant equivalent of official loan disbursements and official grants. In contrast to Official Development Assistance ('aid'), this picks up the grant component in concessional lending, which derives from the World Bank via the IDA. The other donors were selected as significant sources of external funds; the addition of other donors with smaller programmes would serve to enhance the disproportionate nature of Bank funding *vis à vis* any other source.
– Figures not available

its own preferences for big-spending programmes on any existing smaller scale incremental projects funded by other donors. DANIDA in Uganda was funding a moderate capacity building project as part of Uganda's decentralization programme, for example funding a Local Government Finance Commission in Rakia district and a Decentralisation Secretariat. DANIDA's approach was to begin with three selected districts and to ensure that local funds constituted at least 50 per cent of project funding (part of the criterion of ownership). The Bank subsequently created its own decentralisation programme for all of Uganda regardless of the institutional capacity of the district (a serious concern of donors and officials alike), and only requiring a 10 per cent local contribution to the projects therein. A DANIDA programme officer saw this as World Bank 'bulldozing', undermining the more cautious approach of DANIDA (interview, July 2000; also interview UNDP Resident Representative, July 2000). The Government of Uganda accepted the Bank project, which involved far larger amounts of money than the Danish one ($13 million). This meant that a small grant project has been over-run by a large World Bank loan-based project, no matter how long term and concessional the loan might be. The same concerns about 'bulldozing' were expressed in Tanzania (interview, Royal Norwegian Embassy, August 2000).[12] A repercussion of this was that often the government of Tanzania had 'too much' money, that is, in excess of its capacity to absorb money. Also in Tanzania, some donors, involved in administrative reform resent the power of the Bank which it enjoys merely by virtue of its control of resources rather than any clear specialism in a reform area (interview, Programme Office, DANIDA (Danish International Development Agency) August 2000). It is of course possible that this resentment is more a result of donor rivalries rather than substantive questions of competence, but it is noteworthy that this concern was also reported to me by a technical advisor on a World Bank contract (confidential interview, August 2000)![13]

'Cherries should not go rotten': the contradictions between governance and showcases

We must recognise that the role and reputation of the Bank ... is at stake in Africa. To be frank, the Bank has 'stuck its neck out a mile' in Africa. We have said publicly on many occasions that we are giving Africa the highest priority among development problems in the world. We have been telling Africa how to reform, sometimes in terms of great detail (*sic*). Now a significant number of these African countries are beginning to follow the Bank's advice. If these programmes fail, for whatever reasons, *our policies will be seen widely to have failed*.

(World Bank briefing sheet, cited in Kapur *et al.* 1997: 730, emphasis added)

As mentioned earlier, governance states are a selective category: they exist in indebted states where the adjustment agenda has been internalised and where economic recovery is at least a statistical reality. In these cases, it appears that the Bank can at long last claim that SAP was worthwhile after all: 'One valuable and hopeful lesson for Africa is that spectacular increases in growth are indeed possible – if the right policies are in place' (World Bank 1994a: 200). We have seen in Chapter 2 how these states have generated a range of glowing appraisals from the international community. Tanzania, Uganda and Mozambique are touted as a justification for the Bank's actions over the last 20 years or so.

Because the World Bank has invested considerable political capital in Uganda, Mozambique and Tanzania, the costs of substantial decline in these states would be high indeed. It would then be incumbent on the Bank to try to extract itself from any culpability concerning whatever crisis faces the indebted state – something it would find extremely difficult bearing in mind the *intimacy* of World Bank involvement, as argued above. This political investment can undermine the Bank's concerns with some aspects of governance, and especially corruption. In Mozambique, the growing fealty of the elite to neoliberalism, coupled with the rapid increase in rates of economic growth (on paper) have led external agencies to soften criticisms concerning corruption and embezzlement (Harrison 1999a). There are similar signs in Uganda and Tanzania. In Uganda, one international consultant applied for a post in a government department and was told, explicitly in a fax, to submit a bribe to the permanent secretary of the ministry if he/she wanted the job. Refusing to pay the bribe, the consultant gave a copy of the fax to the Bank's offices and asked what action the consultant should take. The person in the Bank's response was that it was not their responsibility, and that they 'didn't want to know about it' (confidential interview). In Tanzania, Raikes and Gibbon note that the recent increase in corruption has been downplayed as donors celebrate Tanzania as a good adjuster (1996: 227). Other donors, enjoying close and routinised working relations with debtor states, are also shy of the sensitive issue of corruption.[14] A number of more candid interviewees said that donors knew about corrupt practice – officials with a row of luxury apartments which they could never have paid for out of a public servant's salary etc. – but demure from acting on these cases in any way because of the repercussions that this would have on a more generalised donor–state relationship.

This is not to say that donors are indifferent to corruption. In both Tanzania and Uganda, donors have financed anti-corruption agencies and raised the issue of corruption at Consultative Group meetings and elsewhere. But the anti-corruption agenda is made more complex by the mutual (albeit still unequal) dependence between donors and debtor state: to identify serious corruption at the highest echelons of the state would be to disrupt the post-conditionality régime, with its image of partnership, progress and powerful claim to showcase status. As a result, public statements of concern about corruption by donors, and funding for anti-corruption bodies are accompanied by a certain shyness among some (but not all[15]) to engage with anti-corruption actions. Another form of 'double standard' relates specifically to Uganda. Uganda has implemented a 'no-party' system which has prohibited active opposition parties. Nevertheless, Uganda is only criticised very mildly for its no party democracy, even though the general political direction that this political form is taking is more towards a single party state (Mamdani 1995; Kasfir 1998; Hauser 1999; Human Rights Watch 1999; Carbone 2000).

Institutional imaginings

An important point, recognised by those involved in administrative reform, is that institutional innovations do not necessarily make the differences expected of them. Some institutions, which might appear to be significant steps in implementing reform, are in fact almost ineffective. In Tanzania, an Ethics Secretariat was created in the President's Office (1995) to ensure the appropriate ethical conduct of politicians and higher-ranking government officials (that is, 'leaders'). Leaders are supposed to submit a declaration of assets to the Secretariat each year, after which the latter ensures that no unexplained enrichment has taken place. The implementation of leadership codes of this kind is seen as a key reform in governance states, and is welcomed by donors. However, the Ethics Secretariat is severely understaffed, and cannot possibly check the 5,000 or so submissions that it is supposed to receive. The Secretariat does not have the power to initiate its own investigations, but passes on information to the President. The public can make a complaint to the Secretariat, but only after paying a fee and giving their full names and address, thus compromising themselves in the process of making a complaint. By 1999, 34 cases had been considered by the Secretariat, and *none* had been passed to the President. Interviewing the Director of the Ethics Secretariat in 2001, I asked if the Secretariat had produced last year's report and was told that they were still working on the report for 1996. In Uganda, a related area of reform – the development of a stronger Leadership Code of Conduct, led to the discovery that only 25 per cent of existing 'leaders' had submitted declarations of assets despite a requirement to do so from 1997 (*New Vision* 30 January 2002).

In other cases, reforms are as much subverted as ineffectual. The following quotation comes from an interview with a Technical Advisor with a remit to introduce staff appraisal techniques into the Tanzanian Ministries:

> Usually Government Departments see appraisal as an annual ritual to be got through ... Departments can set convenient targets for themselves or modify criteria to engineer an improvement. New systems can be ignored or manipulated. There is a need for a change in the ethics. Do donors care if systems are being modified and so on in any case?

Part of the answer to this interviewee's question is that donors heavily support workshops in both Tanzania and Uganda, with the purpose not only of improving the skills levels of officials, but also of inculcating new approaches to – or ethics of – administration. This is particularly the case with anti-corruption programmes. Workshops vary in their intent and their success. There is no clear form of workshop evaluation in many cases, although those concerned with technical skills do have forms of monitoring, such as the training workshops in Uganda's Institutional Capacity Building Programme (interview, Training Manager, July 2000). Workshops are also a means to distribute 'perks' within a department; in some cases public employees vie to attend workshops because they come with an allowance, a stay in a prestigious venue (an international hotel or conference centre) and a good buffet or meal. If department heads plan to reduce the cost of workshops by reducing allowances or holding the sessions within their own buildings, it is far more difficult to get people to attend. Workshops funded out of World Bank money can be quite expensive affairs because the Bank has no accounting methods applied to criteria of value for money at local costs: a workshop in an international hotel at perhaps $300 per person is not exceptional for the Bank – as long as all the money is accounted for (interview, Civil Service Technical Advisor, July 2000). Another related example:

> The poorly attended workshop [in Uganda] ... was funded by the Association of European Parliamentarians for Africa. [Ugandan] MPs signed for 100,000 [Ugandan] shillings each as transport charges but some of them disappeared after lunch, causing lack of quorum.
>
> (*New Vision* 19 April 2002)

It is difficult to say how representative this example is, but it is clear that workshops are only partly about capacity building and a new administrative ethos; they are also about perks and patronage, and have in fact created their own 'development culture' (Green 2003) with their own discursive and performative protocols, removed from the realities of development and poverty (ibid.: 134).

Structured limits to reform

Interviewees in both Uganda and Tanzania stated that some of the highest level bureaucrats, including those directly involved with donors and governance-related reforms, were accumulating substantial amounts of wealth in opaque ways. Dan Wandera Ogalo, MP and Chair of the Ugandan Parliamentary Committee on Legal and Parliamentary Affairs, which reviews reports from the Inspector General of Government, states that 'the real corruption involves millions of dollars and goes on at the highest levels' (interview, July 2000). In Mozambique, Uganda and Tanzania, popular attitudes towards corruption make a distinction between the 'big fish' (in Mozambique called *tubarões* or sharks) and 'small fry', the latter referring to so-called petty corruption. In each country, there is the sense – backed up by fragmentary evidence – that there is a cabal at the highest levels of government which embezzles millions of dollars and acts to all intents and purposes with immunity from the law. Perhaps one aspect of high level corruption which has been under-emphasised is the centrality of violence to accumulation.[16] Interviewees who spoke of high level corruption sometimes remarked that to mention the names of the worst offenders (it seems that the scams of these people was no secret within certain boundaries) would be to risk threats, violence and perhaps death.

Accumulation and class formation in many parts of sub Saharan Africa has relied on extra economic coercion, that is, the direct use of state violence (Mamdani 1987). Often, state power and accumulation are unified in a single process (Bayart 1993). In the era of governance, donor funded programmes and post-conditionality politics, some still use these 'old fashioned' methods to enrich themselves, employing the threat of violence to ensure that they remain 'untouchable' in the face of new governance agendas. And if a 'big fish' is brought to court, it is possible that both the velvet glove of bribes will accompany the iron fist of violence to ensure that justice is not done (confidential interview, Tanzania, August 2000).

Conclusion: evaluating post-conditionality administrative reform

The previous section has set out a series of contradictions within the post-conditionality frontier, mainly associated with administrative reform. One can see that these contradictions do not correspond to any internal-external dichotomy, but instead sit within the complex *internal* politics of governance states' sovereign frontiers. The post-conditionality sovereign frontier encompasses the 'governance ministries' of finance and public service as well as the World Bank, leading other donors. Clearly the social dynamics of the sovereign frontier are strongly shaped by the material preponderance of the Bank. This chapter has shown the salience of various incentivising or proactive forms of lending, based in expanded capacity to survey and reform. But, one can also identify a tentative and uneven kind of 'mutuality' – a product of the selectivity of governance states and their 'showcase' status in international perceptions. In sum, governance states maintain a key range of institutional innovations, underpinned by the pervasive financial underpinning of external donor-creditors. The apparent paradox – of a revived sovereignty within governance states directly as a result of external and proactive funding – is sutured through a specific discourse of intervention articulated by external agencies, and most notably (again) the World Bank. This is the concern of the next chapter.

6 Liberalism and the discourse of reform in governance states

The legitimation of the imperial machine is ... reproposed ceaselessly by developing its own languages of self-validation.

(Hardt and Negri 2000: 33)

Ideologically 'inclusive' liberal approaches are held together by polysemous, apparently apolitical catchwords such as participation, partnership, and community.

(Craig and Porter 2003: 54)

Introduction

Chapter 5 outlined some concrete mechanisms of very stark intervention in governance states by external agencies, most prominently, the World Bank: sectoral donor groups, large amounts of expatriate external assistance, pervasive ideological 'power projection' and so on. The World Bank is also 'arguably the most prestigious and ... most powerful producer ... of international development knowledge' (Berger and Beeson 1998: 487). During my fieldwork in Uganda and Tanzania, reading the daily papers, I was struck by how quickly I became familiar with the faces of World Bank resident representatives before almost all Tanzanian or Ugandan ministers. The daily papers[1] provide a window into the level of political presence of the Bank in another way. Many of the development projects and investment schemes announced in the paper are accompanied by pictures of Bank personnel or soundbites from Bank personnel who are involved in the funding of the project.

Moving away from media evidence, the Bank's involvement in administrative reform clearly reveals how the Bank is involved in the most 'intimate' aspects of governance states' operations. As has been suggested in Chapter 3, the Bank has represented its profound involvement in governance states through liberal discourse, a foundation of its self-representation and ontology. This chapter investigates this aspect of Bank involvement in governance states in more detail.

In doing so, we will demonstrate how the general discursive field of liberalism has been modified into a more specific set of references and tropes. This discourse allows the Bank to involve itself in governance states and represent this involvement in a way that largely denies the power of the Bank. As such, liberal discourse evokes a politics of positive-sum games, interdependency and rational dialogue. This kind of politics is clearly one that fits well with governance states' international image – as 'showcases' and 'good reformers' who have achieved their 'graduated' status by taking the 'driver's seat' and embracing 'partnership' with the Bank and other external agencies.

Administrative reform and liberal discourse

> The principal challenge of [administrative] reform is human: how to create a consciousness that the reforms are necessary in the public functionaries? To change mentalities, culture, poor behaviour for public service, is in fact the principal issue of the reform process.
>
> (Interview, Adelino Jaime da Cruz, Director of Technical Unit for Public Sector Reform, Mozambique, 2002)[2]

Because administrative reform provides the Bank with a remit to support programmes that aspire to re-engineer governance states at their foundations, it has been clothed quite heavily in the 'grammar' of liberal governance: in a sense, it is here that this form of discourse is most required. Administrative reform programmes aim to change the very 'mindsets' of bureaucrats (Williams and Young 1994; Williams 1996); they attempt to tackle corruption, which inevitably moves the Bank's focus on to a most controversial area of politics; and they aspire to realise the normative goals of good governance within the machinery of the state itself. As we saw in Chapters 4 and 5, governance states have achieved a degree of 'internalisation' of the governance agenda and this is crucially the result of administrative reform programmes.

The Bank's interest in administrative reform spans a longer period than just that of governance states (mid 1990s onwards). Between 1981 and 1991, the World Bank funded civil service reform programmes in 25 sub Saharan African countries. Seventeen of these countries began their programmes in 1987 or after (Nunberg 1994: 122–3). Thirty-one of the 56 programmes (55 per cent) in these 25 countries constituted part of a SAP. Technical assistance to sub Saharan Africa (which involves institutional reform and is not directly linked to SAP) was estimated to involve $4 billion per year in the late 1980s (World Bank 1995a: 5). This level of technical assistance represents a precipitous increase over the last twenty years: in the 1970s lending for technical assistance totalled $40 million in the 1970s but rose to $700 million for the 1980s (Mistry 1989: 14).[3] SAPs also involve a component of institutional/administrative reform. By 1988, public sector management components were present in all 59 SAPs in Africa (Nunberg 1990: 3).

Thus, we can see that aspects of administrative reform were part of structural adjustment, the 'first face' of administrative reform outlined in Chapter 4. These reforms were very much focussed on first generation concerns – of scaling down, cutting back and increasing efficiency. It is the *separation* of administrative reform from structural adjustment that is significant for our interests here. The Bank and other external agencies continue to fund administrative reform as part of other programmes – macroeconomic and sectoral. But, the implementation of self-standing administrative reform programmes signals the prominence of 'second generation concerns'; the state's capacity matters in itself, not solely as an adjunct to some other economic target. As such, 'third phase' administrative reform programmes have become significant parts of donor funding in all governance states.[4] As separate administrative reform programmes have been designed and implemented, so has the language of liberal interventionism consolidated.

Administrative reform and liberal intervention

Liberalism as a grammar of reform

Chapter 3 considered Williams's depiction of the Bank as 'liberalism in action'. His analysis relied on the assumption that the philosophical properties of liberalism 'drove' the Bank to act in certain ways. The value of Williams's work is that it highlights the centrality of liberalism as an intellectual and cultural tradition that both pushes a kind of imperial project while representing this project in self-serving ways. The intuition of this argument is taken on board here, and will be given more detail in the section below on 'common sense'. But, we do not take on Williams's perspective in its entirety. Although Williams has a hostility to the notion of 'interests', we shall relate liberal interventionism as a discursive means to allow the Bank pervasive remit over governance states' politics. As Cox notes, 'theory is always for someone and for some purpose. All theories have a perspective' (Cox and Sinclair 1996: 87). The interests of the Bank to finesse its overbearing intervention explains to a significant extent the reasons why the general ontology of liberalism is 'pinned down' to a quite limited set of phrases and references, specifically applied to the sovereign frontier within governance states.

We shall also endeavour to make some suggestive associations concerning the relations of liberalism in this context to changes in governance states' political economy, in other words, the intermingling of liberalism with economic liberalisation. This is not to attempt a structuralist reading of liberal governance discourse; rather it is to tease out the commonalities and mutual references which ensure that no significant contradictions between economic liberalisation and liberal politics occur. In summary, our understanding of liberalism as a discourse is focussed on the specific political dispensation of administrative reform in governance states. Furthermore, this discourse is also inter-related with both the interests of the agencies propounding it and involving themselves in reform.

The topology of governance discourse

Before we proceed to look at the 'nuts and bolts' of governance discourse, we shall make some remarks on its internal logic. Here, we are interested in the structuring of the discourse; the ways in which specific words connote a broader understanding of politics which allows distinct words to 'work' together. The properties of liberal governance discourse emphasise three aspects of liberal political economy more generally.

In the first place, this is an equilibriating discourse. The World Bank and IMF have always worked on the premise that the task is to bring economies into a state of 'normality' or equilibrium (Harris 1986: 84). Politics is understood as a set of processes which tend towards a state of affairs which is balanced. The notion of opposing political forces working against each other to achieve a 'balance' derives from classical liberal political theory and political economy and post-war American political science. In this view, effective democracy relies on a balance between state power and civil society, or a more diffuse set of checks and balances. In respect to the latter, the locus classicus is Dahl's *Polyarchy* (1971). Liberal governance discourse takes this tendency towards equilibrium as an implicit property of political relations and processes; this is why politics is often named as 'consultation' or 'dialogue'. The significance of this understanding of politics is that it locates political conflict or contradiction within specific and relatively limited boundaries. The political 'problems' faced by a governance state are not irreconcilable or 'structural' in nature; rather, they are expressions of an information failure[5] or a lack of effective institutionalisation.

Second, liberal governance constructs a polity that is composed of individuals, officials and 'the poor'.[6] These social categorisations serve the Bank's operational purposes. Following Pincus' (2002) insightful work, one can say that these categorisations make society 'legible'[7] for the Bank in governance states and thus provide a categorisation that is constant with the Bank's operational objectives. Clearly, officials are the group that occupy the sovereign frontier, the interface within which the Bank works. Governing elites are the 'principals' who implement governance reform.

Individuals are represented in liberal fashion, what Williams (1999) calls *homo oeconomicus*, the Economic Man associated most closely with the work of Adam Smith, where human nature is built on a tendency to 'truck, barter, and exchange' (Smith 1986: 117). Representations of society as composed of individuals with key singular interests and behavioural traits effaces social groupings and structured relations. These same individuals are also – and most publicly – named as 'the poor'. But, once agglomerated effectively as 'the poor', a different kind of 'liberal argument' is made. Populist politics since pre-Marxist socialism (Kitching 1982) has referred to 'the people' 'the masses' or 'the poor' as a corporate social group who have a generic set of interests in economic improvement (Roxborough 1979). Populism represents society as having a general common interest in the public good; it 'sutures' any other social difference for example along the lines of class, gender or ethnicity. Populism is most closely associated with the military régimes of Latin America during the 1970s, but we can also identify a similar kind of political viewpoint in the Bank's constant references to the poor, even if shorn of *Latino* nationalist and leftist rhetoric. In other words, 'the masses' have been re-packaged as 'the poor' and integrated into a neoliberal menu of socio-economic reform rather than a national-corporatist one. This leads Gore to remark on a key word in the liberal governance vocabulary: 'participation . . . can be easily fused with a kind of neoliberal populism' (2000: 786).

Third and finally, liberal governance discourse is pervasively optimistic. Reading the Bank's *World Development Reports*, one gets a sense that, if everyone would sit down, work through all the development problems of the day, agree a common set of decisions based on the mutual concessions made by all parties, then a rosy future for all would be imminently reachable. The Bank itself seems implicitly to share this conviction – how else can it seriously be declaring to half poverty and achieve other international development targets by 2015? This optimism is based on a deep foundation of liberal political economy – the mechanism of the positive sum. In other words, social and economic intercourse tends to work to everyone's benefit. This is established by Ricardo's *Principles of Political Economy* and Adam Smith's *Wealth of Nations*. In the latter, Smith starts the first volume by detailing the way in which trade and specialisation have improved productivity in a truly startling fashion. His portrayal of the world and its rich and poor regions is essentially a geography of communication links: Africa's poverty is a result of its land mass and lack of navigable rivers (Smith 1986: 125). The corollary is that denser networks will ameliorate inequalities. Related concepts within liberal economics include 'trickle down', cumulative causation, and within economic geography notions of diffusion or 'spread effects'. The Bank's prospective is linear and 'accelerative'; the effects of increases in trade and social intercourse more generally are greater than any investments in social infrastructure which promote these ends. One can see this most clearly in the Bank's approach to rural development: it is quite simply a project to expand the infrastructure of trade and social provision with a view to stimulating higher levels of visible economic activity (World Bank 2000/2001: Chapter 4; World Bank 2000b: 12).

In sum, the 'topology' of liberal governance discourse draws key liberal nostrums into a specific political milieu. Governance states' politics is one of moving towards a stable equilibrium based on social interaction, dialogue and mutual concession. The outcome of these deliberations is intrinsically progressive and not subject to any structural contradictions as one might imagine would emerge from class relations or ethnic-clientelist politics. The politics of these deliberations is also positive-sum in the sense that any increase in social intercourse will produce 'accelerative' further benefits. This topology has been outlined here to draw out the liberal bases of Bank discourse on governance states. The next section takes the more specific components of the liberal governance discourse and relates them to Bank publications.

A vocabulary of liberal governance discourse

This section will review the key phrases of liberal governance discourse. It will take each phrase (italicised) and elaborate its meaning with respect to the Bank's publications on administrative reform,[8] and in relation to other words in the discourse. This serves to give a sense of how the Bank has acted discursively to represent its actions in governance states; it also provides the detail to back up the points made in the previous section. In order to emphasise the involvement of African governments, and more recently civil society in programmes of governance reform, *participation* has become perhaps the most pervasive reference. In a World Bank discussion paper titled 'Participatory development and the World Bank', Bhatnagar and Williams define participation dryly as 'a process by which people ... influence decisions that affect them' (1992: 177). In fact Bhatnagar and Williams, who are writing at this stage as rapporteurs for a Bank seminar[9] contributing to a 'Bank-wide learning process', begin with the term popular participation,[10] but quickly render this term as broad an anodyne as possible – not referring to any specific category, but 'a broader range of people who are disadvantaged' (ibid.). In other words, 'the poor'. Participation then becomes a verb related to a liberal ideal of equal opportunities: an open polity and a 'level playing field' would allow all, including 'the poor' to participate in development and in the process reduce inequalities.

By creating such a bland, parsimonious, and generalised notion of participation, the Bank has been able to 'mainstream' participation into its language and operations since the early 1990s. One reason for this is the increasing pressure on the Bank in Washington from NGOs and pressure groups, especially in the wake of the Wappenhans Report and 'scandal' projects such as the Narmada Dam (Mehta 1994). Within governance states, participation serves to represent the massive profusion in external funding as something other than imposition.

Other organisations, especially NGOs which have been using 'participation' as part of their operational vocabulary for far longer, have been wary of the Bank's championing of participatory development. Schneider (1999) supportively picks up the way in which 'participation' has become the province of the OECD, World Bank and the governance agenda. He defines participation as 'participatory governance' to remove the word from its previous 'popular empowerment'-NGO meaning. In his hands, participation becomes a signifier of all the liberal desires noted in the previous section: 'more complete and better information, with the potential of more effective decision making and more efficient outcomes' (page 523). Schneider intersperses participation with other key words of the liberal governance vocabulary, which we will deal with below: accountability, empowerment, transparency and efficiency (Cleaver 1999). These words form a network of inter-related liberal norms and images; they justify each other; and each word gains greater ideological purchase for being embedded in a set of mutually supporting terms. Perhaps this is why the Bank discussion paper mentioned above explicitly sets out a participation 'Common Vocabulary' in one of its annexes. By 'expanding' to involve almost everyone involving themselves in development, participation can encompass a great deal, giving it an ability to incorporate any development agenda into its remit: 'can one possibly be "against" participation?' (Harriss 2002: 118). The Bank's participation sourcebook quotes a Bank official remarking of indigenous NGOs 'we had to let them into our tent ... not only because it does better projects [*sic*] but ... to convince the[ir] partners in the North that we're doing a reasonable job' (in Fox and Brown 1998: 7). Thus, one can read the Bank's references to participation as part of its desire to control development processes while speaking about the need for all to be involved. The corporatist effects of this are betrayed in a Bank discussion paper on popular participation:

> Fostering popular participation is a deeply serious matter, but it is not rocket science ... we development professionals sense intuitively that participation is a good thing, and we know how to foster it.
>
>   (World Bank discussion paper, quoted in Schmitz 1995: 57)

A word closely associated with participation is *ownership*. This can relate to a desire to ensure that target groups relate to Bank-funded projects as their own, rather than brought from the 'outside'. Thus, ownership and participation are powerful liberal signifiers of a consensual politics: 'if we come and try and impose something, it won't work. What works is participation' (Wolfenson in Miller-Adams 1999: 69). Ownership is also closely related to cost-sharing, that is, the financial contribution of the targets of the project to the latter's funding. In doing this, target populations are deemed to have a deeper interest in the project and therefore a stronger sense of custodianship (Rietbergen-McCracken 1996; Fox 1997: 965). Ownership is a concept that aspires to work around the pre-eminence of the Bank in project design, but it is also strongly related to project efficacy

– if target groups ('communities') contribute to the costs of a project, they are less likely to let it fail: 'in these projects as in most World Bank discussions, participation is not a process of joint planning and accountability but a measure to mobilise those whom the project planners aim to benefit' (Fox and Brown 1998: 167). As such, ownership is a 'more sophisticated means of ensuring implementation' (Fine 2001: 12). The Bank also relates ownership directly to aid effectiveness (World Bank 2000/2001: 193; World Bank 1997: 141).

Furthermore, and more germane to governance states in particular, ownership connotes processes through which governments relate to reform programmes as their own (Nunberg 1990: 11; Klitgaard 1995: 9, 14).[11] The World Bank has elaborated a veritable 'architecture of ownership' within governance states. All states that are part of the HIPCs debt relief schedule have to have Poverty Reduction Strategy Papers (PRSPs) that are owned by the government, and (supposedly) produced with the participation of civil society. At the time of writing, Mozambique, Uganda and Tanzania have all completed full PRSPs – three of six African states to have done so at the time of writing. Even further, governance states are also required to generate their own reforms under the more removed tutelage of the Bank and other donors. This is most advanced in Uganda, where budgetary reform and resource management are increasingly in the hands of the government, or more accurately, the presidency and the Ministry of Finance Planning and Development.[12]

The Comprehensive Development Framework (CDF), which all governance states and others have generated, defines development programme scheduling in all areas, producing a 'matrix' of specific reforms. James Wolfenson introduces the CDF thus:

> It is ... clear to all of us that ownership is essential ... The matrix ... is a tool to have greater cooperation, transparency, and partnership. The matrix is open to all.
>
> (quoted in Cammack 2001)

One can readily see that Bank initiatives such as the CDF and PRSP are strongly represented not as 'clandestine attempt[s] on the part of the Bank to dominate' (ibid.) but as part of a desire to expand the ownership of governance. Wolfenson also powerfully embeds the argument concerning ownership in liberal governance discourse more broadly – co-operation, transparency and partnership. *Partnership* relates closely to ownership and participation.[13] Partners participate in governance reform and by doing so, gain ownership in it: the opposite of the compulsion implied by conditionality (Kayizzi-Mugerwa 1998). Another frequent reference here is *stakeholder*, which brings us to the Bank's representations of individuals in governance states.[14]

Citizenship depicts a specific behavioural-political agent within African societies: an individual, with a strong self-interest to engage with the polity. The aggregate manifestation of citizenship is a society of individuals whose interests are best served by a programme of good governance which will consolidate their rights and duties as citizens. The Bank sees 'citizens as co managers of governance reform' (World Bank 1997: 118). Citizenship is often linked to theories of rational interest/public choice and institutional economics in which politics is mainly about individuals acting in their private best interests (Picciotto 1995). This links the conceptualisation of the citizen to the above-mentioned stakeholder (Paul 1992) which associates politics with liberal theories of positive-sum games; that is, participation in the polity by all citizens will ensure the most socially-beneficial outcome (much like the idea of a fully-clearing market producing social optimality). The notion of citizenship is most prominent in the Bank literature on anti-corruption reform, where citizens are a key 'check and balance' to corrupt activity within the state. Thus one can see how citizenship evokes concerns with access to information, governmental transparency and freedom of expression. The production of a 'public sphere' will create better governance as a result of the disciplining of the state by citizenries (Williams 1996, 2001). As such increasing citizen participation is seen in thoroughly positive-sum terms; citizen participation can only improve governance. This point relates closely to our next term, and others already mentioned, as the Bank ably demonstrates: 'participation creates a virtuous circle. Participating ... helps build civil society and ensure that majority needs are heard and goals are achieved' (World Bank 2000/2001: 108).

The association of civic participation and improved governance is more explicitly encapsulated in the term *civil society* which depicts a mass of private associations which check the actions of the state, and have the potential to participate in the process of reform. Civil society is particularly relevant to considerations of corruption, as it is depicted as the vanguard of any anti-corruption strategy, especially through the media and human rights organisations (Schloss 1998). Civil society expands the notions of ownership and partnership beyond the state and into the societies of governance states. As a result, indigenous NGOs and civil society organisations (CSOs) such as human rights advocacy groups have engaged in the sovereign frontiers of governance states.

The term civil society relates citizenship more closely to government action because it gives the political demands of individuals a collective 'voice'. This association is encapsulated frequently in the notion of *accountability*. In the Bank's words: '[A]ccountability ... means holding public officials responsible for their actions. Political leaders are ultimately responsible to their populations for government actions, and this means there has to be accountability within government' (quoted in Cahn 1993: 188). This is as close as the Bank can get to an explicit endorsement of liberal democracy, although it remains very unclear exactly what kind of

processes the Bank is thinking of regarding accountability, beyond financial reporting (Shihata 1991: 90).

Ownership notwithstanding, these Lockean political dynamics are
underpinned by the preponderance of donors in the sovereign frontier. All
politically active NGOs and CSOs are externally funded; many have yet to
demonstrate any robust embedding in a domestic constituency; and by and
large, these organisations engage in agendas set by donors.[15] This is why
Mercer dubs the participation of CSOs in Tanzania a 'performing partnership' (2003; Kelsall 2002b)

An associated word employed occasionally is *customer* (Rietbergen-
McCracken 1996: 37), commonly employed to define the user of public
services. Customers marry the notion of empowered individuals with cost
recovery – surely the perfection of liberal governance discourse. Rogerio
Pinto, a Bank researcher, coins the term 'citizen-users' to make a mutual
affirmation between individual rights and consumerism (1998: 389). In the
words of a World Bank/Government of Tanzania document on the MTEF,
'the public will ... be empowered to demand their due rights by way of
quality services from public servants' (World Bank/Government of Tanzania 1999: 39).

How does the notion of citizenship relate to administrative reform? Citizenship and civil society portray a society of individuals whose interests are
best served by a programme of good governance which will facilitate administrative efficiency in the minimal services that they require. State and society
work in harmony according to the same liberal logic: citizenship provides the
natural counterpart to the ideology of the free market: both are arenas of
free association, producing positive sum gains, and generating socially-
optimal outcomes. This ideology filters into administrative reform in the
belief that citizens and associations will reinforce and monitor progress in
administrative reform, most clearly the case in Bank thinking on corruption,
in which professional associations, the media and citizens (as whistleblowers)
all have a stake in ensuring that anti-corruption reform is effective. Another
example is the Bank's funding of Service Delivery Surveys which involve
mass interviews with citizen-customers concerning their experiences in using
public services.[16] As customers, citizens should demand better public services
from the state; much of the focus of second generation administrative reform
rests on facilitating this demand, or 'voice' (Paul 1992).

This may not be an exhaustive compendium, but any omissions are likely
to fit within the contours of liberal governance discourse established in this
section. The condensed and stylised representation of the sovereign frontier produced by this discourse is as follows. The World Bank engages with
its partner governance state in order to encourage better governance in
policy making. This is achieved through the participation of stakeholders
such as citizens and civil society organisations. Participation is facilitated
through greater transparency and accountability which is achieved through

consultations, SDSs and generally the provision of 'voice' top civil society. This produces better circuits of political information and improved political engagement as all have their best interests encapsulated in governance reform. Clearly, reform is owned by governance states and their citizenries – the Bank is merely a 'partner' in the process, and a partner in the 'passenger seat' rather than the 'driver's seat'.[17] Motivations coincide, agencies complement each other, and common goals are achieved; equilibrium is in sight. Or is it? The next section considers liberal governance discourse in the context of the Bank's attempts to embed neoliberalism.

Politics without power?

The anaesthetisation of politics

Liberal governance discourse defines a realm of politics which is by and large unproblematic. In place of the inequalities of the creditor-state relation are relations of partnership, participation and stakeholding. Governments should 'own' their reform programmes, particularly in respect to governance and administrative reform, where political sensitivities run highest and it is relatively difficult to couch Bank involvement in technical language. It is worth reflecting on this point a little more.

Neoliberal economic reform has been 'normalised' or naturalised (Williams 1999: 82) and represented through a powerful economic doctrine concerning the social optimality of the free market. Economic reforms with quite radical and unpredictable social consequences can be set out as uncontroversial and necessary components of fiscal and monetary management. Economic theory is a realm of technical and logical thinking, of equations that tend towards equilibrium and which rely on a set of *ceteris paribus* assumptions. In the Bank's vision, markets serve as *the* developmental tool (World Bank 2002: 26), leaving public institutions the role of serving to enhance their smooth functioning (ibid.: 5 *et seq.*). Administrative reform – and governance reform more broadly – does not lend itself nearly so easily to the language of technical-scientific policy making as does economic modelling. Administrative reform literature does make references to principal-agent theory and new public management (second face administrative reform), but these references have failed to encapsulate the entirety of the Bank's desire to embed neoliberalism. This requires some form of normative statement concerning the 'political good'. Thus, as we have seen, liberal governance discourse produces a range of positive-sounding words which work to support each other and produce a vision of liberal progressive political development. It is striking that, after a profusion of research identifying the ways in which SAP produces political conflict, struggle and protest, the Bank should become a leading source of a vision of politics which is evacuated of conflict and in fact produces an anaesthetisation of politics.

The social perturbations which derive from SAP are *externalised* from the analysis, and in its place emerges the enlightened citizen, aware of her rights and willing to support or join associations to express or promote her interests and desires. Unions (once properly 'refined' – see Beckman 1993), professional associations, cultural associations etc. are grouped together as part of the same civilian politics with little or no reference to the differential impacts of neoliberal economic reform upon different groups, their relations with the state, and with no concern for divisions between leaderships and members. Liberal governance discourse connotes an associational polity in which *participation* is the key to politics, not struggle and differentiation, and much less class relations.

But an understanding of class relations is central to a full understanding of the possibilities for administrative reform in governance states. Most African political economies are characterised by a strong unity of private and state power. Accumulation requires the direct and factionalised support of the state. This structural dispensation and the class forces which reproduce it are outside the scope of liberal governance. As Szeftel states: 'corruption has survived ... despite efforts at institutional political reform precisely because such change has not affected the structural forces which give rise to it and, frequently, has not even addressed it' (1998: 283).

In Tanzania, administrative reform and the heavy involvement of donors has led high-ranking civil servants to resign, hire themselves out as consultants (gaining a huge hike in salary), and return to the bureau in which they were previously working. This has allowed some to build blocks of flats to rent out mainly to expatriates, earning themselves thousands of dollars per month. This has subsequently made the execution of the policy to reduce the number of consultancies (on grounds of cost) particularly difficult as these consultant-bureaucrats defend their lucrative existing state of affairs (interviews, Dar es Salaam, August 2000). In Uganda, loans are 'skimmed off' at various levels, to the extent that an expenditure tracking survey found that in 1991 only 2 per cent of intended non-wage funding for schools reached its intended destination, although this subsequently improved dramatically (Reinikka 2001: 344).[18] In Mozambique, infamously, donors ensured transparency in the management of governmental funds, but ignored the fraudulent manipulation of financial reform within the banking sector, carried out by well-connected members of the ruling elite (Hanlon 2002). In other words, elite groups within governance states have found opportunities to accumulate significant wealth illicitly using public authority, but none of this shows up in the liberal governance register. If it did, this would constitute a refutation of the formal separation of 'politics' from 'economics' that liberal theory often relics upon; and it would mean that the Bank would have to assume that both realms might not be driven entirely by positive sums, and tendencies towards equilibria. It would not produce a discourse to embed neoliberalism; it would produce one that would problematise it.

Bolder and more shallow

Relatedly, liberal governance discourse constitutes a paradox in that it is both more bold in its employment of terms associated with a political language, but less politically analytical in its deliberation. The Bank has always made some political account for its actions. Riddell, in a review of aid policy, recalls the 1974 Bank publication *Redistribution with Growth* and its forthrightness concerning the problems of political will and vested interests. He concludes that contemporary 'efforts to enhance the capacity and efficiency of the administration of government ... either do not address or only marginally touch these core issues of power and self interest' (1999: 328). In this sense, embedding neoliberalism requires a more *political* language – under the rubric of good government – but a 'dumbed down' analysis in which conflict, interests and political economy are substantially outside the frame. One related example (mentioned earlier) of this is the rejection of the term 'popular participation' in favour of 'participatory development', explained as follows:

> The concept of participation should not just be limited to disadvantaged people ... Focussing on *disadvantaged people,* as opposed to *all people* results in a class-biased definition. It has been suggested that the core team drop the reference to *popular* and replace it with *people,* or *participatory development.*
> (Bhatnagar and Williams 1992: 180, Annexe 2, emphases in the original)

The Bank clearly feels awkward about its advocacy of participation in general – a manifestation of its desire for 'shallow' concepts of political action that can be easily 'programatised' and incorporated into its own project to embed neoliberalism. This is explored in respect to anti-corruption reform by Heather Marquette, who quotes the Bank as follows:

> While this comprehensive popular participation or democratisation is indeed an important goal which developing countries are generally trying to achieve, it is not clear how this goal may ... become an operational concern for the Bank. There may be *extreme* cases where the Bank staff reach the firm conclusion that compliance with rules relevant to Bank operations in a given community is not possible without a measure of popular participation in the making of such rules.
> (2001: 399, emphasis added)

This approach can lead some Bank-related work to give an impression of 'virtual reality', as all that is important is relegated to passing brief commentary with abstract and depoliticised analysis in prime place.

How should we make sense of this? Embedding neoliberalism requires an explicitly political normative statement, one that relates to forms of governance and relations between states and citizens. It is precisely the problematic relations between states and their population as the former implemented structural adjustment that led the Bank to embrace issues of governance in the first place. But, this political 'boldness' is accompanied by a 'shallow' representation of politics, one which evades deeper questions of history and structure in preference to one of dialogue and statement making.

Governance states and the 'driver's seat'

> Countries must be in the driver's seat and set the course. They must determine the goals and the phasing, timing and sequencing of programmes.
>
> (Wolfenson quoted in Pincus 2002: 97)

> To foster 'genuine partnership' with its borrowers, the Bank will hold workshops and trumpet 'broad, meaningful participation' in its projects. But this attempt to counter accusations of unaccountability is belied by the Bank's actions.
>
> (Adams 1994: 147)

If there is one component of liberal governance discourse which is pivotal to administrative reform, it is ownership. Contained within the rubric of ownership, and associated phrases, is the idea of an equality of participation between the IFIs and indebted states. It is this equality of participation which allows the Bank to involve itself in a state's politics without appearing to be intervening, interfering or imposing. Rather, there is a dialogue, or an exchange of ideas. But can this be the case when a partnership is forged between two agencies which detain such unequal amounts of power (however defined)? Between debtor and creditor, evaluated and evaluator, between the intervened and the intervener? Clearly, there is good reason to believe that the ownership of a programme of reform by the weaker partner will extend only as far as is required by the more powerful party.

Because of the inequality of power between Bank and state, and the fact that post-conditionality sovereign frontiers are premised on the establishment of a neoliberal orthodoxy, participation in administrative reform can sometimes take on a rather paradoxical appearance.

> The 'lending hiatus' [from creditors] was found to have been a useful means for securing agreement to [SAP] ... , but it was noted, apparently without irony, that Tanzanian 'ownership' of the programme was low. It was thus recommended that both the external pressure for adjustment and the level of Tanzanian 'ownership' be increased!
>
> (Raikes and Gibbon 1996: 225)

This same relation was affirmed during an interview this author carried out with a public sector specialist in a major donor organisation in Tanzania, in which he explained the laggardly behaviour of one ministry in which the donor was funding a sectoral administrative reform programme as a result of the fact that 'ownership has not been planted in this ministry' (interview, August 2000). It is also worth bearing in mind that administrative reform programmes are executed with large sums of donor money, with the government as a 'contributor', in Tanzania's case not contributing as much as the donors. As one UNDP official in Tanzania put it: 'how can you own what you do not pay for?' (interview, August 2000).

This evidence reveals something more akin to a *limited custodianship* rather than ownership, and it also suggests an implicit desire by the Bank and others to maintain forms of compulsion even if these are less easily discernible. Another Bank research paper on Technical Assistance Loans (TALs, which are used for the purposes of capacity building and administrative reform) reveals how important this underlying relation of inequality and coercion is:

> The ... dilemma is that TALs not linked to SAL [structural adjustment loan] conditionality were viewed as 'toothless' and implementation of these free-standing programmes [i.e. not cross-conditioned with structural adjustment] was made that much more difficult.
>
> (Nunberg and Nellis 1990: 32)

In other words, state ownership of administrative reform programmes enjoys an uneasy existence – partly real, partly theatre – atop of a longer, more durable, and well-established relationship of domination between the state and the IFIs. The neoliberal imperatives of FGR give 'bite' to SGRs in administration and governance. The terms upon which partnership, participation and ownership are operationalised have been established during the previous period of adjustment and liberalisation. Nevertheless, as argued in Chapter 4, the apparent force of policy conditionality has been reduced, and succeeded by post-conditionality politics, oriented far less clearly along the internal/external distinction. It is important to recognise here that although governance reforms are not so closely integrated with the 'teeth' of structural adjustment conditionality, other teeth (to stretch the metaphor) have an equally powerful bite to lock reforms into potential material sanctions.

The basis for the shift from policy-based conditionality to post-conditionality is the HIPC scheme.[19] Being accepted as a HIPC enables a country to received a write-off of outstanding debt and capital stock to what international finance organisations judge as a 'sustainable' level.[20] Gaining HIPC status revolves around donor evaluations of an indebted country, and these evaluations are based on the level of indebtedness, social indicators of poverty, and the track record of a country in implementing structural adjustment programmes. These evaluations are led by the World Bank and IMF, and in fact, the key criterion is a country's previous performance in Bank and Fund adjustment policies. Uganda, Tanzania and Mozambique – Africa's first three countries to gain HIPC status – have each been through a broadly similar process: each has introduced structural adjustment, weathered the social and political turbulence that this has created and subsequently managed to 'lock in' neoliberal fundamentals, mainly associated with the IMF's macroeconomic concerns with budget deficits and rates of inflation.

Thus, HIPCs represent a selective engagement by the Bank and IMF in Africa, although a fairly restrictive list of HIPCs is expanding (13 states in 2003). HIPC is premised on a 'secure' macroeconomic environment that makes the outright freezing of programme lending unlikely. But, HIPC is also the starting point for a new raft of lending programmes (which might make heavily indebted countries *more* indebted in the medium term). The World Bank manages an expansive lending portfolio, detailed in its Country Assistance Strategy (CAS) documents. The CAS reviews the Bank's lending in various sectors of public action. There are two noteworthy aspects of the CAS in terms of the nature of the 'teeth' to lock in governance reforms. First, Bank lending is often formulated as a Sector Investment Programme (SIP). Broadly consonant with Sector-Wide Approaches (SWAP) which many bilateral donors now adopt to some extent, the Bank lends money to a specific sector – say, Education or Roads – without making any specific project intervention with specific conditionalities. The idea behind this is that it allows government Ministries to take 'ownership' of reform: a ministry provides a detailed programme of projects and donors/creditors, perhaps collectively through 'basket funds', for the general purpose of funding the sector-wide plan.

But, the second point strongly revises the extent to which government's can be said to own their sectoral plan. The Bank and other donors continue to monitor very closely sectoral development. In fact, there is often more surveillance of public action than before. The Bank's CAS contains mechanisms of 'displaced conditionality': specific project demands made as conditions for the release of funds are played down, while performance indicators are emphasised, triggers for the release of money detailed, and benchmarks established.[21] The CAS also bases its funding projections on 'high' and 'low' cases: if a government implements reforms speedily and efficiently, it receives more money more quickly; if it fails to implement reforms according to performance indicators and the targets they establish, a government might lose substantial amounts of concessional lending. Collectively, mechanisms such as these hardly betray a loosening of external control over reform; it is rather a stronger sense of local custodianship.

The CAS provides a schedule of the creation of Poverty Reduction Strategy Papers (PRSPs). This is the key government document within the architecture of governance. The PRSP defines, in substantial detail, a draft of programmatic reforms and projects to implement a pro-poor development strategy. PRSPs key into the Millennium Development Goals and often make ambitious claims concerning the improvement of social well-being. It is supposed to be country-driven, results-oriented (rather than based in indicative spending targets), and deal with public action in all its aspects. The PSRP is based on previous Comprehensive Development Frameworks (CDFs) and, like CDFs, the PRSP aims to establish a 'shop window' for donors: to demonstrate a concerted and well-thought-through strategy to combat poverty. Countries might produce an interim PRSP or a full PRSP, the former allowing limited debt relief (write-off of interest but not debt stock).

A PRSP is the prerequisite for HIPC status. Some PRSPs have been based on previously existing programmes and some are entirely new. They involve detailed plans to develop new monitoring and surveillance techniques, new forms of statistical processing, new forms of budgetary management, logical frameworks of spending and output scheduling and a long and detailed 'matrix' of execution. The Bank has produced a PRSP sourcebook to 'assist' countries in developing PRSPs. Each PRSP is then evaluated by a Joint Staff Assessment (JSA), held by the World Bank and IMF. Only JSA approval will lead to HIPC status, debt write-off and access to new waves of external credit and loan. HIPC decision point is given, after which (either by 'fast' or 'slow' track) a HIPC is closely monitored and awarded completion point.

PRSPs are financed by the World Bank through Poverty Reduction Support Credits (PRSCs) and by the IMF through Poverty Reduction and Growth Facilities (PRGFs). The PRSC is the funding schedule for the CAS; the credit is on 'IDA' terms; it is multi-sectoral; and it is focussed on 'pro-poor' reforms. The aim is to synchronise both the PRSP and the CAS around the PRSC, and to present the PRSC as a single programme to co-ordinate other donor lending.

Thus, as shown in Figure 6.1, one can see that governance reform is set within an ongoing material context of financial vetting by the World Bank and other organisations. Financial support through HIPC has brought with it an inter-related web of procedures and requisites that, if not observed, would undermine the steady flow of money. As with structural adjustment, a weak economy and high levels of indebtedness overdetermine other kinds of reform. As mentioned earlier, donors have used their influence to endow Tanzania with more ownership. Having now taken that ownership to heart, the government has devised a PRSP and is now a 'fast track' HIPC. But still, 'in Tanzania, the most advanced of our countries in PRSP terms, those in the know are concerned that the "HIPC factor" has been a strong force driving the PRSP process, and that the energy devoted to it will certainly wane as soon as completion is achieved' (ODI 2001, no page number).

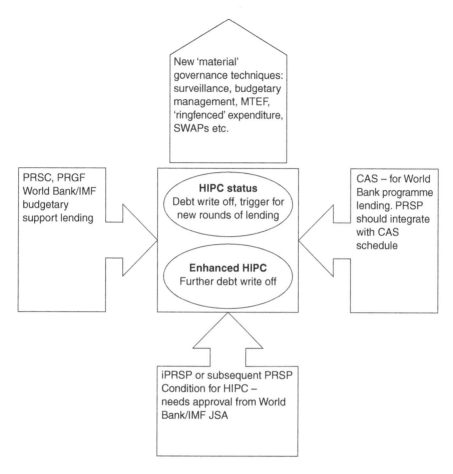

Figure 6.1 A representation of the World Bank's governance 'teeth'.

Conclusion

Many have been struck by the strong discursive elements of the Bank's recent innovations in development lending: the post-Washington consensus (Fine *et al.* 2001; Pincus and Winters 2002), governance (Abrahamsen 2000), liberalism (Williams 1996) and capitalist ideology (Cammack 2002a). This chapter has focussed in a relatively detailed fashion on the workings of liberal governance discourse as a representation of the sovereign frontier in governance states. One can readily see how this representation integrates well with the institutional forms of intervention in governance states analysed in Chapters 4 and 5: post-conditionality institutional development and liberal governance discourse portray a form of intervention by the World Bank that appears far removed from the starker 'conditionality' sovereign frontier of the previous period.

There are powerful ideological effects to this state of affairs. These institutional and discursive interventions reconstruct debt-ridden states as legitimate and purposeful developmental actors. Endowed with a new set of instruments of public action and a progressive narrative to account for them, governance states can work to render the neoliberalism of our age as a socially-embedded project. We have noted a range of contradictions within the coupling of neoliberalism with governance reform in the previous two chapters which raise themes we will return to in the summary. But, there is another, more immediately 'political' tension that we need to deal with first. This tension is, in fact, a secular one in modern history: new liberal orders need to be purposefully forged and subsequently policed. This is the focus of the next chapter.

7   Securing governance states

Introduction

Governance states are important for the World Bank and others because they appear to demonstrate that African states can 'develop' through largely non-coercive processes. Post-conditionality relations within the sovereign frontier, and an emerging and ebullient discourse of liberal governance provide little space for considerations of processes that at least contain elements of compulsion and authoritarianism, if not bare-faced war-making: state construction, modernisation and the deepening of capitalist social relations. But, of course, these processes are hardly absent from the cases considered here.[1]

Perhaps the best way to explore the relationship between governance states as the harmonious reconciliation of external intervention and immanently conflict-riven projects of national development is to consider Polanyi's writing. As mentioned in Part I of this book, the notion of embedding a certain disposition of market social relations in a national society is instructive in understanding the rise of governance states after a succession of less stable forms of intervention by the IFIs, and it derives from Polanyi's writing about the relationship between markets and broader socio-cultural relations. But it is also important to bear in mind that Polanyi was in the first place an anthropologist with an interest in the culture of markets and trading. The notion of embedding refers specifically to modern European societies in which market relations had become pre-eminent in almost all realms of social intercourse. In this situation, existing national states developed ways to ameliorate the socially corroding effects of the rise of markets over cultures in order to render them minimally legitimate. Polanyi saw forms of trade in non-Western societies as *aspects* of existing cultures; capitalist markets in Europe threatened to subordinate cultures and replace them solely with the laws of supply and demand. In this sense, effective public action might discipline markets to embed them in national cultures. It is fortunate that Polanyi wrote about societies outside Europe as it draws our attention to the specific assumptions Polanyi made about state capacity and market relations when he speaks of embedding in Europe which do not pertain in much of Africa. Few states in Africa enjoy the kind of hegemony and capacity that modern European states did; few African societies have the same forms of market relations that Europe did after the war.

What does this mean for our argument that the World Bank is acting to construct governance states in Africa in order to embed a neoliberal market model? It highlights a complexity to post-conditionality and liberal governance which can produce sharp dilemmas for the Bank and other donors that have bought into the governance state project. In essence: the Bank wishes governance states to prosecute a certain legitimising development project, the former simultaneously acting to construct that latter agency. By and large, the governance reforms that are supported and celebrated by the Bank are undertaken by state agencies that have been created (in large part by the Bank) *for the purpose of those specific reforms*. Governance states are both in-action and in-construction. Thus, the agency charged with embedding is not – as Polanyi assumed for Europe – unproblematically 'in existence'; it is in fact 'in construction' and the construction of governance states has its own repercussions on processes of embedding and legitimation.

Thus, one cannot accuse the Bank of miserly ambition. But one should expect that a project of state construction might betray the compulsion in the foundations of governance states at certain moments. This chapter explores this tension and gives particular attention to the way in which the Bank resolves its own actions in this context.

The search for stability

Who can invest in Somalia today?

This quotation belongs to Uganda's President Yoweri Museveni, speaking to the Consultative Group (CG) donors' meeting held in Kampala in 2000. This rhetorical question addresses the tension set out above directly to Uganda's donors. From 2000, bilateral donors became increasingly concerned about the actions of the Uganda Peoples Defence Forces (UPDF) in the Democratic Republic of Congo (DRC). It is clear that parts of the military have been systematically plundering minerals from the DRC, as UN and Ugandan investigative commissions have shown (Clark 2001; Reno 2002). Furthermore, bilateral donors and the Bank have been concerned about the proportion of the budget that is dedicated to military expenditure. These concerns have been enhanced by the ongoing development of pro-poor expenditure mechanisms in Uganda's budgetary management, and the opacity of military budgets, even to the most intrusive of MoFPED institutions. These concerns were all voiced at the CG meeting of 2000.[2] Museveni's response is to remind external agencies of the underlying security demands of state construction. Implicit in Museveni's question is a reminder that Uganda's economic recovery has been based in the first place on the re-establishing of centralised order (Mutibwa 1992; Brett 1995b; Hansen and Twaddle 1995), not the profusion of liberal governance techniques.

Uganda, Tanzania and Mozambique each face security risks of varying degrees. Uganda appears to have the greatest security problems. Since the NRM/A came to power the government has had to address armed resistance in the north from retreating armies and new warrior formations, notably the Lord's Resistance Army (Behrend 1998, 2000; Doom and Vlassenroot 1999). It also faces tensions on its borders in all directions (Khadiagala 1993): concerning war and migration from the DRC, the rear-bases of anti-Museveni forces in Sudan, occasional tension with Kenya, and a cold political relationship with Rwanda (ICG 2000). Tanzania faces less pressing border tensions but has had to deal with a massive influx of refugees from Rwanda since 1994. The Tanzanian government has also deployed an increasingly heavy security apparatus in Pemba and Zanzibar islands since 1995 (Cameron 2002). Having commenced structural adjustment during a civil war, Mozambique has managed to create a post-conflict military and establish a basic state presence over its territory (Borges Coelho and Vines 1995), but the rejection of the 1999 elections by Renamo has left a legacy of political uncertainty.

Nevertheless, each of the three cases can be read as a relatively successful process of stabilisation. Tanzania has won itself an enduring image of stability since the days of Nyerere. Conversely, in post-colonial Uganda and Mozambique, profound instability has been the norm, making the post-conflict governments noteworthy for achieving something most state models take for granted: a minimum of state authority in all national territory and a degree of civic order that allows regular transport, security of investment, and a civilianisation of politics.[3] The stability of donor-state relations within the sovereign frontier is premised on the projects of post-conflict stabilisation prosecuted by Uganda and Mozambique. Each state has accrued an enhanced capacity to act within its own national territory, the better to execute neoliberal policy reform, and to do so in an institutionalised and ordered fashion.

If this seems rather obvious a point to make, there are plenty of counter-examples which make an apparently mundane concern with a basic Weberian state capacity more significant, and in ways that return to the theme of selectivity mentioned in Chapter 1. Two 'good reformers' of the 1980s were Zimbabwe and Kenya. Both had economies that were far more developed than our three governance states, as well as effective and ordered state institutions. But, each state used external assistance as part of a strategy to shore up power, while also purposefully to *destabilising* national societies in the process. In the 1990s, another governance state contender, gaining HIPC accession shortly after Uganda, was Côte d'Ivoire. A *coup* and civil conflict have abruptly removed Côte d'Ivoire from this categorisation. Ethiopia and Eritrea, perceived as part of a 'new generation' of pragmatic African leaders,[4] went to war over a contested boundary, although the former presently maintains close donor relations. All these important examples of aspiring or actual governance states, each receiving large amounts of external loans and credit, only serve to emphasise the salience of persistent stability in our three cases, especially for Uganda. Museveni might have asked: who can invest in Côte d'Ivoire or Zimbabwe today?[5]

If the World Bank is searching for stability and order in sub Saharan Africa, it has found it most strikingly in governance states. In Chapter 1, it was emphasised that the Bank's notion of development is based in the ideal of *stable* capitalist economic growth. The same chapter also defined sub Saharan Africa as a region that evoked most pressingly concerns with stabilisation by the Bank and others. As such, one would expect concerns of stability and order to remain not far from the surface in the Bank's relations with governance states.

Stability and risk

Stability contains both an intrinsic and extrinsic good for the Bank and others. Intrinsically, stability might allude to the security of a society or of the person, which recent expanded definitions of development have brought to the fore. Extrinsically, it alludes to risk assessment and the stability of conditions for investment. This latter sense is addressed by Collier (1999) who sees risk assessment by institutional investors as dependent on policy credibility. Policy credibility here means the capacity of a government to 'lock in' neoliberal foundations for all subsequent reform; Collier also goes on to argue that these foundations cannot be assured by external agencies through conditionality. In other words, Collier is referring to the conditions within governance states: SGR and a post-conditionality sovereign frontier ushered in by a re-established polity. Furthermore, the Bank's operationalisation of governance to its lending policy has led it to conceive of political stability as a legitimate area of concern in its lending (Shihata 1991: 75–6). Thus, stability matters for two important reasons: first, it will impact directly on the ability of the Bank to intervene in policy making with any degree of certainty and predictability; second, stability relates to risk assessment and therefore the ability of countries to attract foreign direct investment (Collier and Pradhan 1998: 28). The promotion of the latter is, of course, an explicit objective of the Bank's Articles of Agreement. But, this is really merely to state that the 'essentials' of the Bank (as outlined in Chapter 1) depend on a minimum of civic order and state capacity. How does this relate to governance states in Africa in particular?

Governance reform as security

> Allow me to be blunt: the political uncertainty and arbitrariness evident in so many parts of sub Saharan Africa are major constraints on the region's development ... I am not advocating a political stance here (*sic*), but I am advocating increased transparency and accountability in government, respect for human rights, and adherence to the rule of law.
>
> (Former World Bank president Barber Conable, in Gillies 1996: 115)

This quotation comes from 1990, and it encapsulates the Bank's incremental development of what it announces as 'governance' in the mid 1990s. One can see the seeds of an emerging concern with state capacity and concepts such as accountability in the report *From Crisis to Sustainable Growth* (1989), but this quotation is especially telling. It demonstrates the Bank's aspirations to evacuate profoundly political concepts and processes of their political content, as discussed in Chapter 6. Perhaps more strikingly, it makes an opaque association between sub Saharan Africa's political instability and the idea that stabilisation can be achieved through better governance. What Barber does not explain is *how* governance reform might lead to more stable political systems.

As argued throughout this book, the World Bank is not merely concerned to impose neoliberal economic models on governance states, involving the roll-back of the state, the opening up of national economies and the promotion of private business. It is also concerned with the *ordering* of the effects of liberalisation, and the *institutionalisation* of market relations. During the 'conditionality' period, the Bank made limited comments on the need for governments to have the political resolve to force through reform, this perhaps requiring a state not subject to the whims of popular accountability (Gibbon *et al.* 1992). But as economic liberalisation produced social disruption, and other international organisations lobbied for a 'human face' to liberalisation, the Bank began to devote more energy to questions of political stabilisation, as well as economic reform. The main result of this shift in perspective can be found in the Bank's publications on good governance (Jeffries 1993; Doornbos 1995). As noted previously, the core of the notion of good governance contains:

- Transparency and accountability
- Stronger rule of law
- Participation in decision making by non-state actors
- Reduced military expenditure (World Bank 1994b).

All of these involve external agencies in efforts to stabilise the state and the social order it oversees. Let us consider these components.

Transparency and accountability

How have general aims such as 'an increase in transparency' or 'account-ability' been effected? Mainly through a dramatic increase in interest and funding for administrative reform and capacity building programmes by the World Bank and bilateral official development agencies, as we have seen in previous chapters. These programmes involve external agencies funding programmes which endeavour to make administration more rou-tinised and predictable through rules-based rather than discretion-based decision making.

All administrative reform programmes funded by external agencies, usually led by the World Bank, involve large-scale retrenchment, the introduction of higher wage levels and greater wage differentials in the public service. The aim of this is to create a smaller (elitist), more stable, motivated and technically competent public sector. Externally-funded administrative restructuring aims to ensure the development of a techni-cally oriented and stable cadre, mainly located in Ministries of Finance, which accord well with the Bank's notion of good governance as stable and predictable administration. This is a key change that has enabled some ministries, departments and agencies to gain relative prominence within post-conditionality régimes. The specific mechanisms through which administrative reform is effected rely on techniques such as the introduc-tion of user surveys for public service 'products', technical assistance to introduce Results Oriented Management, and new technologies of information management and tighter budgeting. Regular reports fix sched-ules of reform, integrated into strategic plans and logical frameworks. Service Delivery Surveys, regular auditing and surveillance all produce more reliable information that allows greater accuracy in planning cycles. Williams conceptualises these components as a programme based on an integrating logic of discipline (1996). The central imperative of this discip-line is a desire to produce order and predictability within policy making and execution. The rise in good governance as a 'policy ideology' for the Bank has manifested itself in an increase in funding for administrative reform which has endeavoured to render the state a fulcrum of order and stability upon the backdrop of rapidly (and unpredictably?) changing societies.

The rule of law

The concern with the rule of law is central to the Bank and IMF's approach to good governance. By rule of law, the Bank is fundamentally interested in the inviolability of private property and the entrenchment of universally-accepted contractarian market regulations, underpinned by an effective system of courts. External donors have been keen to fund spe-cialised institutional reform and capacity building for judiciaries and police forces in governance states. This reveals a desire for stability based on a faith in the market as a harmonious social institution and reveals a focus on society as well as the state. David Moore's analysis of the Bank's *The State in a Changing World* (1997) argues that

> [a key] component of the Bank's analysis is the stern admonition that the most basic task of the state is the establishment of the 'pure public good' of property rights. It is as if that is the holy grail from which all blessings will flow. If the state can get the property rights right, its main task will be done: it will have blended its society with the 'single world marketplace' that the [World Bank] Report sees as an 'international public good' of equal provenance with world peace, a sustainable environment and 'basic knowledge'.
>
> (Moore 1999: 66)

The Bank's concern is to promote the creation of market relations which are regulated through the institutional supremacy of the rule of law and property rights. Faced with a complex and diverse set of social relations of trade, production and accumulation sketched in Chapter 1, the state is exhorted to forge a regulated market: not in the sense of selective subsidy, minimum wages and tariffs (a 'social market' *à la* Polanyi), but rather a market which is based on contractual rules, legislated property and a 'Hayekian neo-statism' (ibid.: 86), that is, a *publicly-enforced* free market. The Bank's concerns here are sharpened by the diversity and expansiveness of forms of 'informal' and 'shadow' economic activity which are associated with a lack of order and regulation, as well as more prosaic concerns with levels of taxation (Moore 1999).

Participation

The Bank's evocation of participation is based on a belief that public decisions will be more effective, or at least binding, if people have broadly participated in the polity during the decision-making process. In respect to specific policy areas, more specific groups, or 'stakeholders', should be brought into the policy-making process in order to ensure policy efficacy. One can see this in the Bank's concern with civil society (Landell-Mills 1992) as well as its funding of development projects through NGOs (O'Brien *et al.* 2000). But, in an early and very perceptive analysis of the relationship between structural adjustment and political liberalisation, Riley and Parfitt identify another dynamic behind the participation agenda:

> The Bretton Woods Institutions focussed upon the mechanics of government rather than ... popular participation. What was needed was ... 'good governance': a mixture of less corruption, more open

decision making, managerial efficiency, and some degree of political pluralism. These ... reforms would assist the neoliberal economic reforms. *Popular participation could do the reverse.*

(Riley and Parfitt 1994: 167, emphasis added)

Riley and Parfitt identify a technicist corporatism to the World Bank's notion of governance in which participation is the means to the end of stable reform. A more 'popular' form of participation is certainly not welcome within the Bank (Harrison 2001).

Stability over governance?

The final component of governance is restricted military spending, which, as Museveni has illustrated, might fit with liberal ideals of peacetime governance, but which contradicts with concerns to maintain stability in a region of the world where many states have recently and tenuously re-established civic order and rebuilt their own capacities to (in some or other) regulate society. The World Bank estimated that in 1992, military expenditure in Uganda amounted to one third of total public spending and one half of recurrent expenditure (in Khadiagala 1993: 251). The World Bank and other donors have set a limit of 20 per cent of GDP to be attributed to military expenditure, which the Government of Uganda has agreed to. It is clear that Uganda has avoided full auditing of its military expenditure, and that millions of dollars of high-value minerals are funnelled through Uganda from the DRC, so it is not clear how closely current expenditures approximate this percentage (*The Monitor* June 21, 2000; Reno 2002). Nevertheless, 'despite Uganda's difficulties with the international community over its involvement in the DRC, relations with the World Bank ... have remained generally good' (EIU 2000: 21).

In Uganda, the World Bank has made no protest about military action and a lack of multi partyism, for as long as the Ugandan state can ensure a minimal national security and oversee a process of economic recovery. In Tanzania, there have been serious and credible allegations of human rights abuses by the Tanzanian police in Zanzibar. From 1995, there have been allegations of foul play during elections and that the police on the islands have been accused of detaining people without cause. The fear of police brutality even produced a wave of migrations to Kenya by about 2,000 Pembans.[6] Although many bilateral donors, led by the US and Sweden, had suspended aid to Zanzibar from 1995, the World Bank continued its lending programme throughout. In Mozambique during the mid 1990s, a number of corruption scandals emerged, including the theft of food aid with the probable collusion of port officials, various forms of over-invoicing, thefts from public banks, and opaque privatisations. Throughout all the scandal, the World Bank maintained its lending programme. In fact, the Bank did not proactively pursue the constitutions of a High Authority

Against Corruption which was explained by one interviewee as a result of the Bank's lukewarm attitude to fully exposing corrupt practice with the state.[7]

Each of these examples is intriguing. The intervention in the DRC, the oppressive police presence in Zanzibar, and the prominence of high-level corruption in Mozambique each ostensibly go against strictures of good governance. One might explain this in terms of the Bank's own constitutional restrictions which prohibit the Bank from concerning itself with internal political systems. Certainly, Bank representatives, when questioned, gave the impression that its apolitical mandate left it unable to act on issues concerning military intervention, police practice or corruption: one interviewee said that these were the preserve of the bilaterals. However, the governance agenda does not allow the Bank such a clear cut distinction. It is the argument of this book that the Bank is involved in deeply political interventions in governance states. Exactly how much more political would it be to act against a state's 'bad governance' than it would be to act to promote its good governance? This is not to say that the Bank does not care about militarism, corruption and human rights: certainly interviewees betrayed a seemingly heart-felt concern to see peace, stability and civic politics in the countries where they worked. But, the Bank's key concerns with stability produce necessary equivocations in the Bank's attitudes. Concerns with a rising militarism in any governance state will be situated in a judgement of the extent to which militarism destabilises the country. The UPDF's intervention in the DRC (now officially over) did not destabilise the governance architecture of the PRSP, IFMS, PSRP and so on. This is the equivocation that Museveni raises for donors in his comparison with Somalia,[8] and it is one he is well-qualified to raise. When Obote's second government introduced an IMF programme in 1981 and SAP in 1982, Museveni's NRM went into the bush. One could convincingly argue that the SAP made some economic gains, but was scrapped by Obote's failure to maintain civic order during the civil war, which led to an inability of the state to execute policy and a massive increase in military expenditure (Berg-Schlosser and Siegler 1990: 105).

Stabilisation, state elites, and the importance of 'politics'

Chapter 2 set out a way of understanding the development of relations between external agencies and governance states through the notion of a sovereign frontier. The sovereign frontier of governance states is characterised by a relatively stable set of relations, based around 'partnership'. Establishing this state of affairs cannot be anything but a political enterprise, undertaken by actors within the sovereign frontier. This draws our attention to the sociology of the ruling elites of governance states and *their* stability. In this sense, the first step of stabilisation and reconstruction concerns the state elite itself, that is, a ruling group within the party and/or state which enjoys a solid hold on the state and which is aligned with the concerns of external agencies This existed in Uganda after 1987 and in Tanzania since independence; it did not exist in Mozambique during the mid 1980s. As a result, the IFIs had an equivocal relationship with Mozambique: both keeping the country's indebted economy afloat, conditioning that assistance on a relatively severe adjustment schedule which served to increase Mozambique's social instability and disruption (Marshall 1990; Hanlon 1991; Harrison 1994) and taking no account of the fact that adjustment was being implemented during a civil war (Wuyts 1991). However, by the early 1990s, the ruling Frelimo government was more or less universally wedded to the neoliberal project (Simpson 1993), and, in fact, much of the ruling elite had done quite well out of the opportunities that economic liberalisation had provided (Bowen 1992; Harrison 1999b). Furthermore, Frelimo had maintained an impressive grip on state power.[9] Once peace had been achieved, the Government of Mozambique's relations with the IFIs improved, bolstered by the economic recovery from 1993 onwards.

In fact, all of the World Bank's 'star adjusters' have important common features in regard to elite stability. Tanzania, Uganda and Mozambique all have elites strongly entrenched in power as a result of a period of authoritarianism. Tanzania and Mozambique's elites have been generated out of a long post-colonial history of party–state fusion under the structures of socialism or Marxism–Leninism; Uganda, as we have already seen, owes its current political configuration to a military victory which has ushered in stability and growth, but no challenge to the 'movement' system. Elections have not proved a serious challenge to long-established elite incumbency, raising important questions about the significance of elections in the African region as a whole (Baker 1998). Uganda's 'no party' elections have made it impossible for the formally-registered but severely restricted opposition parties to challenge the NRM; elections in Tanzania were marred by substantial police violence in Zanzibar but on the mainland the CCM faced little challenge from a factious opposition; in Mozambique the opposition boycotted the Assembly of the Republic in protest of alleged malpractice. In all cases, donors have made quiet protests and have carried on with 'business as usual'.[10]

The point here is that 'politics' matters: stable régimes with close relations to the IFIs that act as official custodians of tentative market-based economic recovery are key to the IFIs' concerns to marry processes of stabilisation with neoliberal reform (Harrison 1999a). Other countries, subject to more turbulent but perhaps more democratic political changes, or countries which contain the vestiges of some form of radical nationalism, experience tangibly more frosty relations with the IFIs.

Both the Beninois and Togolese governments underwent pressure to democratise through the institution of *Conferences Nationales* in the early 1990s. In Benin, the CN declared sovereignty and pushed forward a new constitution and elections, leading to the ouster of President Kérékou (Allen 1992). In Togo, the CN was marginalised by an altogether stronger state response, which allowed President Eyadema to control the democratisation process and civilianise his régime. External responses during the democratisation process were crucial. In brief, France and the IFIs gave little support to Kérékou, increasing his vulnerability during transition, but they maintained support for Eyadema. In comparing the two transitions, Nwajiaku concludes:

> In Togo, by way of contrast [with Benin], the weight of external pressures in provoking fundamental change was negligible. In spite of the pro-democracy stance taken by Washington-based financial institutions, their primary concerns in Africa were economic. They sought to support those régimes that were considered to be most capable of implementing adjustment programmes.
>
> (Nwajiaku 1994: 439)

It is within the realm of 'politics', that is, the working relationships established between elites and IFI missions, in which personalities and 'politicking' can become important, that concerns with the stability of ruling elites and security and neoliberal agenda become intertwined. Clearly, it is difficult to know much about these high level and secretive interactions, but one example is revealing.[11] In Tanzania, the Bank has been very complimentary about the direction of reform since the mid 1990s. In recent meetings, this supportive attitude was apparently reinforced by assurances that if Tanzania remained disengaged from the creeping war within the DRC, its applications for funding would be looked on more favourably.[12] Tanzania was chosen as the venue for a high-level World Bank and IMF meeting on regional integration held in March 2001 attended by the World Bank President and the IMF Managing Director.

Conclusion

The motif of stability runs through Bank-supported reform in governance states. Governance states are not strongly constrained by the Bank as their operations compel groups to adhere to state fiat – in fact this might connote stabilisation and order even if it is experienced by some as oppression. The Bank is certainly keenly concerned to ensure the stability of ruling elites. The notion of 'ownership' takes on a different meaning in this respect: close supportive relations between the Bank and ruling elites that push through neoliberal reform, even if that same purposiveness that allows governments to push reform through turbulent moments is the same as that which leads the government to use the police or military for less edifying ends.

8 Neoliberalism's revenge?

Summary

There are two key features to the general shaping of Bank action in sub Saharan Africa since the early 1990s: a desire to stabilise the perturbations of neoliberal imposition via conditionality mechanisms, and a related tendency to engage selectively with individual states. The Bank's secular concerns with ordered capitalist development are most closely met in governance states, defined largely by their close and stable relations with external donors and their ability to demonstrate palpable progress along the Bank's development model. Throughout the 1990s and 2000s, the Bank has constructed a particular form of intervention, posed here as a form of sovereign frontier. This frontier is characterised by post-conditionality reforms, liberal governance discourse and an underlying concern with the state's ability to maintain order and stability.

But, as we have seen, the project is not as harmonious as one might expect from the representations of the Bank. New institutional innovations have been undermined by the unity of accumulation and political power, which has allowed corruption to flourish among the transparency and 'integrity' reforms favoured by the Bank. Notions of partnership finesse, but do not overcome the preponderance of the Bank within the sovereign frontier. Ultimately, if the concept of ownership had real purchase, one would expect after a decade of reform, to see some signs of an emerging independence from the World Bank and other donor-creditors. There are no such signs in any of the governance states; in fact one might argue that quite the reverse is happening.[1] Nevertheless, governance reforms proceed apace, and new mechanisms of development programming, financial management and institutional reform emerge year-on-year, all with heavy external funding. One might expect this to continue for as long as (a) rates of economic growth maintain a relatively high level, and (b) governance states can ensure a close control of the state and police a minimal civic order. If (b) involves the violation of liberal notions of rights and civility (as opposed to militarism), it is not straightforward how the Bank and other external credit-donors might react.

It is important to understand the World Bank's project in governance states as a project of social engineering – coined here in the phrase embedding neoliberalism. It is not sufficient to review the Bank's lending profile, the statements at 'Paris Club' meetings, nor the mechanics of enhanced HIPC. The Bank's involvement is more profound and intimate than any separate component betrays. As we have seen, the Bank proactively pursues a project to shape the methods by which government policy is made and executed; it funds administrative reform to build up new techniques of administration, it leads major funding initiatives, it aggressively shapes the discursive limits of the 'politics of the possible', and it locks governance states into a powerful 'transparency' by imposing matrices and 'logframes' of policy reform, frequently based in sectoral projects.

It is the intimacy of the Bank's intervention that allows it to represent its actions not as external intervention but as a 'partner' within sovereign frontiers that are pervaded with governance discourse and reform. The economic fragility of governance states and the effusive largesse from external agencies produce the 'grease' (to borrow from the corruption literature – not entirely inappropriately, perhaps) that allows African elites to embrace the governance model as part of their own desires for enrichment and social ascendance.

Embedding neoliberalism and international régimes

So, is this neoliberalism's revenge? That is to say, has governance reform in these selected states produced a form of public authority that has answered the central problem of the 1980s: how to liberalise African economies without destabilising them? There is real evidence of a movement in this direction. Earlier, we saw how governance 'champions' have emerged within governance states, how a powerful discursive intervention had 'de-ideologised' the representation of the Bank's interventions. Economic growth in governance states manages (albeit marginally in some cases) to exceed population growth, and there is some evidence that social well-being is improving, although the figures and their meaning are contested strongly (UNDP 2002).

As we have seen, each moment of governance reform often betrays a contradiction in the politics of the sovereign frontier, and we can draw a broader meaning from these contradictions. In order to do so, let us return to Table 3.1. This table demonstrates that embedded liberalism worked as an international régime; that is, a set of structures and norms that worked within states and between them. The national development models maintained by many African states were underpinned by a certain global political economy, in which the Bank played a key part. For the current period, the three columns – global régime, national context and World Bank policy – have been covered thus far. We have looked in detail at the latter two, but, if we find a congruence in the ways the Bank and governance states think about development within the sovereign frontier, we need to understand if there is a third congruence at the global level.

Currently, the international context is severely limiting to governance states. The founding tenets of governance, liberal politics and free markets, do not work globally. The World Bank and IMF are not run according to any rules of good governance (Woods 2000).[2] In the words of Skogly,

> There is, however, one unfortunate gap in this [governance] approach. It seems to be applied to recipient countries only, and the components of the 'governance' concept are not applied to the Bank's activities themselves.
>
> (Skogly 1991: 57)

More broadly, the centres of global capitalism continue to maintain forms of economic protectionism: First World countries impose import barriers 50 per cent higher for Third World countries than they do between each other; Stiglitz argues that Africa's income fell by 2 per cent as a result of the Uruguay Round of GATT (2001: 61); subsidies to OECD farmers amounted to 40 per cent of their gross income in 1999 – the same proportion as during the 1980s (Gibbon 2002: 106); the European Union and the United States spending an average of $1 billion per day to protect agriculture from external competition (Owusu 2003: 1668); the American government paid its cotton farmers $3.7 billion in subsidies in 2001–2002, which was three times its total aid budget for Africa (*Africa Confidential* September 2003). One might contest the accuracy of any of these figures, but together they make a powerful case that developed states maintain a regulative framework which is not open or liberal but rather guarded and structured.

If one can make a case that the global political economy is structured by powerful states and concentrated economic interests – what Wade calls 'clustering' (Wade 2004) – then it remains to be seen how enduring the sovereign frontier of governance states will be. To be fair, this is something that the Bank is aware of and in some senses actually criticises. The negotiations for HIPC debt relief have sometimes involved the Bank working to extract the requisite financing from some bilateral donors in a general context of declining ODA.[3] But, it is also undeniable that the Bank is a product of powerful states' ambitions. Thus, the Bank might prosecute a liberalising agenda in the indebted regions of the world while those states that are not in the thrall of conditionality and other mechanisms of policy reform can maintain or even introduce protectionist measures. The Bank then becomes an institutionalisation of the double standards of the major capitalist blocs: 'do as I say not as I do'.

These comments require more detail to do them justice, but they do illustrate the fact that there does not exist a reasonably clear global régime that is constant with the governance states' sovereign frontier. In essence, governance states remain extremely small and vulnerable economies in a world structured by the West: liberal political relations are replaced by something more akin to an oligarchy. In this respect, it is surely significant that governance states remain highly indebted with no real prospect of escaping their reliance on external funding. Even after Enhanced HIPC processes are completed, the fiscal imbalances that allow external intervention in the sovereign frontier will remain.

Embedding neoliberalism and national societies

A contradictory set of dynamics at an international level urge caution concerning the prospects for an integrated international régime of SGR. One might also urge caution regarding the robustness of the governance sovereign frontier in its relations with national societies. We have seen throughout this book how a sovereign frontier has been constructed to render governance reform hegemonic, internalised by ruling elites, donors and some intellectuals. But, of course, a deeper project of embedding and legitimation requires the harmonisation of this 'new politics' with a broader social formation.

Here, we should note two salient developments. In the first place, a certain kind of civil society has emerged to engage with governance reform in governance states. Organisations to lobby for anti-corruption reform, stronger human rights protection, a mainstreaming of gender concerns into policy, and a concern with 'the poor' have emerged over the last ten years (Dicklitch 2001; Kelsall 2001; Mercer 2003). Second, Poverty Reduction Strategy Papers require that there is a degree of participation by civil society. Thus, Oxfam is monitoring the PRSP in Uganda as part of the Structural Adjustment Participatory Review Initiative.

These developments constitute a kind of broader socialisation of governance reform, but it is severely limited. First, most CSOs rely on external funding for their operations. They receive finance from certain donors (mainly Scandinavian) who are relatively concerned to promote democratisation and, as a result, they work to produce visible lobbying and political activities that fit closely with the donor agenda. Second, by and large, these CSOs are urban-focussed, elite organisations that clearly express themselves using the liberal governance discourse outlined in Chapter 6. This discourse might be more or less genuinely felt, but it would be naïve to imagine that it is not performed to some extent to please external sources of finance. The presence of CSOs outside the main urban areas is negligible, and many processes of participation have been weak even within this remit (Evans 2001). Third, CSOs' integration into participatory mechanisms of governance is at best partial, and at worst a form of political manipulation by governance elites and donor-creditors (Nyamagusira and Rowden 2002).

This means that the social realm of governance is very narrow. It does not extend beyond the urban centres and the educated few. Once we recognise this, we see a similarity with the period we are considering comparatively from Table 3.1, but this similarity is not encouraging. The national development model pursued in the 1960s was often executed through top-down measures by centralised states institutions, especially in Mozambique (1979–) and Tanzania (1967–).[4] The failure of these projects had a lot to do with the fact that they were not embedded in national societies outside the political elites that controlled the state (Scott 1985).

Once we look beyond the province of CSOs, governance elites, donors and university lecturers and researchers, we enter a complex terrain that raises many difficult questions: does governance reform integrate in any way with existing and pervasive views of politics, or norms of power and rule? Can governance draw on existing repertoires of political morality to embed itself more broadly? Does the governance project ultimately require the state to fashion an authoritarian project of social engineering? Have newly-rehabilitated governance states the capacity to execute such a project, and would donors support it?

These questions require further research, but they do demonstrate the social limits of governance reform. Researching in the cities of all three countries, this author often got a sense of a specific 'world view' shared in the cities which took almost no cognisance of its own narrow compass; working in villages in Mozambique produced very different notions of power and 'governance' indeed (Harrison 2000). Governance states represent a relatively successful stabilisation of neoliberal reform within the sovereign frontiers of selected states: the 'immanent' contradictions of governance might be 'sutured' by continuing economic growth; the broader prospects for governance states will depend on global structural change and the complex interplay of state–society relations in each domestic sphere. The World Bank, champion of governance reform, has thus far greeted both of these with a resounding silence.

Notes

1 The road to governance

1 The notion of 'responsibility' is quite a significant motif in state relations. It has often been the reference made by US government officials to justify interventions in various parts of the world, right from Truman to the present day. The idea of 'rogue states' invented during the post-Cold War period and embraced most fully by George W. Bush can be seen as the counter-position to a responsible state. In Chapter 7, we will see how international concerns with security directly intermesh with governance states.

2 The terms 'World Bank' and 'Bank' will be used interchangeably. Other banks will be referred to by name, and lower case 'banks' will refer to the banking system of a particular country. Where appropriate, specific institutions within the World Bank will be specified: the IBRD, MIGA, IFC or IDA.

3 We will explore this further in Chapter 2.

4 The term 'governance' is used by the Bank, but is closely associated with the notion of 'good governance' which is propounded mainly by bilateral donors and encompasses a more explicit adherence to multi-party democracy. On good governance, see Baylies 1995; Blunt 1995; Doornbos 1995; Minogue 2002.

5 The main bone of contention is the extent to which this statement is undermined by American state power.

6 The World Bank has been strongly influenced by the strategic and economic imperatives of the American state (Mosley *et al.* 1995: 48; Wade 1996; Caufield 1998: 43, 49, 80, 197; Thacker 1999). The repercussions of this for governance states will be addressed in Chapter 6.

7 Relatedly, see Cammack (1997).

8 Note here the infamous works of Deepak Lal: 'a courageous, ruthless and perhaps undemocratic government is required to run roughshod over . . . interest groups' (in Sandbrook 2000: 75).

9 Although it is worth noting that O'Brien *et al.* stress the internal complexities of the Bank earlier in the book (pages 26 *et seq.*)

10 The Bank manages capital raised from bilateral members' contributions, its own returns on previous lending and bond issues.

11 Something John Maynard Keynes and Harry Dexter White, the intellectual 'founding fathers' of the Bretton Woods institutions, both shared in spite of their different viewpoints in some respects.

12 From a very large body of literature, see Ghai 1991; Olukoshi 1993; Tarp 1993; Mkandawire and Olukoshi 1995; Engberg-Pedersen *et al.* 1996; Mohan *et al.* 2000.

13 There is no space to investigate the processes involved in what is generally described as Africa's 'crisis', but see *inter alia* Davidson 1992; Leys 1994; Allen 1995; Berman 1998.

14 Of course, there are other forms of economic activity, not least of which is the emergence of an 'official' capitalist class, often under the wing of the state's regulative structures (Baylies and Szeftel 1982), but sometimes more independent from political patronage (Forrest 1995; Berman and Leys 1994).

15 Observers have noted the increasing willingness of other international actors to follow the World Bank's indications, notably bilateral donors – not just the most obvious ones (USA, Germany, UK) but also the so-called 'like minded' donors of Scandinavia.

16 This is mainly the third sense in which Pastor and Wise use the term SGR in the context of Latin America (1999: 35).

17 This is most clearly expressed in World Bank (1981).

2 Governance states in Africa

1 See Museveni 1997. Mugabe's statements from 2000 represent a more terse and defensive symbolism of sovereignty against the West.

2 TANU became *Chama cha Mapinduzi*, CCM or Communist Party after its unification with the Afro-Shirazi Party of Zanzibar in 1964.

3 The three parties were the Ugandan Peoples Congress, Kabaka Yekka and the Democratic Party.

4 Machel succeeded Frelimo's first president, Eduardo Mondlane, who was assassinated in 1969.

5 Obote's 'Common Man's Charter' was a weak reflection of Nyerere's Arusha Declaration (Berg-Schlosser and Siegler 1990: 103).

6 And many more besides – see Bayart 1993; Allen 1995.

7 Although we should maintain a scepticism concerning claims by post-colonial states that they were defending national interests against imperialism, it remains clear that much intervention from Western governments *was* imperialist. See Mamdani 1983; Austin 1994; Minter 1994.

8 The first Uganda Development Plan ran from 1961–1966; in Tanzania 1964 to 1969; in Mozambique there were three year plans and the grandiose Decade for the Victory over Underdevelopment (1980–1990).

9 A mass expulsion of Ugandan Asians was commenced in 1972, followed by the so-called Economic War in 1973.

10 Indeed, the British army was required to quell a coup attempt against Nyerere in 1964. The coup was partly a result of discontent with the large numbers of expatriates in the post-colonial Tanzanian state.

11 The Tanzania–Zambia railway was funded by the Chinese and represents a 'prestige' development project *par excellence.* During the 1970s, Tanzania relied on China for one third of its aid (Yeager 1982: 104–8).

12 Between 1973 and 1976, 80 per cent of Tanzania's rural population was forced into *ujamaa* villages (Barkan 1994: 20).

13 The best account of the rise and fall of Mozambique's 'high modernism' is Pitcher (2003).

14 Tanzania and Mozambique also received a large number of politically-motivated expatriates (co-operantes) who worked in state institutions to support socialist development in Africa.

15 In fact, the Ten Year Plan was never published.

16 There are debates concerning the interaction of the Renamo war and Frelimo's collapsing national developmentalism. See Clarence-Smith 1989; Roesch 1992; Cahen 1993.

17 Tanzania's first credit from the IMF was in 1974.

18 Mozambique's first loan from the World Bank was approved in 1985.

19 There was also an IMF programme in Uganda from 1981.
20 Museveni studied at the University of Dar es Salaam in the 1970s. He also visited the liberated zones of Mozambique, writing a chapter afterwards on the revolutionary properties of violence. Interestingly, the book was edited by Nathan Shamuyarira, who went on to be a Minister in Mugabe's government.
21 In fact, the lack of rule of law and protracted nature of conflict had pulled a substantial amount of Uganda's economy into the informal sector (Meagher 1990).
22 If the IMF declares its programme off-track, this produces the effect of representing the debtor country as a reform failure, leading many other external providers of finance to cut back or abandon lending/aid schedules.
23 Jeffrey Sachs, for some the architect of 'shock therapy', also refuted Leite's judgement.
24 Less strong contenders for the status of governance state, 'good reformer' and so on would be Ghana, Burkina Faso and perhaps others that have attained HIPC status (which Ghana doesn't have). But none of these reaches our three cases' level of 'affirmation' by the Bank *et al.*
25 Highly Indebted Poor Countries: the first three HIPCs in Africa were, in succession: Uganda, Tanzania and Mozambique, the latter two 'fast-tracked' by the Bank and IMF.
26 Relatedly, see Duffield (2001: 122–3).
27 The report is co-authored by a researcher who has written consultancies for the World Bank, precisely to locate Tanzania and Uganda within the Bank-inspired league table of policy effectiveness described above. See Bigsten *et al.* 1999, 2001.

3 Conceptualising the World Bank

1 The overbearance of the Bank as a source of intellectual production has increased, especially once it re-packaged itself as the 'knowledge Bank' with a lavish 'development gateway' in cyberspace. A recruiting drive for political scientists in the 1990s, the widening opportunities for Bank-funded consultancies in the premier universities of the West, and the general ideological atmosphere of the Washington consensus has made the Bank powerful indeed in the minds of others. Relatedly, see Fine (2001: Chapter 9).
2 The main exception in the 'early' literature on the Bank is the seminal Payer (1982).
3 Hence the drive by the Bank to recruit more 'political scientists'.
4 These writers will be referred to in passing but not individually as they have not engaged centrally with a theorisation of the Bank.
5 An obvious and simple definition, but the term has been used in different ways in different literatures, so opening it up would unnecessarily divert this chapter.
6 Williams' former co-author calls liberalism the 'armed wing of the Enlightenment' (Young 2002).
7 A related and more general argument is Hopgood (2000).
8 This is not to say that Williams crudely asserts the pre-eminence of liberalism as a theoretical starting point; rather it is that in practice he cleaves exclusively to this concern, occasionally implying that other factors or 'interests' might be relevant.
9 Two recent and key contributions are Muthu (2003) and Mehta (1999).
10 One feels a tangible unease at this ahistoricism when Williams writes that 'governance is part Hobbes ... part Locke, Smith and de Tocqueville ... with a

healthy dose of contemporary management theory thrown in' in Williams (1996: 170).

11 This is evident in Williams's eloquent exploration of agency and ideology in which he finally comes to argue that methodologically, we should assume that language, norms etc. pre-exist us as individuals and that these norms are essential to explain why certain actions take place (1996). Williams deserves credit for tackling epistemological issues concerning our understanding of the Bank in far greater depth than the other authors reviewed here.

12 Although Mill implies earlier that this separation is more complex (Mill 1982). See also Pitts (2003) which compares Bentham and both Mill senior and junior on the question of empire.

13 The WDR is an annual Bank publication which, although ostensibly written by academics outside the Bank, constitutes a central statement of Bank development ideology. See Wade 2001b.

14 Although Cammack clearly steers away from this kind of analysis.

15 Writers such as Rosenburg (1994), Meiksins Wood (1999) and Bromley (1991) have addressed the relationship between capital and the nation-state.

16 Perhaps the *World Development Reports* are better interpreted not as a capitalist manifesto but as a powerful hegemonic claim by capital on the concept of development.

17 For a strong version of this argument, see Kitching 2001.

18 In respect to Mozambique, see Cramer and Pontara 1998.

19 Ruggie's notion has generated a growing secondary literature. See for example: Keohane 1991; Hart and Prakash 1997; Lacher 1999.

20 Consider the period from 1968 to 1975: the Vietnam War, the rise of West Germany and Japan, the wave of revolutions in the global South, the structural trade deficit of the US and the changes in oil markets in the US.

21 The end of the Vietnam War put an end to the brief period of rising primary commodity international prices. During the Vietnam War, world trade increased by 8 per cent per year, giving a significant boost to primary exports.

22 The Wapenhans Report was commissioned by the Bank to evaluate lending policy, rudely awakening the Bank to a poor level of return on investments, as well as a severely underdeveloped concern for the social and environmental repercussions of Bank-supported projects. See for example: Danaher 1994.

23 In fact, the Bank fell from the fourth largest international bank in 1960 to the sixty-second (excluding the concessional IDA) in 1997 (Kapur 2002: 71).

24 Although new development agendas were fed into it.

25 The base year is 1995 (1995 = 100). Table 5.17 in World Bank (2000a). Subsequent figures in this paragraph are from the same source unless otherwise stated.

26 SAL is one name for a variety of conditioned packages of economic reform generically titled SAP throughout this book.

27 There are many condemnatory narratives of neoliberalism's impact on Africa during the 1980s, evoking telling statistics. To pick ones I have recently come across: from 1986 to 1989 cocoa exports increased by 25 per cent, but global cocoa prices fell by 33 per cent (McMichael 2000: 158); during the 1980s, sub Saharan Africa's total debt trebled (Mohan *et al.* 2000: 12); between 1984 and 1991, developing countries made a net payment of $209 million to 'northern creditors' (Hanlon 2000: 877).

28 From the creation of the World Bank and IMF at New Hampshire to the delinking of the dollar from a fixed value in gold. See also Helleiner 1994.

29 The Regulation School's original interest lay in interpreting the interactions of accumulation and regulation within Keynesian-type societies.

30 Serious consideration of the emergence of the global South is absent from the model of embedded liberalism.
31 Consider the Atlantic Treaty, the Marshall Plan and the denouement of the Suez Crisis.

4 Introducing post-conditionality

1 The indices by Freedom House International, and Transparency International.
2 Kenya's image as a poor reformer has been replaced by a significant warming by donors since Mwai Kibaki replaced Moi as president after elections in 2002. One might speculate that this constitutes the 'new beginnings' for Kenya that might see it move towards the governance state category, but this will depend on many other factors.
3 In this sense, the PRSP structure replaces conditionality with 'triggers'; that is, policy outputs enable the further release of funds.
4 Much of the monitoring has recently been displaced from central foci to sector wide basket funds. On the example of Tanzania, see D. Holtom 2003.
5 For more detail, see Chapter 2.
6 See page 63.

5 The mechanics of post-conditionality

1 As the 'pro-poor' agenda has grown stronger from the late 1990s, the social provision line ministries of health and education have also been substantially rehabilitated by donor funds, ploughed into Sector Wide Approaches. See for example Jeppson 2002.
2 1992 ushered in a reduction in tension between donors and the Government.
3 The Poverty Eradication Action Plan was Uganda's interim PRSP.
4 Confidential interview and documentation.
5 Mozambique has donor groups – *grupos de trabalho*. For the Public Sector Reform Programme, the *grupo* is chaired by the Director of the Technical Unit for the Reform of Public Sector, with the group of donors led by DFID.
6 This has lessened recently as most donors (with the significant exception of the USA) have begun to pool their resources as part of the new sector wide approach (SWAP). The Bank is also keen on SWAP, developing sector investment programmes which are broadly similar (Jones 2000).
7 A sobering contextual statistic is that by the end of the 1980s there were 100,000 expatriate advisors employed in African public sectors and that expatriates are paid an average of $10,000 per month or about one hundred times the salary of a senior civil servant (*Financial Times* 2 December 1993).
8 The IFC is especially active in Mozambique.
9 The first page of the Uganda country director's visitors book had a message from a certain Yoweri Museveni: 'thanks for all the help', it read. The country director in Tanzania was teased by other donor personnel because he was frequently in the press, photographed next to the Tanzanian President. On another occasion, the country director in Tanzania upset other donors by giving them 'orders' concerning a particular area of reform. The country director acknowledged that he had 'given orders', to bilaterals, but debated that he had meant this in an imperious and entirely serious-minded fashion.
10 The apparent inconsistency of this figure with those in the paragraph above are to some extent a result of discrepancies between pledges and disbursements, and the fact that this figure includes grants and loans. Any residual errors are the result of unexplained differences in Bank figures.

11 Oloka-Onyango and Barya (1997). But see refuting comments of Robert Blake, the World Bank's country director in Uganda (*New Vision* 6 March 2001). Blake does not mention that Uganda is now making greater debt repayments than it was when it began HIPC (Mosley 2000: 222).

12 There was a strong perception within the CSD that the Bank's own cumbersome procedures regarding the releasing of funds had slowed aspects of the reform programme.

13 See also Pincus (2002: 94–5) for a similar case in Indonesia.

14 Research into corruption in Tanzania, Mozambique and Uganda suggests that incumbent elites manage to find avenues for personal enrichment through neoliberal reform itself. See Harrison 1999b; Tangri and Mwenda 2001; Kelsall 2002b.

15 In Uganda in 1998, DANIDA passed on the names of those suspected of corrupt practices in projects with Danish funding.

16 See also Chapter 1.

6 Liberalism and the discourse of reform in governance states

1 More specifically: *The Monitor* and *New Vision* in Uganda, and *The Guardian* and *The African* in Tanzania. Another good source is *The East African*, which covers Kenya, Tanzania and Uganda. One World Bank resident representative was teased by some within the donor community for seeming to appear in the newspapers as often as the President!

2 Interview carried out via email. Original Portuguese text (translated by the author) is: *O principal desafio da Reforma é o factor humano: como criar nos funcionários públicos a consciência de que as reformas são necessárias? Mudar mentalidades, cultura, comportamentos menos apropriados para funcionários públicos, é de facto a questão principal deste processo de reforma.*

3 There is an obvious inconsistency in the figures here. Neither figure gives detail as to how it was calculated. They are reproduced here merely to illustrate that funding for technical assistance has risen quickly to high levels. On the general reliability of World Bank statistics, see Raikes (1988) and Wade (2004).

4 Tanzania and Uganda have been reviewed in some detail in Chapter 4; Mozambique's administrative reform programme commenced in 2002. This relative lateness is largely a result of a recalcitrant Ministry, the politics of language (Portuguese versus English) and the exceptionally strong grip of the ruling party over the state.

5 Since the mid 1990s, some Bank reports have been influenced by the then Chief Economist Joseph Stiglitz, who has been a key innovator of information theoretic economics. Compare, for example Stiglitz (1999a) and World Bank (1998).

6 Reference has been made to the categorisation of 'the poor' in Chapter 3.

7 Pincus takes the concept of legibility from Scott (1998).

8 The sources here are mainly World Bank discussion papers, or scholarly publications on governance by those who have worked for the Bank recently.

9 The Bank held two seminars – in 1991 and 1994 – as part of its 'learning process' with regards to participation, involving other international organisations as well as the Bank.

10 This term is not actually very prevalent in the Bank's literature because the term 'popular' is often associated with left-wing politics. This disquiet is noted in the discussion paper. Most Bank literature refers to 'participation'.

11 Recall the quotation from Tumusiime-Mutebile on page 71.

12 See Chapter 4.

13 An insightful case study of 'partnership' in Burkina Faso – in many ways a contender for the categorisation of governance state – is given by Samoff (2003).

14 The notion of 'stakeholders' also applies to the member states of the World Bank. Here stakeholding is oligarchic rather than polyarchic. See Woods (2000, especially page 831) and Kapur (2002).

15 On Tanzania's civil society and donor dependence, see Kelsall (2001). On Uganda, see Dicklitch (1998; 2001).

16 These are most developed in Uganda, but are also being mainstreamed into Tanzania's governance.

17 On Mozambique, see Tibana (1995).

18 By 1995 this had increased to 20 per cent; by 1999, thanks to expenditure tracking systems and the gazetting of the releasing of funds, the percentage had increased to 90 per cent (Collier and Reinikka 2001: 9).

19 The rest of this section is based on governance states' PRSPs, CASs and the World Bank's HIPC web pages, mainly at www.worldbank.org/poverty/strategies/.

20 Mainly – but with exceptions – a debt to export ratio of 150 per cent.

21 Triggers and benchmarks are also present in other funding and programme documents (ODI 2001).

7 Securing governance states

1 See Chapter 2.

2 But, not by the World Bank.

3 The salient exception is the north of Uganda. See for example: Woodward 1991; Amnesty International 1999.

4 Along with Uganda – consider the salience of stability to the branding of these régimes as 'new': In Africa, Clinton officials enthused in the mid 1990s over the soft authoritarian régimes in Uganda, Rwanda and Ethiopia, seizing upon the ... concept of 'New African leaders' *in the hope that they could deliver régime stability and order.* (Carothers 2000: 3, emphasis added).

5 In fact, foreign investment does not stop when war starts, as one can see even in Somalia. What does change is that investments are either of the quick-return/plunder variety, or that investors must politically negotiate private or factionalised security for their property. The pitfalls of this can be seen in the run-up to the succession of Mobutu by Laurent Kabila (Taylor 2003).

6 Pemba is one of the Zanzibari islands.

7 Confidential interview, 1997.

8 The dilemma is not new. See Schatzberg 1990.

9 Having researched in Mozambique a number of times, it became obvious that – at least in the capital city Maputo – state employees were *Frelimistas*.

10 See, for example the Tanzanian case (*The Express* 1–7 February 2001, 22–28 February 2001); *Africa Confidential* 28 May 1990: 4. For the democratisation period more generally, Vener (2000) finds that aid levels and democratic progress are unrelated for Tanzania.

11 See also Bresser Pereira 1995: 224 *et seq.* Bresser Pereira was Brazil's Finance Minister. More generally, see Thacker 1999.

12 The Tanzanian military intervened in Uganda's civil war to ouster Amin, and has recently been host to large numbers of Rwandan refugees. The donor assurances were related to me by a confidential source.

8 Neoliberalism's revenge?

1 See, for example various issues of *Bretton Woods Update* on the PRSP.
2 A notorious example of Bank internal realpolitik is the 'resignation' of Ravi Kanbur. See Wade (2001a).
3 Public expenditure on development has fallen by 22 per cent over the period 1990–1999 (Jordan 1999: 2)
4 For the latter case, see especially Havnevik 1993.

Bibliography

Abrahamsen, R. (2000) *Disciplining Democracy: Development Discourse and Good Government in Africa* London: Zed Press.

Abrahamsson, H. and Nilsson, A. (1995) *Mozambique, the Troubled Transition: From Socialist Construction to Free Market Capitalism* London: Zed Books.

Adam, C. and Gunning, J. (2002) 'Redesigning the aid contract: donors' use of performance indicators in Uganda', *World Development* 30 (12): 2045–56.

Adamolekun, L. and Pinto, R. (1995) 'Governance and civil service reform: a regional programme', in *Civil Service Reform in Anglophone Africa*, Langseth, P., Nogxina, S., Prinsloo, D. and Sullivan, R. (eds) Somerset West, South Africa: EDI/South Africa Management and Development Institute/ODA.

Adams, P. (1994) 'The World Bank's new rules (same as the old ones)', in *Fifty Years is Enough. The Case Against the World Bank and IMF*, Danaher, K. (ed.) Boston, MA: South End Press, 146–7.

Administrative Reform Secretariat, Government of Uganda (1997) Public service 2002. The Public Service Reform Programme 1997–2002. Kampala, Uganda: Ministry of Public Service.

Africa Confidential, monthly news bulletin, London.

Allen, C. (1992) 'Restructuring an authoritarian state: democratic renewal in Benin', *Review of African Political Economy* 54: 43–59.

Allen, C. (1995) 'Understanding African politics', *Review of African Political Economy* 22 (65): 301–20.

Allen, T. and Weinhold, D. (2000) 'Dropping the debt for the new millennium: is it such a good idea?', *Journal of International Development* 12 (6): 857–75.

Altvater, E. (2002) 'The growth obsession', in *Socialist Register: A World of Contradictions*, Panitch, L. and Leys, C. (eds) London: Merlin Press, 73–92.

Amnesty International (1999) *Uganda*, London: Amnesty International.

Anderson, D. (2002) 'Vigilantes, violence and the politics of public order in Kenya', *African Affairs* 101: 405.

Apter, D. E. (1997) *The Political Kingdom in Uganda: A Study in Bureaucratic Nationalism*, London: Frank Cass.

Armstrong, P., Glyn, A. and Harrison, J. (1991) *Capitalism Since 1945*, Oxford: Blackwell.

Arrighi, G. (2002) 'The African crisis', *New Left Review* Series II (15): 15–39.

Ascher, W. (1983) 'New development approaches and the adaptability of international agencies: the case of the World Bank', *International Organization* 37 (3): 415–39.

Austin, K. (1994) *Invisible Crimes: US Private Intervention in the War in Mozambique*, Washington, DC: Africa Policy Information Centre.

Ayres, R. (1983) *Banking on the Poor. The World Bank and World Poverty*, Cambridge, MA: The MIT Press.

Baker, B. (1998) 'The class of 1990: how have the autocratic leaders of sub-Saharan Africa fared under democratisation?', *Third World Quarterly* 19 (1): 115–27.

Barkan, J. D. (1994) *Beyond Capitalism Versus Socialism in Kenya and Tanzania*, Boulder, CO: L. Rienner.

Barry, B. (2001) *Culture and Equality: An Egalitarian Critique of Multiculturalism*, Cambridge: Cambridge University Press.

Bartton, M. and Rothchild, D. (1992) 'The Institutional Bases of Governance in Africa', in *Governance and Politics in Africa*, Hydén, G. and Bratton, M. (eds) Boulder, CO: Lynne Rienner, 263–84.

Bayart, J. F. (1986) 'Civil society in Africa', in *Political Domination in Africa*, Chabal, P. (ed.) Cambridge: Cambridge University Press, 109–29.

Bayart, J. F. (1993) *The State in Africa: The Politics of the Belly*, London: Heinemann.

Bayart, J. F. (2000) 'Africa in the world: a history of extraversion', *African Affairs* 99 (395): 217–69.

Baylies, C. (1995) 'Political conditionality and democratisation', *Review of African Political Economy* 22 (65): 321–37.

Baylies, C. and Szeftel, M. (1982) 'Zambia's economic reforms and their aftermath: the state and the growth of indigenous capital', *Journal of Commonwealth and Comparative Politics* XX (3): 235–64.

Bayliss, K. and Fine, B. (1998) 'Beyond bureaucrats in business: a critical review of the World Bank approach to privatisation and public sector reform', *Journal of International Development* 10: 841–55.

Beckman, B. (1993) 'The liberation of civil society: neo liberal ideology and political theory', *Review of African Political Economy* 58: 20–34.

Behrend, H. (1998) 'War in Northern Uganda: the Holy Spirit movements of Alice Lakwena, Severino Lukoya, and Joseph Kony (1986–1997)', in *African Guerrillas*, Clapham, C. (ed.) Oxford: James Currey.

Behrend, H. (2000) *Alice Lakwena and the Spirits: War in Northern Uganda, 1985–96*, London: Athens: J. Currey, Ohio University Press.

Berger, M. (2001) 'The rise and demise of national development and the origins of post-Cold War capitalism', *Millennium: Journal of International Studies* 30 (2): 211–34.

Berger, M. and Beeson, M. (1998) 'Lineages of liberalism and miracles of modernisation: the World Bank, the East Asian trajectory, and the international development debate', *Third World Quarterly* 19 (3): 487–504.

Berg-Schlosser, D. and Siegler, R. (1990) *Political Stability and Development: A Comparative Analysis of Kenya, Tanzania, and Uganda*, Boulder, CO: Lynne Rienner Press.

Berman, B. 1998 'Ethnicity, patronage, and the African State: the politics of uncivil nationalism', *African Affairs* 97 (388): 305–43.

Berman, B. and Leys, C. (eds) (1994) *African Capitalists in African Development*, Boulder, CO: Rienner.

Bernstein, H. (1981) 'Notes on the state and the peasantry: the Tanzanian case', *Review of African Political Economy* 21: 44–63.

Bernt Hansen, H. and Twaddle, M. (1998) 'Introduction', in *Developing Uganda*, Bernt Hansen, H. and Twaddle, M. (eds) Oxford: James Currey, 1–26.

Berry, S. (1993) *No Condition is Permanent. The Social Dynamics of Agrarian Change in Sub-Saharan Africa*, Madison, WI: University of Wisconsin Press.

Bhatnagar, B. and Williams, A. C. (eds) (1992) *Participatory Development and the World Bank*, Washington, DC: World Bank Discussion Papers, 183.

Biel, R. (2000) *The New Imperialism. Crisis and Contradictions in North/South Relations*, London: Zed Press.

Biermann, W. and Campbell, J. (1989) 'The chronology of crisis in Tanzania, 1974–86', in *The IMF the World Bank and African Debt Vol. 1*, Onimode, B. (ed.) London: Zed Press, 69–87.

Biermann, W. and Wagao, J. (1986a) 'The quest for adjustment: Tanzania and the IMF 1980–1986', *African Studies Review* 29 (4): 89–103.

Biermann, W. and Wagao, J. (1986b) 'The IMF and Tanzania: a solution to the crisis?', in *World Recession and the Food Crisis in Africa*, Lawrence, P. (ed.) London: James Currey: 140–8.

Bigsten, A. and Kayizzi-Mugerwa, S. (2001) 'Is Uganda an emerging economy?', Nordiska Afrikainstitutet Research report 118.

Bigsten, A., Mutalemwa, D., Tsikata, Y. and Wangwe, S. (1999) *Aid and Reform in Tanzania*, Dar es Salaam: World Bank.

Bigsten, A., Mutalemwa, D., Tsikata, Y. and Wangwe, S. (2001) 'Tanzania', in *Aid and Reform in Africa: Lessons from Ten Case Studies*, Deverajan, S., Dollar, D. and Holmgreen, T. (ed.) Washington, DC: World Bank, 289–360.

Bird, G. (2000) 'Reforming the IMF', *New Economy* 7 (4): 214–18.

Birmingham, D. (1992) *Frontline Nationalism in Angola and Mozambique*, London: Africa World Press.

Block, F. (1977) *The Origins of International Economic Disorder*, Berkeley, CA: University of California Press.

Blunt, P. (1995) 'Cultural Relativism, "good governance" and sustainable human development', *Public Administration and Development* 15 (1): 1–9.

Booth, D. (1985) 'Marxism and development sociology: interpreting the impasse', *World Development* 13 (7): 761–87.

Borges Coelho, J. and Vines, A. (1995) *Pilot Study on Demobilization and Re-integration of Ex-combatants in Mozambique*, Oxford: RSP.

Bowen, M. (1992) 'Beyond reform: adjustment and political power in contemporary Mozambique', *Journal of Modern African Studies* 30 (2): 255–81.

Bracking, S. (1999) 'Structural adjustment: why it wasn't necessary and why it didn't work', *Review of African Political Economy* 26 (80): 207–26.

Bracking, S. (2003) 'Regulating capital accumulation: negotiating the imperial "frontier"', *Review of African Political Economy* 30 (95): 11–32.

Bratton, M. and Rothchild, D. (1992) 'The institutional bases of governance in Africa', in *Governance and Politics in Africa*, Hydén, G. and Bratton, D. (eds) Boulder, CO: Lynne Reinner, 263–84.

Brenner, R. (1998) 'The economics of global turbulence', *New Left Review* Series I (229): 1–265.

Brenner, R. (2001) 'The world economy at the turn of the millennium: toward boom or crisis?', *Review of International Political Economy* 8 (1): 6–44.

Bresser Pereira, L. C. (1995) 'Development economics and the World Bank's identity crisis', *Review of International Political Economy* 2 (2): 211–49.

Brett, E. A. (1994) 'Rebuilding organisational capacity in Uganda under the National Resistance Movement', *Journal of Modern African Studies* 32 (1): 53–80.

Brett, E. A. (1995a) 'Uganda', in *Limits of Adjustment in Africa*, Engberg-Pedersen, P. G., Raikes, P. and Udsholt, L. (eds) Oxford: James Currey, 309–40.

Brett, E. A. (1995b) 'Neutralising the use of force in Uganda: the rôle of the military in Politics', *Journal of Modern African Studies* 33 (1): 129–52.

Bretton Woods Update, bi-monthly new bulletin from Bretton Woods Monitor (London). Available at: http://www.brettonwoodsproject.org/update/.

Bromley, S. (1991) *American Hegemony and World Oil: The Industry, the State System, and the World Hegemony*, Cambridge: Polity Press.

Brown, A., Foster, M., Norton, A. and Naschold, F. (2001) 'The status of sector wide approaches', *ODI Working Paper 142*, London.

Bullard, N., Bello, W. and Mallhotra, K. (1998) 'Taming the Tigers: the IMF and the Asian crisis', *Third World Quarterly* 19 (3): 505–55.

Burnside, C. and Dollar, D. (2000) 'Aid, growth, the incentive régime and poverty reductions', in *The World Bank. Structures and Policies*, Gilbert, C. and Vines, D. (eds) Cambridge: Cambridge University Press, 210–27.

Cahen, M. (1993) 'Check on socialism in Mozambique – What check? What Socialism?', *Review of African Political Economy* 57.

Cahn, J. (1993) 'Challenging the new imperial authority: the World Bank and the democratisation of development', *Harvard Human Rights Journal* 6 (Spring): 159–94.

Callaghy, T. (2001) 'Networks of governance in Africa: innovation in the debt régime', in *Intervention and Transnationalism in Africa. Global-local Networks of Power*, Callaghy, T., Kassimir, R. and Latham, R. (eds) Cambridge: Cambridge University Press, 115–49.

Cameron, G. (2002) 'Zanzibar's turbulent transitions', *Review of African Political Economy* 29 (92): 313–30.

Cammack, P. (1990) 'Statism, new institutionalism and Marxism', in *Socialist Register*, Miliband, R., Panitch, L. and Saville, J. (eds) London: Merlin Press, 147–71.

Cammack, P. (1997) *Capitalism and Democracy in the Third World: The Doctrine for Political Development*, London: Leicester University Press.

Cammack, P. (2001) *The Mother of all Governments: The World Bank's Matrix for Global Governance*, Manchester.

Cammack, P. (2002a) 'Attacking the global poor', *New Left Review* 2 (13): 125–34.

Cammack, P. (2002b) 'Neoliberalism, the World Bank and the new politics of development', in *Development Theory and Practice: Critical Perspectives*, Kothari, U. and Minogue, M. (eds) Basingstoke: Palgrave, 157–78.

Cammack, P. (2002c) 'Making poverty work', in *Socialist Register: A World of Contradictions*, Panitch, L. and Leys, C. (eds) London: Merlin Press, 193–211.

Cammack, P. (2004) 'What the World Bank means by poverty reduction', *New Political Economy*, forthcoming.

Campbell, H. and Stein, H. (1992) 'Introduction: the dynamics of liberalization in Tanzania', in *Tanzania and the IMF: The Dynamics of Liberalization*, Campbell, H. S. H. (ed.) Boulder, CO: Westview Press, 1–19.

Carbone, G. (2000) *Disguising Partisanship and Hegemony: The Organisational Bases of 'Movement Democracy' in Uganda*, unpublished manuscript, London.

Carothers, T. (2000) *The Clinton Record on Democracy*, Washington, DC: Carnegie Working Paper 16.

Carr, E. H. (1938/1995) *The Twenty Year's Crisis*, Basingstoke: Macmillan.

Casal, A. (1988) 'A crise da Produção Familiar e as Aldeias Comunais em Moçambique', *Revista Internacional de Estudos Africanos* 8/9: 157–91.

Caufield, C. (1998) *Masters of Illusion: The World Bank and the Poverty of Nations*, Houndmills, Macmillan.

Charney, C. (1987) 'Political power and social class in the neo-colonial African state', *Review of African Political Economy* 38: 48–65.

Chingono, M. (1996) *The State, Violence, and Development. The Political Economy of War in Mozambique, 1975–1992*, Aldershot: Avebury.

Christie, I. (1989) *Samora Machel, a Biography*, London: Panaf.

Clapham, C. (1996) *Africa and the International System*, Cambridge: Cambridge University Press.

Clarence-Smith, G. (1989) 'The roots of the Mozambican counter-revolution', *Southern African Review of Books* April/May: 7–10.

Clark, J. (2001) 'Explaining Ugandan intervention in Congo: evidence and interpretations', *Journal of Modern African Studies* 39 (2): 261–87.

Cleaver, F. (1999) 'Paradoxes of participation: questioning participatory approaches to development', *Journal of International Development* 11 (4): 597–612.

Cohen, J. (1993) 'Importance of public service reform: Kenya', *Journal of Modern African Studies* 31 (3): 449–76.

Collier, P. (1999) 'Learning from failure: the International Finance Institutions as agencies of restraint in Africa', in *The Self-Restraining State. Power and Accountability in New Democracies*, Schedler, A., Diamond, L. and Plattner, M. (eds) London: Lynne Rienner, 313–30.

Collier, P. and Pradhan, S. (1998) 'Economic aspects of the transition from civil war', in *Developing Uganda*, Bernt Hansen, H. and Twaddle, M. (eds) Oxford: James Currey, 19–37.

Collier, P. and Reinikka, R. (2001) 'Introduction', in *Uganda's Recovery. The Role of Farms, Firms, and Government*, Reinikka, R. and Collier, P. (eds) Kampala, Uganda: Fountain Press, 1–11.

Commins, S. K. (1988) *Africa's Development Challenges and the World Bank: Hard Questions, Costly Choices*, Boulder, CO: L. Rienner.

Cooper, F. (2001a), 'What is the concept of globalisation good for? An African historian's perspective', *African Affairs* 100: 399.

Cooper, F. (2001b) 'Networks, moral discourse, and history', in *Intervention and Transnationalism in Africa. Global-local Networks of Power*, Callaghy, T., Kassimir, R. and Latham, R. (eds) Cambridge, Cambridge University Press, 23–47.

Coulson, A. (1982) *Tanzania: A Political Economy*, Oxford: Oxford University Press.

Cowen, M. and Shenton, R. (1996) *Doctrines of Development*, London: Routledge.

Cox, W., with Sinclair, T. (1996) *Approaches to World Order*, Cambridge, Cambridge University Press.

Craig, D. and Porter, D. (2003) 'Poverty reduction strategy papers: a new convergence', *World Development* 31 (1): 53–69.

Cramer, C. and Pontara, N. (1998) 'Rural poverty and poverty alleviation in

Mozambique: what's missing from the debate?' *Journal of Modern African Studies* 36 (1): 101–39.

Crane, B. and Finkle, J. (1981) 'Organizational impediments to development assistance: the World Bank's population program', *World Politics* 33 (4): 516–53.

Dagger, R. (1997) *Civic Virtues: Rights, Citizenship, and Liberal Republicanism*, Oxford: Oxford University Press.

Dahl, R. (1971) *Polyarchy: Participation and Opposition*, London: Yale University Press.

Danaher, K. (1994) *50 Years is Enough: The Case Against the World Bank and the International Monetary Fund*, Boston, MA: South End Press.

Danielson, A. (2001) 'Can HIPC reduce poverty in Tanzania?', paper, WIDER conference, Helsinki, August.

Das Gupta, M. (1999) Liberté, égalité, fraternité: exploring the role of governance in fertility decline. Policy research working paper 2126, Washington, DC: World Bank Development Research Group Regulation and Competition Policy.

Davidson, B. (1992) *The Black Man's Burden: The Curse of the Nation State*, London: James Currey.

Desai, M. (2002) *Marx's Revenge. The Resurgence of Capitalism and the Death of Statist Socialism*, London: Verso.

Deverajan, S., Dollar, D. and Holmgren, T. (eds) (2001) *Aid and Reform in Africa: Lessons from Ten Case Studies*, Washington, DC: World Bank.

Dicklitch, S. (1998) *The Elusive Promise of NGOs in Africa: Lessons from Uganda*, New York, NY: St Martin's Press.

Dicklitch, S. (2001) 'NGOs and democratisation in transitional societies', *International Politics* 38 (1): 27–46.

Doom, R. and Vlassenroot, K. (1999) 'Kony's message: a new koine? The Lord's resistance army in Northern Uganda', *African Affairs* 98 (390): 5–37.

Doornbos, M. (1995) 'State formation processes under external supervision: reflections on "good governance"', in *Aid and Political Conditionality*, Stokke, O. (ed.) London: Frank Cass: 377–91.

Doornbos, M. (1996) 'Uganda: a Bantustan?', *Review of African Political Economy* 23 (69): 429–37.

Duffield, M. (1993) 'NGOs, disaster relief and asset transfer in the Horn: political survival in a permanent emergency', *Development and Change* 24 (1): 131–57.

Duffield, M. (2001) *Global Governance and the New Wars: The Merging of Development and Security*, London: Zed Press.

Economist Intelligence Unit (2000) *Uganda Country Report*, London: EIU.

Egerö, B. (1990) *Mozambique, a Dream Undone: The Political Economy of Democracy, 1975–84*, Uppsala: Nordiska afrikainstitutet.

Elgstrom, O. (1999) 'Giving aid on the recipient's terms: the Swedish experience in Tanzania', in *Agencies in Foreign Aid. Comparing China, Sweden, and the United States in Tanzania*, Hydén, G. and Mukandala, R. (eds) Houndmills: Macmillan, 116–56.

Elson, D. (1994) 'People, development, and international financial institutions: an interpretation of the Bretton Woods System', *Review of African Political Economy* 62 (21): 511–24.

Engberg-Pedersen, P., Gibbon, P., Raikes, P. and Udsholt, L. (eds) (1996) *Limits of Adjustment in Africa*, London: James Currey.

Escobar, A. (1995) *Encountering Development: The Making and Unmaking of the Third World*, Princeton, NJ: Princeton University Press.

Evans, A. (2001) Institutionalising the PRSP approach in Tanzania, ODI PRSP Institutionalisation Study, final report, chapter 9.

Fanon, F. (1990) *The Wretched of the Earth*, London: Penguin.

Fauvet, P. (1984) 'Roots of the counter-revolution: the MNR', *Review of African Political Economy* 29: 108–21.

Ferguson, J. (1994) *The Anti-politics Machine. 'Development', Depoliticisation and Bureaucratic Power in Lesotho*, London: University of Minnesota Press.

Fieldhouse, D. K. (1967) *The Theory of Capitalist Imperialism*, London: Longmans.

Fine, B. (1999) 'The developmental state is dead: long live social capital?', *Development and Change* 30 (1): 1–19.

Fine, B. (2001) *Social Capital Versus Social Theory. Political Economy and Social Science at the Turn of the Millennium*, London: Routledge.

Fine, B., Lapvitsas, C. and Pincus, J. (eds) (2001) *Development Policy in the Twenty-first Century: Beyond the Post-Washington Consensus*, London: Routledge.

Finnemore, M. (1997) 'Redefining development at the World Bank', in *International Development and the Social Sciences*, Cooper, F. and Packard, R. (eds) California: California University Press, 203–28.

Forrest, T. (1995) *Politics and Economic Development in Nigeria*, Boulder, CO: Westview Press.

Fowler, A. (1992) 'Distant obligations: speculations on NGO funding and the global market', *Review of African Political Economy* 55: 9–29.

Fox, J. (1997) 'The World Bank and social capital: contesting the concept in practice', *Journal of International Development* 9 (7): 963–71.

Fox, J. and Brown, L. (eds) (1998) *The Struggle for Accountability: The World Bank, NGOs, and Grassroots Movements*, London and Cambridge, MA: MIT Press.

Fox, R. (1996) 'Bleak future for multi party elections in Kenya', *Journal of Modern African Studies* 34: 4.

Freund, B. (1998) *The Making of Contemporary Africa*, Houndmills: Macmillan.

Frischtak, L. (1994) *Governance Capacity and Economic Reform in Developing Countries*, World Bank technical paper no. 254. Washington, DC: World Bank.

Geffray, C. (1991) *A Causa das Armas, Antropologia da Guerra Contemporânea em Moçambique*, Porto: Afrontamento.

Geffray, C. and Pederson, M. (1986) 'Sobre a guerra na província de Nampula. Elementos de análise e hipóteses sobre as determinações e consequências socio-económicas locais', *Revista Internacional de Estudos Africanos* 4/5: 303–18.

Germain, R. (1997) *The International Organisation of Credit*, Cambridge: Cambridge University Press.

Ghai, D. (ed.) (1991) *The IMF and the South: The Social Impact of Crisis and Adjustment*, London: Zed Press.

Gibbon, P. (1992) 'The World Bank and African Poverty, 1973–91', *Journal of Modern African Studies* 30 (2): 193–221.

Gibbon, P. (1993) 'The World Bank and the New Politics of Aid', *European Journal of Development Research* 5 (1): 35–62.

Gibbon, P. (1995) 'Towards a Political Economy of the World Bank', in *Between Liberalisation and Oppression: The Politics of Structural Adjustment in Africa*, Mkandawire, T. and Olukoshi, A. (eds) Dakar: CODESRIA, 116–57.

Gibbon, P. (2002) 'Present-day capitalism, the new international trade régime and Africa', *Review of African Political Economy* 29 (91): 95–112.

Gibbon, P., Bangura, Y. and Ofstad, A. (eds) (1992) *Authoritarianism Democracy and Adjustment*, Uppsala: Scandinavian Institute of African Studies.

Giddens, A. (1995) *The Nation-State and Violence*, Berkeley, CA: University of California Press.

Gill, S. (1995) 'Globalisation, market civilisation, and disciplinary neoliberalism', *Millennium* 24 (3): 399–423.

Gill, S. and Law, D. (1993) *The Global Political Economy: Perspectives, Problems, and Policies*, London: Harvester Wheatsheaf.

Gillies, D. (1996) 'Human rights, democracy, and good governance: stretching the World Bank's policy frontiers', in *The World Bank. Lending on a Global Scale*, Griesgraber, J. and Gunter, B. (eds) London: Pluto, 101–42.

Gore, C. (2000) 'The rise and fall of the Washington consensus as a paradigm for developing countries', *World Development* 28 (5): 789–95.

Gould-Davies, N. and Woods, N. (1999) 'Russia and the IMF', *International Affairs* 75 (1): 1–23.

Gowan, P. (1995) 'Neo liberal theory and practice for Eastern Europe', *New Left Review* 1 (213): 3–61.

Gowan, P. (1999) *Global Gamble: Washington's Faustian Bid*, London: Verso.

Green, D. (1996) 'Latin America: neoliberal failure and the search for alternatives', *Third World Quarterly* 17 (1): 109–22.

Green, M. (2003) 'Globalising Development in Tanzania', *Critique of Anthropology* 23 (2): 123–43.

Gros, J. (1996) 'Towards a taxonomy of failed states in the new world order: decaying Somalia, Liberia, Rwanda, and Haiti', *Third World Quarterly* 17 (3): 455–71.

Hanlon, J. (1990) *Mozambique: The Revolution Under Fire*, London: Zed Books.

Hanlon, J. (1991) *Mozambique: Who Calls the Shots?*, London: James Currey.

Hanlon, J. (2000) 'How much debt must be cancelled?', *Journal of International Development* 12 (6): 877–901.

Hanlon, J. (2002) 'Bank corruption becomes site of struggle in Mozambique', *Review of African Political Economy* 29 (91): 53–4.

Hansen, H. B. and Twaddle, M. (1995) *From Chaos to Order: The Politics of Constitution-Making in Uganda*, Kampala, Uganda: Fountain Publishers.

Hardt, M. and Negri, A. (2000) *Empire*, Cambridge: Cambridge University Press.

Harris, L. (1986) 'Conceptions of the IMF's role in Africa', in *World Recession and the Food Crisis in Africa*, Lawrence, P. (ed.) London: James Currey, 83–96.

Harris, N. (1986) *The End of the Third World*, Harmondsworth: Penguin.

Harrison, G. (1994) 'Mozambique: an unsustainable democracy', *Review of African Political Economy* 21 (61): 429–40.

Harrison, G. (1999a) 'Clean-ups, conditionality, and adjustment: why institutions matter in Mozambique', *Review of African Political Economy* 26 (81): 323–33.

Harrison, G. (1999b) 'Corruption as "boundary politics": the state, democratisation, and Mozambique's unstable liberalisation', *Third World Quarterly* 20 (3): 537–51.

Harrison, G. (2000) *The Politics of Democratisation in Rural Mozambique: Grass-roots Governance in Mecúfi*, Lewiston, NY: Edwin Mellen.

Harrison, G. (2001) 'Administering market-friendly growth? Liberal populism and the World Bank's involvement in administrative reform in sub-Saharan Africa', *Review of International Political Economy* 8 (3): 528–48.

Harrison, G. (2004) 'Africa', in *The New Regional Politics of Development*, Payne, T. (ed.) Houndmills: Palgrave.

Harriss, J. (2002) *Depoliticising Development. The World Bank and Social Capital*, London: Anthem Press.

Harriss, J., Hunter, J. and Lewis, C. (eds) (1995) *The New Institutional Economics and the Third World*, London: Routledge.

Hart, J. and Prakash, A. (1997) 'The decline of embedded liberalism and the rearticulation of the welfare state', *New Political Economy* 2 (1): 65–79.

Hauser, E. (1999) 'Ugandan relations with Western donors in the 1990s: what impact on democratisation?', *Journal of Modern African Studies* 37 (4): 621–43.

Havnevik, K. (1993) *Tanzania. The Limits to Development from Above*, Motala: Nordiska Afrikainstitutet.

Helleiner, E. (1994) *States and the Re-emergence of Global Finance: From Bretton Woods to the 1990s*, Ithaca, NY: Cornell University Press.

Helleiner, G. (1999) *Changing Aid Relationships in Tanzania*, mimeograph, Dar es Salaam.

Helleiner, G., Killick, T., Lipumba, N., Ndulu, B. and Svendsen, K. (1995) Report of Independent Advisors on Development Cooperation Issues between Tanzania and its Donors. Dar es Salaam.

Hibou, B. (1998) 'The social capital of the state as an agent of deception', in *The Criminalization of the State in Africa*, Bayart, J. F., Ellis, S. and Hibou, B. (eds) Oxford: James Currey, 69–87.

Higgott, R. and Phillips, N. (2000) 'Challenging triumphalism and convergence: the limits of global liberalisation in Asia and Latin America', *Review of International Studies* 26 (3): 259–380.

Himbara, D. and Sultan, D. (1995) 'Reconstructing the Ugandan state and economy: the challenge of an international Bantustan', *Review of African Political Economy* 22 (63): 85–93.

Hodges, T. (2001) *Angola: From Afro-Stalinism to Petro-Diamond Capitalism*, Oxford: James Currey.

Holtom, D. (2003) *Coercion and Consent: The World Bank in Tanzania*, PhD, CDS, Swansea.

Hope, K. R. (2001) 'New public management: context and practice in Africa', *International Public Management Journal* 4 (1): 119–34.

Hopgood, S. (2000) 'Reading the small print in global civil society: the inexorable hegemony of the liberal self', *Millennium: Journal of International Studies* 29 (1): 1–25.

Hopkins, R., Powell, A., Roy, A. and Gilbert, C. (2000) 'The World Bank, conditionality and the comprehensive development framework', in *The World Bank: Structure and Policies*, Gilbert, C. and Vines, D. (eds) Cambridge: Cambridge University Press, 282–98.

Human Rights Watch (1999) *Hostile to Democracy*, Washington, DC: HRW.

Hydén, G. (1980) *Beyond Ujamaa in Tanzania. Underdevelopment and an Uncaptured Peasantry*, London: Heinemann.

Hydén, G. (1999) 'Top down democratisation in Tanzania', *Journal of Democracy* 10 (4): 142–55.

International Conference Group (2000) *Uganda and Rwanda: Friends or Enemies?*, Nairobi/Brussels: ICG Report 14.

Isaacman, A. and Isaacman, B. (1983) *Mozambique: From Colonialism to Revolution, 1900–1982*, Boulder, CO: Westview Press.

Jackson, R. (1990) *Quasi States: Sovereignty, International Relations and the Third World*, Cambridge: Cambridge University Press.

Jackson, R. and Rosberg, C. (1982) 'Why Africa's weak states persist: the empirical and the judicial in statehood', *World Politics* 35 (1): 1–24.

Jeffries, R. (1993) 'The state, structural adjustment and good government in Africa', *Journal of Commonwealth and Comparative Politics* 31 (1): 20–35.

Jennings, M. (2001) ' "Development is very political in Tanzania" Oxfam and the Chuunya integrated development programme', in *The Charitable Impulse: NGOs in East and Northeast Africa*, Barrow, O. and Jennings, M. (eds) Oxford: James Currey, 109–30.

Jeppsson, A. (2002) 'SWAP dynamics in a decentralised context: experiences from Uganda', *Social Science and Medicine* 55 (11): 2053–60.

Jones, S. (2000) 'Increasing aid effectiveness in Africa? The World Bank and sector investment programmes', in *The World Bank: Structure and Policies*, Gilbert, C. and Vines, D. (eds) Cambridge: Cambridge University Press, 266–81.

Jordan, B. (1983) 'Mission Mozambique', *Soldier of Fortune* January: 82–8.

Jordan, L. (1999) *The Death of Development? The Converging Policy Agendas of the World Bank and the WTO*, New York: Bank Information Centre.

Joseph, R. (1999) 'Africa, 1990–1997: from *Abertura to Closure*', in *The Self-Restraining State. Power and Accountability in New Democracies*, Schedler, A., Diamond, L. and Plattner, M. (eds) London and Boulder, CO: Lynne Rienner, 3–18.

Kaplan, R. (1994) 'The Coming Anarchy', *Atlantic Monthly* February: 44–66.

Kapur, D. (2002) 'The changing anatomy of governance of the World Bank', in *Reinventing the World Bank*, Pincus, J. and Winters, J. (eds) New York: Cornell University Press, 54–76.

Kapur, D., Lewis, J. and Webb, R. (eds) (1997) *The World Bank: Its First Half Century Vol. 1*, Washington, DC: Brookings Institution Press.

Kasekende, L. and Atingi-Ego, M. (1999) 'Uganda's experience with aid', *Journal of African Economies* 8 (4): 617–49.

Kasfir, N. (1998) 'No party democracy in Uganda', *Journal of Democracy* 9: 2.

Kay, G. (1975) *Development and Underdevelopment: A Marxist Analysis*, London: Macmillan.

Kayizzi-Mugerwa, S. (1998) 'Africa and the donor community: from conditionality to partnership', *Journal of International Development* 10 (1): 219–25.

Kelsall, T. (2001) 'Donors, NGOs and the state. Governance and "civil society" in Tanzania', in *The Charitable Impulse: NGOs in East and Northeast Africa*, Barrow, O. and Jennings, M. (eds) Oxford: James Currey, 133–48.

Kelsall, T. (2002a) 'New political struggles and democracy in mainland Tanzania', paper, African Studies seminar, Edinburgh.

Kelsall, T. (2002b) 'Shop windows and smoke-filled rooms: governance and the repoliticisation of Tanzania', *Journal of Modern African Studies* 40 (4): 597–621.

Keohane, R. (1991) 'The theory of hegemonic stability and changes in international economic régimes', in *The Theoretical Evolution of International Political Economy*, Crane, T. and Amani, A. (eds) Oxford: Oxford University Press, 245–62.

Khadiagala, G. (1993) 'Uganda's domestic and regional security since the 1970s', *Journal of Modern African Studies* 31 (2): 231–55.

Killick, T. (1997) 'Principals, agents, and the failings of conditionality', *Journal of International Development* 9 (4): 483–95.

Kitching, G. (1982) *Development and Underdevelopment in Historical Perspective*, London: Methuen.

Kitching, G. (2001) *Seeking Social Justice Through Globalisation*, Pennsylvania: Penn State Press.

Klitgaard, R. (1995) 'Institutional Adjustment and Adjusting to Institutions', Washington, DC: World Bank Discussion Paper 303.

Krasner, S. (1990) *Sovereignty: Organized Hypocrisy*, Princeton, NJ: Princeton University Press.

Krugman, P. (1995) 'Dutch tulips and emerging markets', *Foreign Affairs* 74 (4): 28–44.

Lacher, H. (1999) 'Embedded liberalism, disembedded markets: reconceptualising the *pax Americana*', *New Political Economy* 4 (3): 343–61.

Lamont, T. (1995) 'Economic planning and policy formulation in Uganda', in *Uganda: Landmarks in Rebuilding a Nation*, Langseth, P., Katorobo, J., Brett, E. A. and Munene, J. (eds) Kampala, Uganda: Fountain Press, 11–26.

Landell-Mills, P. (1992) 'Governance, cultural change and empowerment', *Journal of Modern African Studies* 30 (4): 543–69.

Langseth, P. (1996) 'The context of civil service reform', in *Post-conflict Uganda: Towards an Effective Civil Service*, Langseth, P. and Mugaju, J. (eds) Kampala, Uganda: Fountain Press, 24–54.

Langseth, P., Katorobo, J., Brett, E. A. and Munene, J. (eds) (1995) *Uganda: Landmarks in Rebuilding a Nation*, Kampala, Uganda: Fountain Publishers.

Latham, R. (2001) 'Identifying the contours of transboundary life', in *Intervention and Transnationalism in Africa. Global-local Networks of Power*, Callaghy, T., Kassimir, R. and Latham, R. (eds) Cambridge: Cambridge University Press, 69–93.

Lawrence, P. (ed.) (1986) *World Recession and the Food Crisis in Africa*, London: James Currey.

Legum, C. and Mmari, G. R. V. (1995) *Mwalimu: The Influence of Nyerere*, Trenton, NJ: Africa World Press.

Lenin, V. I. (1916/1975) *Imperialism: Highest Stage of Capitalism*, Peking: Foreign Language Press.

Leys, C. (1994) 'Confronting the African tragedy', *New Left Review* 204: 33–47.

Lindauer, D. and Nunberg, B. (eds) (1994) *Rehabilitating Government: Pay and Employment Reform in Africa*, Washington, DC: World Bank.

Littlejohn, G. (1988) *Rural Development in Mueda District, Mozambique*, Leeds: Southern African Studies, No. 9.

Loxley, J. (1989) 'The Devaluation Debate in Tanzania', in *Structural Adjustment in Africa*, Campbell, B. and Loxley, J. (eds) London: Macmillan, 13–36.

Loxley, J. (1995) 'A review of adjustment in Africa: reforms, results, and the road ahead', *Canadian Journal of African Studies* 29 (2): 266–71.

Loxley, J. (2003) 'Imperialism and economic reform: NEPAD', *Review of African Political Economy* 30 (95): 119–28.

MacGaffey, J. (1987) *Entrepreneurs and Parasites: The Struggle for Indigenous Capitalism in Zaire*, Cambridge: Cambridge University Press.

MacGaffey, J. with Mukohya, V., ye Beda, M., Gundfest Schoepf, B., wa Nkera, N. and Engundu, W. (1991) *The Real Economy of Zaire*, London: James Currey.

Machel, S. and Munslow, B. (1985) *Samora Machel: An African Revolutionary: Selected Speeches and Writings*, London: Zed.

Malima, K. (1986) 'The IMF and World Bank conditionality: the Tanzanian case', in *World Recession and the Food Crisis in Africa*, Lawrence, P. (ed.) London: James Currey.

Mamdani, M. (1976) *Politics and Class Formation in Uganda*, London: Heinemann Educational.

Mamdani, M. (1983) *Imperialism and Fascism in Uganda*, London: Heinemann Educational Books.

Mamdani, M. (1987) 'Contradictory class perspectives on the question of democracy: the case of Uganda', in *Popular Struggles from Democracy in Africa*, Anyang' Nyong'o, P. (ed.) London: Zed, 78–93.

Mamdani, M. (1990) 'Uganda: contradictions of the IMF programme and perspective', *Third World Quarterly* 21 (3): 427–69.

Mamdani, M. (1995) *And Fire Does Not Always Beget Ash: Critical Reflections on the NRM*, Kampala, Uganda: Monitor Publications.

Manning, C. (1998) 'Constructing opposition in Mozambique: Renamo as a political party', *Journal of Southern African Studies* 24 (1): 161–91.

Marquette, H. (2001) 'Corruption, democracy, and the World Bank', *Crime Law and Social Change* 36: 395–407.

Marshall, J. (1990) 'Structural adjustment and social policy in Mozambique', *Review of African Political Economy* 47: 28–43.

Marshall, J. (1992) *War Debt and Structural Adjustment in Mozambique: The Social Impact*, Ottawa: North-South Institute.

McCourt, W. and Minogue, M. (eds) (2001) *The Internationalisation of New Public Management*, Cheltenham: Edward Elgar.

McMichael, P. (2000) *Development and Social Change: A Global Perspective*, California: Pine Forge Press.

Meagher, K. (1990) 'The hidden economy: informal and parallel trade in northwestern Uganda', *Review of African Political Economy* 47: 64–84.

Mehta, P. (1994) 'Fury over a river', in *Fifty Years is Enough. The Case Against the World Bank and IMF*, Danaher, K. (ed.) Boston: South End Press, 117–21.

Mehta, U. S. (1999) *Liberalism and Empire. A Study in Nineteenth-Century British Liberal Thought*, Chicago, IL: University of Chicago Press.

Meiksins Wood, E. M. (1999) 'Unhappy families: global capitalism in a world of nation-states', *Monthly Review* 51 (3).

Mercer, C. (2003) 'Performing partnership: civil society and the illusions of good governance in Tanzania', *Political Geography*, forthcoming.

Milder, D. (1996) 'Foreign assistance: catalyst for domestic coalition building', in *The World Bank. Lending on a Global Scale*, Griesgraber, J. G. B. (ed.) London: Pluto, 142–92.

Mill, J. S. (1982) *On Liberty*, Harmondsworth: Penguin.

Miller-Adams, M. (1999) *The World Bank: New Agendas in a Changing World*, London: Routledge.

Ministry of Public Service, Government of Uganda (1993) *Management of Change: Improved Service Delivery*, Report on the Proceedings of the Seminar of Ministers and Permanent Secretaries at the International Conference Centre, Kampala, Uganda: 19–20 August.

Ministry of Public Service, Government of Uganda (1995) *Civil Service Reform Programme: Restructuring Report*, Kampala, Uganda: Ministry of Health.

Minogue, M. (2002) 'Power to the people? Good governance and the reshaping of the state', in *Development Theory and Practice: Critical Perspectives*, Kothari, U. and Minogue, M. (eds) Houndmills: Palgrave, 117–35.

Minter, W. (1994) *Apartheid's Contras: An Inquiry into the Roots of War in Angola and Mozambique*, London: Zed Books.

Mistry, P. (1989) 'The present role of the World Bank in Africa', *Institute for African Alternatives*, lecture, London.

Mkandawire, T. (1999) 'Crisis management and the making of "choiceless Democracies"', in *State, Conflict, and Democracy in Africa*, Joseph, R. (ed.) Boulder, CO and London: Lynne Rienner, 119–36.

Mkandawire, T. and Olukoshi, A. (eds) (1995) *Between Liberalisation and Oppression: The Politics of Structural Adjustment in Africa*, Dakar: CODESRIA.

Mkandawire, T. and Soludo, C. (2000) *Our Continent Our Future: African Perspectives in Structural Adjustment*, Trenton, NJ and Asmara, Eritrea: Africa World Press.

Mohan, G., Brown, E., Milward, B. and Zack-Williams, A. (2000) *Structural Adjustment: Theory, Practice and Impacts*, London: Routledge.

Mondlane, E. (1983) *The Struggle for Mozambique*, London: Zed Press.

Moore, D. (1999) '"Sail on O Ship of State": neo-liberalism, globalisation, and the governance of Africa', *Journal of Peasant Studies* 27 (1): 61–97.

Moore, D. and Schmitz, G. (eds) (1995) *Debating Development Discourse*, Houndmills Basingstoke: Macmillan.

Mosley, P. (2000) 'Britain's Aid Policy', *New Economy* 7 (4): 219–23.

Mosley, P. and Weeks, J. (1993) 'Has recovery begun? "Africa's adjustment in the 1980s" revisited', *World Development* 21 (10): 1583–606.

Mosley, P., Harrigan, J. and Toye, J. (1991) *Aid and Power: the World Bank and Policy Based Lending*, London: Routledge.

Mosley, P., Subasat, T. and Weeks, J. (1995) 'Assessing Adjustment in Africa', *World Development* 23 (9): 1459–73.

Mozambiquefile, monthly news bulletin, Maputo, Mozambique.

Mueller, S. (1981) 'The historical origins of Tanzania's ruling class', *Canadian Journal of African Studies* 15 (3): 459–97.

Munslow, B. (1983) *Mozambique: The Revolution and Its Origins*, London and New York, NY: Longman.

Museveni, Y. (1997) *Sowing the Mustard Seed. The Struggle for Freedom and Democracy in Uganda*, London: Macmillan.

Muthu, S. (2003) *Enlightenment Against Empire*, Princeton, NJ: Princeton University Press.

Mutibwa, P. (1992) *Uganda Since Independence. A Story of Unfulfilled Hopes*, London: Hurst.

Nabuguzi, E. (1995) 'Popular initiatives in service provision in Uganda', in *Service*

Provision Under Stress in East Africa, Semboja, J. and Therkildsen, O. (eds) Oxford: James Currey, 192–200.

Naim, M. (2000) 'Fads and fashion in economic reforms: Washington consensus or Washington confusion?', *Third World Quarterly* 21 (3): 505–29.

Nelson, P. (1995) *The World Bank and Non-Governmental Organisations. The Limits of Apolitical Development*, Houndmills: Macmillan.

New Vision, Ugandan daily newspaper, Kampala, Uganda.

Nunberg, B. (1990) *Public Sector Management Issues in Structural Adjustment Lending*, Washington, DC: World Bank Discussion Papers, 99.

Nunberg, B. (1994) 'Experience with civil service pay and employment reform: an overview', in *Rehabilitating Government: Pay and Employment Reform in Africa*, Lindauer, D. and Nunberg, B. (eds) Washington, DC: World Bank.

Nunberg, B. and Nellis, J. (1990) *Civil Service Reform and the World Bank*, Washington, DC: Policy Research and External Affairs, 422.

Nwajiaku, K. (1994) 'The national conferences in Benin and Togo revisited', *Journal of Modern African Studies* 32 (3): 429–47.

Nyamugasira, W. and Rowden, R. (2002) 'Do the new IMF and World Bank loans support countries' poverty reduction strategies? The case of Uganda', report, Kampala, Uganda.

Nyerere, J. K. (1967) *Freedom and Unity: Uhuru na umoja; A Selection from Writings and Speeches, 1952–65*, London and Nairobi: Oxford University Press.

O'Laughlin, B. (1996) 'From basic needs to safety nets: the rise and fall of urban food rationing in Mozambique', *European Journal of Development Research* 8 (1): 200–23.

O'Brien, R., Goetz, A. M., Scholte, J. A. and Williams, M. (2000) *Contesting Global Governance: Multilateral Economic Institutions and Global Social Movements*, Cambridge: Cambridge University Press.

Oliver, R. (1975) *International Economic Co-operation and the World Bank*, Houndmills: Macmillan.

Oloka-Onyango, J. and Barya, J. (1997) 'Civil society and the political economy of foreign aid in Uganda', *Democratization* 4 (2): 113–38.

Olowu, B. (1999) 'Redesigning African civil service reforms', *Journal of Modern African Studies* 37 (1): 1–23.

Olukoshi, A. (ed.) (1993) *The Politics of Structural Adjustment in Nigeria*, London: James Currey.

Omara-Otunnu, A. (1987) *Politics and the Military in Uganda (1890–1985)*, New York, NY: St Martin's Press.

Overseas Development Institute (2001) *PRSP Institutionalisation Study. Final Report*, London: ODI.

Owusu, F. (2003) 'Pragmatism and the gradual shift from dependency to neoliberalism: the World Bank, African leaders, and development policy in Africa', *World Development* 31 (10): 1655–72.

Palan, R. (2000) *Global Political Economy: Contemporary Theories*, London: Routledge.

Pastor, M. and Wise, R. (1999) 'The Politics of Second Generation Reform', *Journal of Democracy* 10: 34–48.

Paul, S. (1992) 'Accountability in public services: exit, voice and control', *World Development* 20 (7): 1047–60.

Payer, C. (1982) *The World Bank: A Critical Analysis*, New York, NY: Monthly Review Press.

Payer, C. (1991) *Lent and Lost: Foreign Debt and Third World Development*, London: Zed Press.

Picciotto, R. (1995) *Putting Institutional Economics to Work. From Participation to Governance*, Washington, DC: World Bank Discussion Papers: 304.

Pincus, J. (2002) 'State simplification and institution building in a World Bank financed development project', in *Reinventing the World Bank*, Pincus, J. and Winters, J. (eds) New York, NY: Cornell University Press, 76–101.

Pincus, J. and Winters, J. (eds) (2002) *Reinventing the World Bank*, New York, NY: Cornell University Press.

Ping, A. (1999) 'From proletarian internationalism to mutual development: China's co-operation with Tanzania', in *Agencies in Foreign Aid. Comparing China, Sweden, and the United States in Tanzania*, Hydén, G. and Mukandala, R. (eds) Houndmills: Macmillan, 156–202.

Pinto, R. (1998) 'Innovations in the provision of public goods and services', *Public Administration and Development* 18: 387–97.

Pitcher, M. A. (2003) *Transforming Mozambique*, Cambridge: Cambridge University Press.

Pitts, J. (2003) 'Legislator of the world? A rereading of Bentham on colonies', *Political Theory* 31 (2): 200–34.

Plank, D. (1993) 'Aid, debt, and the end of sovereignty: Mozambique and its donors', *Journal of Modern African Studies* 31 (3): 407–30.

Polanyi, K. (1957) *The Great Transformation*, Boston: Beacon Press.

Raikes, P. (1988) *Modernising Hunger*, London: James Currey.

Raikes, P. and Gibbon, P. (1996) 'Tanzania', in *Limits of Adjustment in Africa*, Engberg-Pedersen, P., Gibbon, P., Raikes, P. and Udsholt, L. (eds) London: James Currey, 215–301.

Reinikka, R. (2001) 'Recovery in service delivery: evidence from schools and health centres', in *Uganda's Recovery. The Role of Farms, Firms, and Government*, Reinikka, R. and Collier, P. (eds) Kampala, Uganda: Fountain Press, 343–71.

Reinikka, R. and Collier, P. (eds) (2001) *Uganda's Recovery. The Role of Farms, Firms, and Government*, Kampala, Uganda: Fountain Press.

Reno, W. (1995) 'Reinvention of an African patrimonial state: Charles Taylor's Liberia', *Third World Quarterly* 16 (1): 109–20.

Reno, W. (1998) *Warlord Politics and African States*, Boulder, CO: Lynne Rienner.

Reno, W. (2002) 'Uganda's politics of war and debt relief', *Review of International Political Economy* 9 (3): 415–35.

Rhodes, I. (ed.) (1970) *Imperialism and Underdevelopment*, New York, NY: Monthly Review Press.

Rich, B. (1994) 'The cuckoo in the nest: fifty years of political meddling by the World Bank', *The Ecologist* 24 (1): 8–13.

Rich, B. (2002) 'The World Bank under James Wolfenson', in *Reinventing the World Bank*, Pincus, J. and Winters, J. (eds) New York, NY: Cornell University Press, 26–54.

Riddell, R. (1999) 'The end of foreign aid to Africa? Concerns about donor policies', *African Affairs* 98 (392): 309–37.

Rietbergen-McCracken, J. (ed.) (1996) *Participation in Practice. The Experience of the World Bank and other Stakeholders*, Washington, DC: World Bank Discussion Papers 333 .

Riley, S. and Parfitt, T. (1994) 'Economic adjustment and democratisation in Africa', in *Free Markets and Food Riots*, Walton, J. and Seddon, J. (eds) Oxford: Blackwell, 135–70.

Rist, G. (1997) *The History of Development*, London: Zed Press.

Robinson, M. and Rosser, A. (1998) 'Contesting reform: Indonesia's new order and the IMF', *World Development* 26 (9): 1593–609.

Rodney, W. (1972) *How Europe Underdeveloped Africa*, London: Bogle l'Ouverture.

Rodrik, D. (2001) 'Trading in illusions', *Foreign Policy* March–April.

Roesch, O. (1992) 'Renamo and the peasantry in Southern Mozambique: a view from Gaza Province', *Canadian Journal of African Studies* 26: 3.

Rosenberg, J. (1994) *The Empire of Civil Society: A Critique of the Realist Theory of International Relations*, London: Verso.

Roxborough, I. (1979) *Theories of Underdevelopment*, London: Macmillan.

Ruggie, J. (1982) 'International régimes, transactions, and change: embedded liberalism in the postwar economic order', *International Organization* 36 (2): 379–415.

Rupert, M. (1995) *Producing Hegemony: The Politics of Mass Production and American Global Power*, Cambridge: Cambridge University Press.

Rutland, P. (1999) 'Mission impossible? The IMF and the failure of the market transition in Russia', *Review of International Studies* 25 (4): 183–200.

Salter, J. (1992) 'Adam Smith on feudalism, commerce and slavery', *Political Theory* XIII (2): 219–41.

Samoff, J. (2003) 'Partnership in aid to education: evolving terminology, persisting patterns', Paper, *Review of African Political Economy conference*, Birmingham, UK.

Sandbrook, R. (2000) *Closing the Circle: Democratisation and Development in Africa*, London: Zed Press.

Saul, J. (1990) 'From thaw to flood: the end of the Cold War in Southern Africa', *Review of African Political Economy* 18 (50): 145–58.

Saul, J. S. (1985) *A Difficult Road: The Transition to Socialism in Mozambique*, New York, NY: Monthly Review Press.

Schacter, M. (1995) 'Recent experience with institutional development: lending in the West Africa department', in *Civil Service Reform in Anglophone Africa*, Langseth, P., Nogxina, S., Prinsloo, D. and Sullivan, R. (eds) Somerset West, South Africa: EDI/South Africa Management and Development Institute/ODA.

Schatz, S. (1994) 'Structural adjustment in Africa: a failing grade so far', *Journal of Modern African Studies* 32 (4): 679–92.

Schatzberg, M. (1990) *Mobutu or Chaos?: The United States and Zaire, 1960–1990*, London: University Press of America.

Schloss, M. (1998) 'Combating corruption for development: the role of government, business, and civil society', in *Transparency International/EDI New Perspectives on Combating Corruption*, Washington, DC: World Bank.

Schmitz, G. (1995) 'Democratization and demystification: deconstructing "governance" as development paradigm', in *Debating Development Discourse*, Moore, D. and Schmitz, G. (eds) London: Macmillan, 54–91.

Schneider, H. (1999) 'Participatory governance for poverty reduction', *Journal of International Development* 11 (4): 521–34.

Scott, J. (1985) *Weapons of the Weak: Everyday Forms of Peasant Resistance*, London: Yale University Press.

Scott, J. (1998) *Seeing Like a State: How Certain Schemes to Improve the Human Condition Have Failed*, London: Yale University Press.

Sender, J. (2002) 'Reassessing the role of the World Bank in sub Saharan Africa', in *Reinventing the World Bank*, Pincus, J. and Winters, J. (eds) New York, NY: Cornell University Press, 185–203.

Sender, J. and Smith, S. (1986) *The Development of Capitalism in Africa*, London: Methuen.

Shao, J. (1986) 'The villagization program and the disruption of the ecological balance in Tanzania', *Canadian Journal of African Studies* 20 (2): 219–39.

Shihata, I. (1991) *The World Bank in a Changing World: Selected Essays*, Dordrecht: Martinus Nijhoff.

Shivji, I. (2003) 'The life and times of Babu: the age of liberation and revolution', *Review of African Political Economy* 30 (95): 109–18.

Silver, B. and Arrighi, G. (2001) 'Workers North and South', in *Socialist Register: Working Classes, Global Realities*, Pantich, L. and Leys, C. (eds) London: Melrin Press, 53–77.

Simpson, M. (1993) 'Foreign and domestic factors in the transformation of Mozambique', *Journal of Modern African Studies* 31 (2): 309–37.

Singh, A. (1986) 'A commentary on the IMF and World Bank policy programme', in *World Recession and the Food Crisis in Africa*, Lawrence, P. (ed.) London: James Currey, 104–14.

Skogly, S. (1991) 'The World Bank and International Human Rights Law: relationship and relevance', in *Democratisation and Structural Adjustment in the 1990s*, Deng, L., Kostner, M. and Young, C. (eds) Wisconsin: African Studies Programme, University of Wisconsin-Madison, 50–8.

Smith, A. (1776/1986) *The Wealth of Nations Books I–III*, Harmondsworth: Penguin.

Southall, R. (1999) 'Reforming the state? Kleptocracy and the political transition in Kenya', *Review of African Political Economy* 79.

Standing, G. (2000) 'Brave new worlds? A critique of Stiglitz's World Bank rethink', *Development and Change* 31: 737–63.

Stein, H. (1992) 'Economic policy and the IMF in Tanzania: conditionality, conflict and convergence', in *Tanzania and the IMF: The Dynamics of Liberalization*, Campbell, H. S. H. (ed.) Boulder, CO: Westview Press, 59–83.

Stern, N. and Ferreira, F. (1997) 'The World Bank as "intellectual actor"', in *The World Bank: Its First Half Century*, Kapur, D., Lewis, J. and Webb, R. (eds) Washington, DC: Brookings Institution Press, 2: 523–609.

Stiglitz, J. (1999a) *Whither Reform? Ten Years of Transition*, Annual Bank Conference on Development Economics, Washington, DC.

Stiglitz, J. (1999b) 'The World Bank at the Millennium', *The Economic Journal* 109 (November): F577–97.

Stiglitz, J. (2001) *Globalisation and Its Discontents*, London: Allen Lane.

Szeftel, M. (1987) 'The crisis in the Third World', in *The World Order: Socialist Perspectives*, Bush, R., Johnston, G. and Coates, D. (eds) Oxford: Polity Press, 87–141.

Szeftel, M. (1998) 'Misunderstanding African politics: corruption and the governance agenda', *Review of African Political Economy* 25 (76): 221–41.

Tangri, R. and Mwenda, A. (2001) 'Corruption and cronyism in Uganda's privatisation in the 1990s', *African Affairs* 100 (398): 117–33.

Tarp, F. (1993) *Stabilization and Structural Adjustment: Macroeconomic Frameworks for Analysing the Crisis in Sub Saharan Africa*, London: Routledge.

Tata, G. (1996) 'Capacity building', in *Post-conflict Uganda: Towards an Effective Civil Service*, Langseth, P. and Mugaju, J. (eds) Kampala, Uganda: Fountain Press, 126–43.

Taylor, I. (2003) 'Conflict in Central Africa: clandestine networks and regional/global configurations', *Review of African Political Economy* 30 (95): 45–55.

Taylor, L. (1997) 'The revival of the liberal creed – the IMF and the World Bank in a globalised economy', *World Development* 25 (2): 145–52.

Thacker, S. (1999) 'The high politics of IMF lending', *World Politics* 52 (1): 38–75.

The Express, weekly newspaper, Dar es Salaam, Tanzania.

The Monitor, daily newspaper, Kampala, Uganda.

Therkilsden, O. (2000) 'Public sector reform in a poor, aid-dependent country, Tanzania', *Public Administration and Development* 20 (1): 61–73.

Thirkell-White, B. (2003) 'The IMF, good governance and middle income countries', *European Journal of Development Research* 15 (1): 99–125.

Tibana, R. (1995) 'Stabilization and structural adjustment in a dual transition: Mozambique in the 1990s', paper, 'Mozambique: post electoral challenges', LSE.

Tilly, C. (1992) *Coercion Capital and European States*, Oxford: Blackwell.

Tumusiime-Mutebile, E. (1995) 'Management of the economic reform programme', in *Uganda: Landmarks in Rebuilding a Nation*, Langseth, P., Katorobo, J., Brett, E. A. and Munene, J. (eds) Kampala, Uganda: Fountain Press, 1–11.

United Nations Development Programme (2002) *Mozambique National Human Development Report 2001*, Maputo: UNDP.

United Republic of Tanzania (2001) *Poverty Reduction Strategy Paper. Progress Report 2000/2001*, Dar es Salaam.

van de Walle, N. (2001) *African Economies and the Politics of Permanent Crisis 1979–1999* Cambridge, Cambridge University Press.

van der Laar, A. (1980) *The World Bank and the Poor*, The Hague: Martinus Nijhoff.

Vener, J. (2000) 'Prompting democratic transitions from abroad: international donors and multi-partyism in Tanzania', *Democratization* 7 (4): 133–62.

Vines, A. (1991) *Renamo: Terrorism in Mozambique*, London: Centre for Southern African Studies University of York in association with James Currey.

Wade, R. (1996) 'Japan, the World Bank and the art of paradigm maintenance: the East Asian miracle in perspective', *New Left Review* 1 (217): 3–36.

Wade, R. (2000) *International Institutions and the US Role in the Long Asian Crisis of 1990–2000*, paper, New Institutional Theory, Institutional Reform and Poverty Reduction DESTIN Conference, LSE, 7–8 September.

Wade, R. (2001a) 'Showdown at the World Bank', *New Left Review* 2 (7): 124–37.

Wade, R. (2001b) 'Making the World Development Report 2000: attacking poverty', *World Development* 29 (8): 1435–41.

Wade, R. (2002) 'US hegemony and the World Bank: the fight over people and ideas', *Review of International Political Economy* 9 (2): 215–43.

Wade, R. (2004) 'Why world poverty and inequality may be increasing and the north–south divide persisting', *New Political Economy* 9: 2, forthcoming.

Wade, R. and Veneroso, F. (1998) 'The Asian crisis: the high debt model vs. the Wall Street–Treasury–IMF complex', *New Left Review* 1 (228): 3–23.

Walton, J. and Seddon, D. (eds) (1994) *Free Markets and Food Riots: The Politics of Global Adjustment*, Oxford: Basil Blackwell.

Warren, B. (1980) *Imperialism: Pioneer of Capitalism*, London: Verso.

Watkins, K. (2000) 'Growth with equity', *New Economy* 7 (4): 189–98.

White, G. (1984) 'Developmental states and socialist industrialisation in the Third World', *Journal of Development Studies* 21 (1).

White, G., Murray, R. and White, C. (eds) (1983) *Revolutionary Socialist Development in the Third World*, Sussex: Wheatsheaf.

Whitehead, A. (2003) *Failing women, sustaining poverty. Gender in Poverty Reduction Strategy Papers*, Gender and Development Network, mimeograph, University of Sussex.

Williams, D. (1996) 'Governance and the Discipline of Development', *European Journal of Development Research* 8 (2): 157–77.

Williams, D. (1999) 'Constructing the economic space: the World Bank and the making of homo oeconomicus', *Millennium* 28 (1): 79–99.

Williams, D. (2000) 'Aid and sovereignty: quasi-states and the international finance institutions', *Review of International Studies* 26 (4): 557–75.

Williams, D. (2001) The liberal project in international relations: the World Bank, state sovereignty and good governance, *ms.*

Williams, D. and Young, T. (1994) 'Governance, the World Bank and liberal theory', *Political Studies* 42 (1): 84–100.

Williams, G. (1994) 'Why structural adjustment is necessary and why it doesn't work', *Review of African Political Economy* 60 (21): 214–25.

Williams, M. (1991) *Third World Cooperation: The Group of 77 in UNCTAD*, New York, NY: St Martin's Press.

Williamson, T. and Canagaraja, S. (2003) 'Is there a place for virtual poverty funds in pro-poor public spending reform? Lessons from Uganda's PAF', *Development Policy Review* 21 (4): 449–80.

Woods, N. (2000) 'The challenge of good governance for the World Bank and the IMF themselves', *World Development* 28 (5): 823–41.

Woodward, P. (1991) 'Uganda and Southern Sudan 1986–9: new régimes and peripheral politics', in *Changing Uganda*, Hansen, H. B. and Twaddle, M. (eds) London: James Currey, 178–87.

World Bank (1981) *Accelerated Development in Sub Saharan Africa: An Agenda to Action*, Washington, DC: World Bank.

World Bank (1989) *Sub-Saharan Africa: From Crisis to Sustainable Growth: A Long Term Perspective Study*, Washington, DC: World Bank.

World Bank (1992) *Governance and Development*, Washington, DC: World Bank.

World Bank (1993) *The East Asian Miracle. Economic Growth and Public Policy*, Oxford: Oxford University Press.

World Bank (1994a) *Adjustment in Africa: Reforms Results and the Road Ahead*, Oxford: World Bank.

World Bank (1994b) *Governance: The World Bank's Experience*, Washington, DC: The World Bank.

World Bank (1995a) *The African Capacity Building Initiative. Toward Improved Policy Analysis and Development Management in Sub-Saharan Africa*, Washington, DC: World Bank.

World Bank (1995b) *World Development Report 1995: Workers in a Changing World*, Oxford: Oxford University Press.

World Bank (1997) *The State in a Changing World*, Oxford: Oxford University Press.

World Bank (1998) *Knowledge for Development*, Oxford: Oxford University Press.

World Bank (1999) *Project Appraisal Document for a Proposed Credit to the United Republic of Tanzania for a PSRP*, Africa Region, Report no. 19216–TA.

World Bank (2000/2001) *Attacking Poverty*, Oxford: Oxford University Press.

World Bank (2000a) *African Development Indicators*, Washington, DC: World Bank.

World Bank (2000b) Memorandum of the President of the IDA and the IFC to the executive directors on a Country Assistance Strategy of the World Bank for the Republic of Mozambique, Report No. 20521MOZ .

World Bank (2002) *Building Institutions for Markets*, Oxford: Oxford University Press.

World Bank (2003) *Sustainable Development in a Dynamic World*, Oxford: Oxford University Press.

World Bank and Government of Tanzania (1999) *Towards a Medium Term Expenditure Framework*, Africa Region report no. 19898.

Wuyts, M. (1991) 'Mozambique: economic management and adjustment policies', in *The IMF and the South: The Social Impact of Crisis and Adjustment*, Ghai, D. (ed.) London: Zed Press, 215–35.

Yeager, R. (1982) *Tanzania: An African Experiment*, Boulder, CO: Westview Press.

Young, T. (2002) ' "A project yet to be realised": global liberalism and a new world order', in *The Globalization of Liberalism*, Hovden, E. and Keene, E. (eds) Basingstoke: Palgrave, 173–92.

Zartman, W. (1995) *Collapsed States: the Disintegration and Restoration of Legitimate Authority*, Boulder, CO: Lynne Rienner.

Index